PISS AND LIGHT

PISS
AND
LIGHT

CRITICAL ESSAYS OF
BARUCH D. KIRSCHENBAUM

WITH COMMENTARIES BY
ELIZABETH G. GROSSMAN

EDITED BY
MICHAEL GNAT

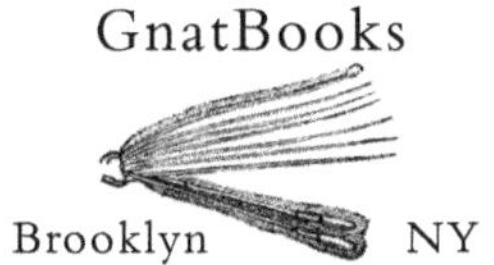

Photo on page 96: © Ed Brown.

"Piss and Light" was first published in *Shop Talk: Essays in Honor of Seymour Slive,* ed. Cynthia P. Schneider, William W. Robinson, and Alice I. Davies (Cambridge, MA: Harvard University Art Museums, 1995).

"Book Reviews: 'The Art Museum: Power, Money, Ethics' by Karl E. Meyer; 'An Anti-Catalog' by The Catalog Committee" was first published in *Winterthur Portfolio* 15.3 (1980): 273–6. © 1980 by The Henry Francis du Pont Winterthur Museum, Inc.

"Photo-Synthesis: The Work of Doug Prince" was first published in 1985 by the Museum of Art, Rhode Island School of Design.

This book was edited and designed by Michael Gnat.

PUBLISHER'S CATALOGING-IN-PUBLICATION DATA
Names: Kirschenbaum, Baruch David, 1931-2024, author. | Grossman, Elizabeth Greenwell, author. | Gnat, Michael, editor.
Title: Piss and light : critical essays of Baruch D. Kirschenbaum / with commentaries by Elizabeth G. Grossman; edited by Michael Gnat.
Description: Includes bibliographical references. | Brooklyn, NY: GnatBooks, 2024.
Identifiers: LCCN: 2024918832 | ISBN: 979-8-218-49628-9
Subjects: LCSH Kirschenbaum, Baruch David, 1931-2024--Knowledge and learning. | Art teachers--United States--Biography. | Art, Renaissance. | Art, Contemporary. | Essays. | BISAC ART / Criticism & Theory | ART / History / European / Renaissance | ART / History / Contemporary (1945-) | ART / Individual Artists / Essays | BIOGRAPHY & AUTOBIOGRAPHY / Educators
Classification: LCC N7445.2 .K57 2024 | DDC 701.18--dc23

TO

BARUCH D. KIRSCHENBAUM

1931–2024

CONTENTS

PREFACE

I UNDERTOOK THIS PROJECT as a way to try to hold on to the remarkable spirit and intellect of Baruch Kirschenbaum (BK). The nine chapters that follow analyze, one by one, nine of his twelve publications. These analyses are in the form of lengthy quotations transcribed from the writings themselves and interspersed in a heterogeneous fashion with my comments. I hope, with my accumulating observations, to explicate the intellectual substance and emotional investment that characterize BK's particular take on art and, by extension, life.

As is evident from my Table of Contents, I do not take up his writings in chronological order. When I started this project in 2022, I had copies of only three of his publications, which make up the first three chapters; yet even these are not arranged chronologically. If I had to offer a rationale for my ordering, I would say it was initially based on personal preference and what was to hand; that sequencing led to the sequencing of the rest.

I started in the fall of 2022 with the essay "Piss and Light" because it seemed more manageable than tackling his book on Jan Steen (which I do address in Chapter II). It also seemed to require less explication than "Private Parts and Public Consideration," which is so very much intertwined with his career at the Rhode Island School of Design (RISD). I finished drafts of my analysis of these three works, the only ones I had to hand, that first winter.

By the time I resumed work on the project again in the fall of 2023, I had acquired, through the help of the RISD Library, six of BK's other writings – which, in the end, were all we could locate. "A Divergent View on Art School Humanities," related as it also is to RISD, appeared to be a good follow-on to "Private Parts." It also seemed, at least on first read, to be pretty straightforward, so I could ease back into the project after the summer's hiatus. I next took up "Primitivism and Impossible Art," as it too was related to his teaching at RISD. That essay raises the issue of art world institutions, so I chose to write next about BK's review for *Winterthur Portfolio* of two books on museums.

None of these works focus on individual works of art, though, which are my favorite type of BK's writings. Happily, the remaining three essays do: "The

Scull Auction and the Scull Film" comes first because it addresses the market for art, and so extends BK's consideration of museum practices. His article on Doug Prince demonstrates in miniature BK's skill at formal analysis. In it he considers the use of metaphor in art, which made it a good antecedent to BK's "Reflections on Michelangelo's Drawings for Cavaliere," in which BK compares these drawings to the artist's sonnets. "Reflections" was BK's first publication. It felt appropriate to end the Part One commentaries with that.

For people who want to read these BK essays for themselves, I have included them all in Part Two of this volume, in the same order as in my commentaries. His book, though out of print, is still available.

I wish to thank particularly: Julia Kirschenbaum, Rebecca Gruber, and Judith Wolin, all of whom read and edited various chapters, and encouraged me to keep on with the writing. I am grateful for their insights, and for their love for the two of us. Emily Coxe, of the RISD Library, tenaciously tracked down the articles I discuss in Chapters IV–IX. Without her help and expertise, this project would not have been possible. This work was edited by Michael Gnat, who was my editor back in the mid-1990s, and then in 2016 edited BK's book of poetry, *Slippage*. BK and I have valued his friendship a lot.

INTRODUCTION

MY FIRST IDEA for this project was in a sense biographical: I wanted to understand for myself, and for those who know him as a part of their circle of family and friends, how Baruch Kirschenbaum's early life underwrote the success of his work teaching decades of students at the Rhode Island School of Design (RISD).

It seemed a pretty compelling story. As he tells it, he grew up on the West Side of Manhattan during the Depression and war years. His family moved from apartment to apartment as they fell behind on the rent. BK was pretty much on his own – a truant from school, a New York street kid when he was young, earning money, which he gave to his mother, by working at a newspaper stand at Columbus Avenue and 72nd Street. and by delivering ice cream cakes to the apartments of the wealthy, among other things. He hung out in Central Park, where he went fishing in "borrowed" boats and played softball in pickup games on the 62nd Street diamond. Later, in his teenage years, he was on the road part of the time, working on a dairy farm in New England, and later on a muck farm in Wisconsin, from which he was drafted into the Marine Corps. He did not ship out to Korea, however, but spent his time as a paymaster in North Carolina. As a teenager he accompanied his sister Frances to folk dances at the New York Society for Ethical Culture on West 64th Street. There he met Blossom Steinberg, whom he would marry while on leave after basic training.

Yet somehow, despite his sketchy early education, BK ended up with a Harvard Ph.D. His thesis on Jan Steen's religious paintings was important enough to be published – first in hardback, later in paperback. He was offered a position at RISD while working on his dissertation. There, BK turned out to have a remarkable ability to earn the admiration and affection of the generations of RISD students he taught – despite the fact that they, almost as an act of self-definition, were often resistant to taking their liberal arts courses seriously.

I started this project by reading BK's publications, which was in itself a bit quixotic for, to this day, he puts minimal value on them. (It is telling, I think, that although BK has kept boxes and boxes of his lecture notes, he had only three of his publications; the rest I had to access with the help of RISD's librarians. Also, his bibliography is quite short: one book and eleven fairly brief articles.)

I soon realized, however, that his writings were key: They reveal BK's attitudes and convictions about art (directly) and life (indirectly). It is these, I think, that made him such an effective teacher. How much these attitudes and convictions may be attributed to his experiences growing up in New York City is less obvious.

So rather than a biography in the larger sense of that word, this project has become an effort to explain the common threads that run through BK's published work. His writings reveal what is really important to him. Directness, humor, and compassion for our flawed humanity are what he underscores in his exemplary discussions of the art about which he chose to write; acceptance of internal contradictions to expose the fallacies of comfortable answers is what his prose style supports; and a knowledge of history and of the realities of life that are inconsistent with institutional verities are what he highlights.

The respect, attraction, and affection that his students showed him, he reciprocated in his teaching and support for them and their work. I hope that my analyses of his writing are convincing. I do realize, however, one could say that these are merely my findings in his publications, and that as his companion (in the largest sense of that word) my findings are suspect by definition. To that I would respond that I can't deny, nor would I wish to, that I found in his writing what I have experienced in my years of sharing life with him.

CODA

Early in April 2023, when I was still poring over his Michelangelo article, BK and I went out for supper. Over Asian tapas, sake, and beer, I asked him about Panofsky. The conversation expanded to a range of topics about art and art history. I tried to commit his words to memory. What follows is a transcription of our conversation as I remembered it when we got home.

EG: Do you think it is right to say that Erwin Panofsky is the most well-known art historian?
BK: Yes, I think so.
EG: What was he famous for?
BK: That was a long time ago, I would have to go back and review …
EG: Was he the one who wrote about iconography and iconology? I know what iconography is, but I always had trouble with iconology.
BK: Iconography has to do with what the subject matter is. Iconology has to do with the larger meaning of the subject matter.

EG: So identifying the drawing as the myth of Ganymede is iconography,
interpreting it is Neoplatonic yearning for spiritual love is iconology.

BK: Yes, you could say that.

EG: So I guess you would give my answer a "B."

BK: No, an "A." … Well maybe an "A–."

EG: *(laughing)* or worse, a B+.

BK: It was Blossom who taught me to be a student.

EG: What does that mean – to be a student?

BK: It means to follow an idea.

EG: And you learned that from Blossom?

BK. Well, and from some of my teachers.

EG: I have read all your publications now … except for a few that we
couldn't find. And I was struck by how consistently you stressed the
complexity of works of art, that their meaning wasn't simply one
thing or the other.

BK: My interest in art is intellectual. Not that I am an intellectual, but
that was my interest in art. Most people aren't interested in that.
They are interested in art as buyers and sellers. After I published my
book on Steen I got lots of phone calls – people wanting me to at-
tribute works. I was not interested in the works as objects to buy
and sell. I was interested in them intellectually. I guess I could have
made more money if I did that. Many scholars did.

EG: After your book on Steen, until you wrote your article "Piss and
Light" you hadn't written any in-depth studies of works of art. Your
articles were all about the insider dealing of the art establishment,
the deals, the museums, et cetera.

BK: At RISD I was more involved with the making of art. I did not want
to have anything to do with the buying and selling. My interest was
intellectual.

EG: I think your interest in art was more than intellectual.

BK: *(silence)*

EG: I think you thought works of art – I mean, works worth thinking
about – were somehow magic things.

BK: I think that is a good way of putting it. … I really loved teaching at
RISD.

PART ONE

COMMENTARIES

I

PISS AND LIGHT (1995)

PERHAPS THE MOST REMARKABLE statement of BK's institutional skepticism and his belief in the power of individual works of art is contained in the last paper he published. The history of his "Piss and Light" is itself rather remarkable. It was first given in 1991 at a symposium at RISD entitled "Images of Power / Images of Rebellion." Then, as "Szczyny i światło," the paper was published in 1993 in Poland, a deeply Catholic country, in the contemporary art journal *Obieg*. That same year, it also appeared in a Festschrift for Seymour Slive, the famed Harvard professor of Dutch baroque art who had supervised BK's Ph.D. thesis.[1] (BK received his Ph.D. in 1966, by which time he had been teaching at RISD for four years.)

"Piss and Light" is BK's analysis of a large, 40×60-inch (w×h) Cibachrome photograph that Andres Serrano himself titled *Piss Christ* (1987). Serrano affixed the title to his photograph of a construction he made in which he submerged a plastic crucifix in urine, "purportedly his own" (134.1). When it turned out that the NEA had supported the exhibition in which *Piss Christ* appeared, it "caused a major uproar … [that] almost brought down the NEA and the whole apparatus of government support of the arts" (133.1). Note BK's language here: the judicious *purportedly* in which BK chooses not join this speculation, and the colloquial *major uproar,* which reads as both an accurate and a minimizing characterization of what went on.

BK explains that he "had become particularly interested in the Serrano photograph for two reasons. First, because at the height of the NEA funding controversy the issue of art attacked and rejected as blasphemous or inappropriate generated some heated discussion in a course on Italian seventeenth-

1 Baruch Kirschenbaum, "Piss and Light," *Shop Talk: Studies in Honor of Seymour Slive,* ed. Cynthia P. Schneider, William W. Robinson, and Alice I. Davies (Cambridge, MA: Harvard University Art Museums, 1995), 133–36; BK, "Szczyny i światło," *Obieg,* nos. 49–50 (1993): 10–16. The information about the symposium is from the article. All quotations are from the 1995 Festschrift version of BK's paper. In addition to page numbers cited in the text in parentheses, I give the column, e.g., (133.1).

century art I was then teaching" (133.1). He goes on to explain that he is referring to class reaction to certain of Caravaggio's religious paintings, which he discusses in the paper at some length as well. BK's interest in the issue of blasphemy as it relates to the making of religious art clearly did not start with Serrano's work. Rather, as he was an expert in baroque art, and especially in its religious iconography, the reverse is obviously true; that is, BK's knowledge of the controversies engendered by works like Caravaggio's *Death of the Virgin* had primed him for the Serrano controversy. By reminding the reader that some of Caravaggio's paintings also were once too controversial for the Catholic Church, literally, to accept, BK positions the Serrano from the start within a lineage of disruptive masterpieces. (His interest in such issues obviously helps explain BK's effectiveness as a teacher of art students.)

But BK's second reason for being interested in the *Piss Christ* is really his motivation for the paper, which is an extended analysis to consider what the meaning of the work might be: "for all the fuss made over the photograph little, if any, consideration was given to the meaning that Serrano's self-conscious blasphemy may have been intended to express" (133.2). This is a classic BK provocation – the diminishment of the fuss while acknowledging that Serrano may well have intended the work to blaspheme.

BK then goes on to give his reasons for dismissing as ignorant grandstanders both those who would be outraged and those who would defend Serrano's work. Whereas the former "simply took its offense as self-evident," the latter "were more concerned with the issues of censorship … than with questions of meaning" (133.2). BK considered both sides to be both disingenuous and exploitative because they ignored the fact that "the serious religious content of Serrano's work had [already] received significant critical consideration" (133.2). BK will rely on some of that writing, by Lucy Lippard, Patrick Finnegan, and Derek Guthrie, in his own paper.

The co-option of art for partisan ends troubles BK – whether he agrees with the cause or not – because it is, at its core, fundamentally dishonest and hypocritical. He requires that Serrano's piece be judged on its own terms. What those terms might be are the subject of "Piss and Light." (When in Chapter III I discuss his article "Private Parts and Public Considerations" we shall see this issue of hypocrisy played out in full.)

After this opening gambit, BK goes on to discuss (with what some might consider unexpected authority, especially given that his strong Jewish identification was more cultural and secular than religious) the role of the "crucifix in Catholic understanding" (133.2). He then underscores Serrano's own Catholicism, noting, "Serrano speaks from the inside of the faith," and though he is a "'lapsed' Catholic, he understands that this only means lapsed from the rituals of the church, not necessarily from personal belief" (133.2). And here BK sets up the key tensions that he will explore for the rest of the paper: blasphemy, private faith, and institutional religion.

BK introduces the subject conditionally by posing a rather simple, or even simplistic, dichotomy: "If the power of the *Piss Christ* photograph, then, is the power of internalized belief and institutional control, the rebellion is expressed in the emphatic challenge to that power through the obscene defamation of its sacred and central icon" (134.1). Note BK's use of that intial "if."

Taking the work apart, BK demonstrates how – from Serrano's use of "a common and cheap plastic crucifix, though one (probably Early Renaissance or Late Gothic in derivation) that presents the body of Christ as delicate and vulnerable," to the urine, to the photograph, to the title of the photograph – Serrano has piled defamation upon defamation (134.1).

Then, having made this case, BK seems to change tack: "That Serrano has some difficulty with authority in general can be seen in his other 'piss works'" (134.1) He points to other Serrano photographs – all Cibachromes – in which not only urine but blood, or urine mixed with blood, is used, and that are all clearly anti-church. BK further asserts, "Serrano is intent on making the association of blood and Catholicism inescapable and physically repulsive" (134.2). So we are left to wonder: Is the *Piss Christ* really a work of blasphemy that, in its intention, merits our consideration? Or is it merely a rebellion against authority, an effort to *épater,* in which case maybe it doesn't?

But having floated the latter possibility, BK seems not only to reject it but to propose an even graver motivation for Serrano's use of body fluids than blasphemy. "The fluids of the body with which Serrano is so fundamentally concerned function in his images, I believe, as indices of the real bodies that endure the suffering of the world" (134.2). And he enlarges this proposition by analyzing still other Cibachromes of Serrano's that use body fluids with more secular connotations – menstruation, the AIDS crisis.

BK is still not done turning the issue around. "In a strange way, all of Serrano's images despite their apparent harshness are saying, 'Yes' and 'No' and then again 'Yes'" (135.1). And with this shorthand we now are able to see the tactical purpose of BK's reversals: All of what BK exposes/reveals in this analysis of the *Piss Christ* is there to be found in the work – the defamation, Serrano's problems with authority, the lament for human suffering, the attack on the Catholic church. BK's argument is that we have to accept all of it to understand the work. BK is not offering us a Hegelian analysis. There is no thesis, antithesis, synthesis – no forward progress. "In *Piss Christ* that 'Yes/No/Yes' can be understood as an expression of Serrano's unresolved conflict with his own Catholicism. The picture is more than a simple power/rebellion opposition, but … affirms the very belief it appears to attack so meanly" (135.1).

With this statement BK both critiques the topic of the symposium at which he first delivered this paper, and also explains his own use of that "If" at the start of his analysis. BK elaborates his "Yes/No/Yes" assertion this way: "To put the issue another way, if the crucifix is the power of Catholicism, the piss is the piss of the corruption and suffering of the world through which the image (the icon) of the crucified Christ shines forth as the promise of ultimate re-demption. And in the picture, the crucifix is light struck in the golden fluid as if by the presence of divine light" (135.1). There it is: crucifix/piss/light; Yes/No/Yes.

BK then places Serrano's work within "the tradition of Christian iconography, [where] the image of the suffering Christ is, of course, very common" (135.1). "*Piss Christ,* I would argue, far from being an obscene blasphemy, can be located within a long iconographic tradition in Christian art the meaning of which Serrano forces us to confront with a renewed understanding and passion by the very obscenity of his gesture" (135.1–2). He goes on to discuss a George Grosz drawing in which Christ is wearing a gas mask and army boots, which he relates to a Barbara Krueger photomontage that uses a variant of this iconography.

But BK is still not finished with us – and I use that pronoun emphatically. "Finally, there is the nagging suspicion that those who reject images like those of Caravaggio or of Serrano do so not out of a lack of understanding, but out of a clear recognition of their potential for radical political meaning. To accept [such images] … might reinforce the potential of Christianity to become a voice for social and political discontent. … Serrano's religious images come at a time when the Catholic church is again challenged for neglecting the call to a social ministry by those who feel marginalized" (135.2). This is no-holds-barred stuff for, with this commentary, BK has aligned himself unequivocally with Serrano the "'lapsed' Catholic." One is left to wonder whether in the bluntness of this statement, BK, who might be called a "lapsed Jew," is also speaking about the condition of his own identity and his own social values.

I would argue that the blow BK lands here is not as an embrace of Bertolt Brecht's claim that "art is not a mirror held up to reality, but a hammer with which to shape it." Rather, through the very structure of his arguments in "Piss and Light," BK seems to be claiming that art's power is more subtle and more significant than that of the hammer. That the meanings of Serrano's work are complex and also contradictory is, in fact, the source of its authority. Art neither shapes nor mirrors reality, but it can allow us to glimpse the conditions of our humanity – if we care enough to do the work we are offered.

II

THE RELIGIOUS AND HISTORICAL
PAINTINGS OF JAN STEEN (1977)

IN 1957, AT THE AGE OF 26, BK graduated summa cum laude, Phi Beta Kappa, from Hunter College. He had gone through Hunter with Blossom Steinberg, having met at Ethical Culture as teenagers and married in 1952 when he was in the Marine Corps, into which he was drafted late in the Korean War).[1] According to BK they were the first couple in the history of Hunter to graduate in the same class together. (Hunter admitted its first male students as freshmen in 1946.) He credits Blossom with teaching him how to be a student, through her remarkable intellect and her own brilliance as a student. However true, this explanation does not fully explain why he acquired the interest and confidence to apply himself to his studies at Hunter, given that he had shown so little predisposition for bookwork as a kid.

BK first encountered art history as a discipline as an undergraduate at Hunter in a course taught by William Rubin, then himself a graduate student at Columbia studying under Meyer Schapiro. One might have thought, given the impact that course had on him, that BK would have also chosen to go on to graduate school at Columbia. But for reasons he himself to this day cannot really explain, he chose not to remain in NYC and study at Columbia with Schapiro, the brilliant Marxist historian of medieval art. Instead, he decided to go to Harvard on his Woodrow Wilson National Fellowship. At the time, Harvard's faculty were known for their connoisseurship approach to art history – in which the formal and iconographic attributes of images were the focus of analysis, and judgments of quality were a primary motivation. He says that he was *educated* at Hunter and *trained* at Harvard.

BK was clearly as accomplished at Harvard as he was at Hunter. He says he could have written his dissertation with Sydney Freedberg – by then an eminent scholar of Italian sixteenth-century art – on the basis of a paper on

---

1 BK told me it was at the Society for Ethical Culture that he learned he had a responsibility to try to make the world a better place. All the biographical herein information is from BK.

Michelangelo BK had written for one of Freedberg's courses. (This paper, selected for a prestigious symposium held at the Frick Collection in New York, was subsequently published in the *Gazette des Beaux-Arts*; see Chapter IX.) However, BK chose instead to work with Seymour Slive on Dutch art of the seventeenth century for reasons, again, that he cannot fully explain. I do know that BK did not take kindly to Freedberg's tutoring him not only on the pronunciation of the Italian words, but also on his English in an effort to tone down his heavy New York accent. He always felt that, fundamentally, it was all meant to spare Freedberg embarrassment when BK read the paper at the Frick symposium.

Slive was only eleven years BK's senior and, at the time, not yet a full professor. He had earned his Ph.D. at the University of Chicago in 1952 and was apparently the first scholar of Dutch art to be trained in the United States. His dissertation, published in 1953 as *Rembrandt and His Critics 1630–1730,* focused not on Rembrandt's art per se, but on the artist's reputation. But there are doubtless other, more positive reasons that led BK to work with Slive. No doubt the field of Dutch art seemed less rarified compared to Italian art. Perhaps, too, seventeenth-century Netherlands interested him because of the visibility of Jewish culture there – a point BK has made in passing.

Even so, ask BK about his years at Harvard and he always will stress how painfully alien its culture felt to him. Perhaps he never really recovered from that first negative impression he'd had when he and Blossom pulled up to their rental apartment in Somerville with all their possessions, and the landlady, when she realized the Black man driving the car was his brother-in-law, refused to honor the rental agreement. (BK's sister, Dorothy, who was connected to the New York theater business, had gone to the Soviet Union with the State Department–sponsored touring production of *Porgy and Bess.* There she met, and subsequently married, John McCurry, the African American actor who played the role of Crown. It was he who was driving the car.) In the end, BK and Blossom found another apartment down by the river on the third floor of a triple-decker. The first landlady refunded their deposit and paid their extra expenses. BK never owned a car until he moved to Providence, though he had learned to drive probably when he was working as a teenager on a muck farm in Wisconsin.

They were economically hard-pressed: Blossom earned money typing, and BK at some point drove a cab evenings when people got off work, and nights after the bars closed, which were when he could get the most fares. He also worked as a docent at Harvard's Fogg Museum. In light of all these demands on his time, I find it the more telling that BK took time from his studies to teach about the art of Picasso at a prison south of Boston. The men there elected to learn about Picasso over Rembrandt. Apparently, this was not an incidental commitment for BK; he did it once a week for two semesters even though it was not remunerated. When I asked BK recently why he did so, he said simply that he loved doing it.

BK completed his dissertation in 1966, by which time he and Blossom had three children, ranging in age from four to nine years old. These facts are important because the determination, stamina, and focus it takes to complete a dissertation at an elite university are considerable, even when one can devote oneself solely to research and writing.

A dissertation, by definition, is supposed to make a significant contribution to its field. In fact, that is a high bar that many, I might say most, cannot clear. However – and this is really to be highlighted – BK's dissertation was important enough to be published in 1977 as *The Religious and Historical Paintings of Jan Steen.*[2] The book is visually impressive: an octavo volume, on heavy cream stock, with wide margins. Although all but one of the photographs are black and white, there are 132 of them, some full-page. It was published both in hardback and paperback. It became, one could say, a seminal work.

It is also a highly specialized one: A considerable portion is devoted to the minutiae of the chronology of Steen's paintings, the facts of Steen's life, and – not surprisingly, given that BK was working under Slive – the critical commentary and accumulated scholarly reputation of Steen's work. It has the apparatus of a dissertation that showcases scrupulous research, and it revises long-standing narratives about Steen's work, demonstrating original thinking.

I do not want to minimize either of these aspects of the book, so I am first going to discuss the apparatus: the catalog of Steen's paintings that forms the appendix, and the lengthy first chapter of the book that establishes a chronology for Steen's religious and history paintings. I will then backtrack to the Introduction and the remaining chapters in which he develops his argument. I do not attempt, in my analysis, to convey the extent of the material that BK controls to shape his points. Instead, I rely on his discussions of just a few paintings – passages that stand out both for the eloquence of his analysis and for the pithiness of the points he makes.

First, the catalog, each of whose eighty-three entries demonstrates BK's mastery of the scholarship: the listing of all known sources relevant to a work's provenance, exhibition history, and critical literature, its present location if extant, and so on, accompanied by his own commentary about its style, iconography, and its place in Steen's oeuvre. The entries reveal his ability to read German, Dutch, and French, his firsthand familiarity with the works he discusses, and his knowledge of the literature not only on Steen but on Steen's Dutch contemporaries.

The appendix serves as proof, as it were, that his argument about Steen's work rests on a solid foundation. It also evinces a tremendous amount of meticulous and time-consuming research, perseverance, and downright hard work. (BK seems to this day to identify with some former grad student who had carved "Grind" in cursive into a carrel in the Fogg Museum Library).

2 Baruch D. Kirschenbaum, *The Religious and Historical Paintings of Jan Steen* (New York: Allanheld & Schram, 1977).

Unless one is a specialist (and maybe even if one is), the first chapter, in which BK develops a six-part chronology for Steen's history and religious paintings – though absolutely necessary for his subsequent argument – is rather slow going. It reads as more about the minutiae of Steen's stylistic development as a history painter, and about the themes he chose to paint, than as a discussion of the significance of the paintings themselves. Yet it is also impressive to see how, by skillfully deploying the art historical conventions of formal and iconographic analysis, as well as his knowledge of the literature on Steen, he builds up his argument. By the end of the chapter, he has laid the ground to make some substantive claims about Steen and his work that, while not assertive in tone, are quite bold in their implications.

(How comprehensive he was required to be in his command of the literature is suggested by a story BK has told about Slive's standards: When he was finally nearing the end of his dissertation writing, BK learned that a Russian art historian had just written about some of the material he was covering. Slive would not let that pass. BK had to acquire a copy of the Russian text, pay someone to translate it, then read it and incorporate the relevant parts into his argument.)

Judging from BK's conclusion to the chronology, its purpose was to demonstrate to skeptics that Steen himself took his history paintings seriously, and therefore so should we. Yet BK seems at first cautious about pushing this idea too hard: "Steen has a permanent place in history as a painter of peasant and middle-class life. One can hardly damage that image by revising it somewhat. The consistency of his interest in historical painting, and the number and quality of the works, do call for something of a reevaluation of his reputation" (56). But then BK pushes a little harder: Steen "was not only one of The Netherlands' greatest genre painters, … but also one of her [*sic*] most accomplished and prolific painters of narrative histories, an occupation which he took with extreme seriousness" (56). This assertion, that Steen could be a master of genre painting and an accomplished history painter as well, will prove to be more radical than it may appear.

BK then elaborates on the claims he is making about Steen's history paintings. His "mature historical paintings are like compendia of all that was best in Dutch painting of the mid-seventeenth century … [a] remarkable mixture of … still life and genre painting, the religious drama of Rembrandt, and the low humor of Haarlem's peasant painters" (56).

But it is not Steen's eclecticism, provocative though any celebration of it might be, that so interests BK. Rather it is something unique to Steen: "[I]n one aspect of his historical imagination he stands alone within the whole sweep of Dutch and European painting of his time. What isolates him is his conscious use of incongruous elements and his sense of historical ridiculousness" (56). In other words, BK is asserting that Steen deliberately challenged the conventions of history painting, and with considerable skill and purpose. Demonstrating how Steen did this is what the rest of the book is about.

The chronology is a demonstration of graduate student erudition. In contrast, the Introduction, which directly precedes it, reveals the scope of BK's ambitions for the work. In fact, the Introduction shows that BK realizes that his analysis of Steen's paintings will challenge the intellectual status quo not only of Steen's paintings, but, more broadly, of art history in general.

BK starts the Introduction, conventionally enough, with a quotation about Steen by Joshua Reynolds, the great eighteenth-century portraitist and academician. Reynolds, for all he clearly admires Steen, also laments his limitations. He finds that despite Steen's extraordinary abilities, because he had been born in Holland and not in Italy, and although he displayed "sagacity and penetration … in his vulgar figures" he was not "equally successful" in painting "what was great and elevated" (19).

BK then considers the implications of Reynolds's reservations. Summarizing the prevailing position, for which Reynolds was a spokesman, BK writes, "Jan Steen was one of the great makers of the 'lower class of art,' from whom students could learn, but whom they should never imitate if they aspired to true greatness" (19). Here, BK is explicating the fact that since the Renaissance, art academies had insisted on a hierarchy of painting subjects. Scenes of everyday life and of lower-class people were on lower rungs of the hierarchy than paintings of subjects taken from mythology, religion, and history, with their heroic protagonists acting as moral or tragic exemplars.

For BK, the implications of this hierarchy were broader than they might appear: "As determined by an accident of birth, Steen could only excel in what was rightly his to paint: family intimacies, tavern jollity, brothel scenes, and the like. To go beyond these limits meant personal failure – and the very degradation of Art" (19). In short, BK argues that it was assumed that history painting required respectability on the part of its artists to protect its elevated status. From that it followed that there was a congruence between the type of subjects painters might paint and the lives they led; to overreach would result in artistic failure.

To show that he has not overstated Reynolds's position BK quotes him again, this time about a specific history painting by Steen, *The Sacrifice of Iphigenia,* regarding which "one would be almost tempted to doubt, whether the artist did not purposely intend to burlesque his [classical] subject" (20). Interestingly, BK seems to agree with Reynolds's negative assessment: "However carefully composed and beautifully painted, the picture nevertheless breaks all the rules of classical decorum, which demanded that serious narrative painting be historically appropriate. Steen seems either unaware of or unconcerned with such canons. He has jumbled the costumes anachronistically … and has hung this finery on radically un-heroic subjects" (20).

BK used Reynolds to establish how Steen's reputation stands. Now the question becomes how BK is going to rectify it, given that he himself allows the truth of Reynolds's criticism by using of phrases like "jumbled the costumes" and "hung this finery." First he has to show that Reynolds is not simply a stalking horse: "It is difficult to say when the denial of 'great subjects' to Steen first began" (20). To do this he takes off, as one might expect of a student of Seymour Slive, on a short survey of the critical literature about Steen. (It is worth observing that Slive's book on Rembrandt's critics was written at a time when virtually everything Rembrandt had produced – works of his youth or old age, paintings or etchings, of subjects secular or religious – was valued, even revered.) BK, in contrast, is working with paintings by Steen, which, at least from the late eighteenth century, had been out of favor. And indeed, even in Steen's lifetime, although critics testified to his popularity, they seemed to have little good to say about Steen's narrative history and religious subjects.

BK, in short, has an open field to rehabilitate Steen's reputation, but the question remains how he is going to do it. He acknowledges that Reynolds and subsequent critics found Steen's history and religious works unacceptable because they viewed the paintings through the lens of Steen the person. "Steen's reputation as a drunkard and a buffoon probably contributed to the moralistic dismissal of especially his religious paintings" (21). Rather than dispute the facts of Steen's character, BK challenges the underlying assumptions concerning the connection between art and the life of the artist. "While stories of Steen's profligacy may have some basis in fact, they came in this case to hide both Steen and his art. Such obfuscation … arose out of the premise … that the life and work of an artist are an inseparable unity" (21). Finally, he goes on to observe that critical approaches have changed, so apparently these old prejudices should no longer be an obstacle: "In our time we have learned to do away with the association of life and work" (21).

Here is where BK makes a quite extraordinary declaration. It turns out that he is no happier with our time's separation of the artist's life and work than he was with the premise that an artist's life and work were inseparable: "Critically, such disassociation allows us to judge work on its own merit, but it also leads to a narrow view in which art is too often thought of as separable either from life in general or from the life of the person who created it" (21–22). And he goes much further: "Because of such separation, our criticism is too often mechanical and bereft of spirit. Our desire must be to discover Steen's vision, and that means a reintegration of his art and his life but without the old moral prejudices" (22).

You can see why I began this project with "Piss and Light." There can be no doubt that, from the very start of his career to that late work of his, BK actively challenged those who would make of art less than what he could see it to be. From the beginning, he rejected both the lens of self-righteous morality and ideology, and also the lens of art for art's sake, by which art is sequestered from life. (Anyone who has dismissed a work of art because of the politics of its maker, or embraced a work despite them, is implicated in his criticism.) Here, at the very beginning of his career as an art historian, he finds himself at odds with the establishment. (This conviction actually can be traced even earlier, as we shall see, to the paper BK gave at the Frick Symposium.)

Despite BK's attacks on the status quo, the Introduction ends quietly. "Steen did mix the vulgar with the elevated, the satirical with the serious, the comic with the tragic; and in so doing, he created an image of historical happening unique in the history of art" (23). His purpose, he declares, is to "reexamine and reevaluate Steen's work in history in the hope of bringing that uniqueness to better definition and to larger attention" (23). What he doesn't insist on at this point is that to do so he will have to expose, if only by indirection, how entrenched the old hierarchical assumptions about history painting have remained.

BK starts to make his case not with a discussion of the paintings themselves but with a discussion of the religious context in which Steen painted. He considers it important that though Steen is believed to have been a Catholic, "both Dutch art and Dutch culture by the mid-century were overwhelming Protestant" (59). Then, after considering some of his religious works, he states that, so too, "essentially Steen's religious paintings are Protestant" (60). Protestantism, it turns out, has direct implications for Steen's choice of subjects and their treatment: It means that the subject matter was primarily taken from the Old Testament. The painter "might tell a story, … but never create sacred images for veneration" (60). The stories from Scripture "were *exempla* teaching the individual how to stand before God as had Abraham and Moses" (60).

BK goes on at some length to discuss the differences between Catholic and Protestant artists' treatment of religious subjects, establishing how in keeping with Protestant conventions Steen's religious paintings were. He goes so far as to state: "His narratives are events out of the history of God's first chosen people, a position the Calvinists believed had passed to them" (61). This phrasing, however oblique, suggests another reason why BK found Dutch painting more congenial than the deeply Catholic Italian art.

But BK admits that "there is something un-Protestant, un-Calvinist, about his work" (61). To make this case, he discusses a late work of Steen's, *Samson Mocked by the Philistines.* BK's analysis of this painting is worth quoting in full:

> [It] was for Steen the excuse for an almost joyful romp and a parade of costly stuffs. Bare-breasted Delilah, about to receive her whore's wages, taunts the anguished Samson, whose shorn weakness is demonstrated by the boy holding the chain around his neck. From the drunken captain, to the summer-soldier brandishing his sword, to the old Jew who clenches his hands in pity, all is exuberance and display even at this moment of Biblical horror. Adding a note of irony, Steen places the barber's bowl and open razor case on the floor beneath the sacks of coin, thus in still life symbolically uniting act and payment. (61)

Note how BK, while on the track of his main point about Protestantism and Catholicism, has used his formal and iconographical analysis to highlight Steen's integration of multiple genres, highlighting, rather than downplaying, the artist's eclecticism.

Then he continues: "This abundance, this delight in human foible, this touch of humorous irony, cannot be held as either strictly Protestant or Catholic; but certainly the ability to celebrate, and to find humor in Scripture, is more a part of the Catholic spirit than the Protestant" (61). And as if that generalization weren't sufficiently grounded, relying on recent scholarship about Steen, he makes an even more sweeping assertion. "Catholicism, less possessed of guilt, and less troubled by individuality, has generally been more open in its acceptance of human weakness" (61).

BK will not pursue this thread, at least not immediately. Rather he takes up another aspect of Steen's painting that he considers "more important than either his Protestant orientation or the possible overtones of a more Catholic spirit. Whether in genre, religious, or historical pictures, one of his major concerns was with themes of love. Contemporary or ancient, he used love to reveal the foibles of men and women when they are both at their most passionate and at their most vulnerable" (62). BK will use this iconography to integrate Steen's disparaged paintings back into his oeuvre. "It is not at all surprising to find that love spurred Steen's historical interest, for it appears strongly as a major theme in his genre work" (62).

He divides Steen's paintings of love into two categories: the sacred and the profane. The division, however, is not between the religious and the secular but "between that which ennobles and that which degrades" (63). Predictably, though, given his demonstrated distaste for simplistic categories, BK insists on the artificiality of the distinction: "Sacred love may include base desires and, contrariwise, what appears only lustful may yet partake of the divine" (63).

It is hard to capture the impact of BK's analysis of Steen's range of treatment of the subject of love, given how many paintings he covers, but his discussion of *Antiochus and Stratonice* suggests how artful he can be. First, he tells the story, which is based on an ancient source:

> There it is told how the prince Antiochus, son of the great Seleucus, fell desperately in love with his stepmother, the young and beautiful Stratonice. From that love, which he struggled to conceal, he fell mortally ill, and was on the point of death. The physician Erasistratus, discovering a reviving pulse upon Stratonice's passing the prince's bed, correctly diagnoses the illness. Hearing the doctor's report, Seleucus, out of love for his son, cedes him the fair Stratonice and thus obtains his recovery. (65)

Notice how easily BK takes up the role of storyteller.

Then he turns to the iconography of Steen's painting, pointing out how it is probably based on a later variant of this source, one in which Stratonice is "an active party, sharing the love of Antiochus" (65). As BK describes the scene that Steen has painted, "Stratonice, passing by a balustrade, looks longingly at the very much revived prince, who seems to have lost – if he ever possessed it – the classical restraint generally given to the hero" (65). Again, notice how BK comments on the story, thereby reminding us, that Steen's Antiochus does not quite fit the bill of hero in a history painting. "It would seem also … that the malady has already been diagnosed. The prince has already a fetching but clearly undesired bedmate, no doubt provided by the procuress who holds a wreath of flowers. Antiochus, however, like all obsessed lovers, seems to have found no satisfaction in the substitute" (65).

BK's description, with its own embedded sense of the ridiculous, makes Steen's approach to the subject the more convincing. And he concludes by underscoring how simultaneously farcical and serious the result is: "Here everybody except old Seleucus seems aware of the difficulty. The story deals with the passions of the young, and Steen has kept the three important elements of the story before us: the bed (as both sickbed and love-bed); the request; and the object" (66).

By means of his pointed analysis of Steen's paintings and his own assured commentary, BK, in this chapter, provides an encyclopedia, as it were, of the many varieties of love that Steen painted. In BK's hands, Steen emerges as a master of history and religious subjects, who orchestrated every aspect of his work: the version of the story he chose to paint; the degree of modesty or abandonment his figures conveyed; the focus on everyday, extravagant, or salacious details; and the appropriate balance of farce and seriousness. BK has also revealed, I think, how much he relishes Steen's approach to history painting.

Having made the case for Steen's brilliance as a history painter, he goes on in the remaining, short chapters to discuss the artist's erudition. Drawing on research on seventeenth-century Dutch theater, commedia dell'arte, and the moralistic literature on love from emblem books, he makes the case for Steen's knowledge of the general culture of his day.

In the final chapter, "Steen's Historical Vision," he returns, as is only appropriate, to his opening concern with the hierarchical distinction between genre and history. Here his focus is on Steen's use of anachronism – that is, his use of contemporary figures in paintings set in the past, which Steen employs to blur the categories of history and genre. Anachronism is key to "Steen's particular historical vision" in which he is able in his paintings "to unite the past with the present" (91).

BK's (re)analysis of works he has already discussed shows how this occurs, emphasizing the slippage not only between past and present but between genre and history in Steen's narrative paintings. For example, of Steen's painting *The Prayer of Tobias and Sarah* he says: "Here we have an ancient action seen in contemporary terms. … He has made a Scriptural love story into a wedding–day spoof and abstracted it out of Biblical time. Love is eternal and the actions that surround it are typically human and for Steen typically humorous" (92).

And this is what is really important for BK's argument: Genre inclusions "serve … as the context of general humanity in which Steen's historical events occur. In their anachronism they symbolize the remarkable continuity and persistence of common life even in the face of great or significant events" (97).

He stresses that it is not anachronism per se that sets Steen apart, for "Anachronism was rife in both sixteenth[-] and seventeenth-century painting" (99). It was Steen's "conscious inclusion in historical scenes of clearly incongruous types and vignettes from contemporary life. … This joining together of incongruities is his means of uniting the high and the low, or better, the elevated and the mundane. Through that union he makes a profound historical statement. History becomes genre in the sense that it is about common human behavior, and genre becomes history in that it is present through historical time" (99).

Then he launches into a remarkable summary:

> Steen chose as a major theme for his historical pictures that passion most open to the mixture of high tragedy and low comedy, and most revealing of human seriousness and folly. Love as the exposure of what is private, love with its titillation of sexual desire, love with its extravagance, love which makes us slaves to our passions and oblivious to the world – love is both elevating and degrading, both poetic and lustful. … For Steen, the lover was always disarmed, revealed by his behavior, open to public jest, and the butt of low humor, even when the love itself might be tragic or destructive. By so placing the great loves in the same context that he might a lovesick girl, or a tavern solicitation, he has put them in a perspective of a universal comedy in which the contemporary and historical are inextricably united. (99–100)

There is a "purposeful irreverence" to Steen's paintings that is "not directed against religion but against the traditional concept of history and history painting. … By breaking the rules of correctness and decorum, by intentionally including sequences out of time and out of place, and by boisterously laughing over the ludicrousness of great actions, … [h]e makes us understand, whether purposefully or not, the artificiality and inhumanness of the grand heroics of much of the history painting of his day" (101).

One senses, in this finale, how much BK not only admires Steen but how much he learned from him, not only about how to think about art, but about how to find the connection between art and life. In fact, in the Preface to the book he revealed how personal was his connection to Steen:

> My interest in Jan Steen as a painter of Biblical and historical narratives began at the Städelsches Kunstinstitut in Frankfurt. It was there that I saw his early painting of *Moses Striking the Rock*. Though I had seen others of his Biblical paintings before that … it was this painting that excited my imagination and curiosity. One detail in particular captured my attention – in the family group at the left, a man bending over places his hand gently on the head of a little girl as he raises a cup to her lips. The girl, seen from the back, drinks eagerly. (n.p.).

The tenderness in that description is touching in itself, but then BK continues: "I was at the time traveling with my wife and small daughter on what was our first and very low-budget trip to Europe. Perhaps it was the painful awareness of our own difficulties that led me to the recognition of that particular motif, and a love of Steen" (n.p.).

I find this statement both moving and informative. It reveals so much about BK: his familiarity with hardship, and not only as a graduate student; how open he was to the connections between art and life, and how appreciative he was of human generosity. At the least, it seems obvious to me that the themes and issues that he will pursue in his later writings, and also in his teachings, are all, in one way or another, to be found in his book on Steen. It may be that if BK was able to claim for Steen his rightful place as a master of what was important in history painting, it was because BK was able to find in Steen's work that which was most meaningful to himself. He dedicated the book, "For Blossom."

CODA

In his Introduction, BK writes, "Our desire must be to discover Steen's vision, and that means a reintegration of his art and his life but without the old moral prejudices" (22). Certainly, he discovered Steen's vision – but did he reintegrate his art and his life? I had anticipated, when I first read this statement, that I would find biographical information about Steen emphatically brought to bear on the paintings. For the most part, however, this was not to be the case.

In fact he reserves, almost to the very end, any direct focus on Steen's life. And even then he achieves this shift by highlighting a subject that is itself anomalous among Steen's religious paintings – because it is taken not from the Old Testament, but from the Gospel of John, and tells of Jesus turning water into wine for guests at a marriage celebration in Cana. BK characterizes Steen as having a "lasting interest in the marriage at Cana, … perhaps from a certain point of view Christ's most questionable miracle" (62).

Steen painted six versions of the marriage at Cana, all of them portraying it obliquely:

> Steen refuses to treat the miracle directly. Though it is not entirely obscured, he loses it in a welter of genre episodes which in their lowness seem to compromise the sacredness of the event. …
>
> The paintings of the miracle actually revolve around the act of drinking in celebration of love. … [I]n these pictures love and drink, or rather love and the act of drinking, are united and sanctified by miracle. The wedding, as Steen understood it, was not more important than the miracle but the ground of its being. (95)

BK describes a number of versions but makes his most extended case for the best known of them, in which Steen "monogrammed the picture IHS on the empty wine-barrel being rolled along by a small boy" (95).

[The] perfectly fitting pun [on Christogram IHS] … too neatly fits the case to be ignored. How appropriate not only for the subject, but for Steen's life as well. Wine and beer must have been important to him. He was first a brewer and later a tavern-owner. … This in itself might explain Steen's love of the subject of the marriage at Cana, for it constitutes a Biblical sanction for purveyance as well as consumption. The "*In Hoc Signo*" pun would indicate that Steen was well aware of the sanction, and used it to his advantage. If this is so, it is yet another indication that through the use of genre vignettes Steen spiced historical subjects with personal concerns, and the reverse as well. That is to say, he used historical events to dramatize personal and contemporary affairs. (95–96)

The entire book, in my opinion, should be read as a demonstration of BK's conviction that to understand the art is to understand the artist – not vice versa, and definitely not one without the other. I think that this conviction goes a long way to explaining his effectiveness as a teacher. Faced with students who viewed art, axiomatically, as self-expression, he turned their focus from themselves to the art. In fact, he used to say: I don't teach students; I teach a subject. Although I intuited his meaning, until I read his book on Steen I did not fully grasp the significance of his laconism.

III

PRIVATE PARTS AND PUBLIC

CONSIDERATIONS (1984)

O F ALL BK'S WRITINGS, his article on the "Private Parts" exhibition of 1978 is the one most intertwined with events at RISD. It is also the one that most directly conveys his engagement with the students and his concern for the making of art. For that reason I am quoting from the article at greater length than might seem warranted by other standards.

BK's article describes an exhibition that is very much of its time. So, in order to define that moment, I begin with a series of overlapping chronologies, constructed variously from facts and recollections, both BK's and my own.

The one that pertains directly to BK spans two decades from 1962, when he first started teaching at RISD, to 1982, when he returned from Rome after a second time there in RISD's European Honors Program (EHP). The 1960s and '70s, as is well known, were a time of antiwar protests, civil rights activism, and general social unrest in the United States, including in Providence and specifically at RISD. In order to clarify the import of some of these larger events for the BK chronology, I first provide a reminder of a small part of what was happening in those two decades. The highlights below are particularly relevant to BK's life:

1954–68 American civil rights movement

1963 John F. Kennedy assassinated, November 22

1965 Malcolm X assassinated, February 21; third Selma-to-
Montgomery march in Alabama, March 21–25

1965–73 U.S. War in Vietnam, with its concomitant conscription

Mid-'60s to mid-'70s Counterculture movement

1967 Anti-Vietnam War March on the Pentagon, October 21

1966–76 Providence Plan to Desegregate the City's Public Schools[1]

1968 Martin Luther King assassinated, April 4; Robert F. Kennedy
assassinated, June 5

---

1 Emilio Abeyta, *School Desegregation in Providence, Rhode Island* (Washington, DC: US Commission on Civil Rights, October 1977), https://files.eric.ed.gov/fulltext/ED166339.pdf.

1969 Family of the Mystic Arts commune in Oregon on cover of
    Life Magazine, July 18; third Harlem Cultural Festival (aka "Black
    Woodstock"),[2] June 29–August 24; Woodstock Festival, August
    15–19
1979 RISD full-time faculty and librarians unionize[3]
1982 RISD unions, full- and part-time, go out on strike, April 5–19[4]

The other thing to keep in mind are the institutional changes that were taking place at RISD, of which BK's hiring was symptomatic. These can be most easily conveyed by a look at the backgrounds of RISD's presidents from John Frazier, who hired him, to Lee Hall, who almost caused him to leave RISD:

1955-62 *John Frazier* was the last of a tradition of RISD presidents
    who were, one might say, of RISD. He had graduated from RISD
    in 1909, eventually became head of the Painting Department, and
    ended his career at the school as president.
1962–68 *Albert Bush-Brown* was a scholar with an established
    reputation as an architectural historian, with a Ph.D. from
    Princeton. He had been on the faculty of various universities,
    including MIT's Architecture Department, before his appointment
    as president.
1969–75 *Talbot Rantoul* came to RISD from Harvard's Business
    School.
1975–82 *Lee Hall* was a painter and professor who had served as
    Dean of Visual Arts at SUNY Purchase.[5]

The variety of backgrounds of these four people reflects what those of us with firsthand knowledge of the Board of Trustees in those years clearly knew: the Trustees wanted change, but they were not sure what that change should look like.

At the time of BK's hiring, RISD was on the cusp of changing from a regional school to one with the national and, eventually, international, reputation it has today. It had been founded in 1877 by Helen Rowe Metcalf and other women associated with Rhode Island's industrial wealth for the purpose of improving the design of the state's manufactured products. The Board of Trustees still retained that connection to local industrial wealth and power. Many of

---

2 See the 2021 documentary film *Summer of Soul (… Or, When the Revolution Could Not Be Televised)*, directed by Questlove.
3 Eileen M. Smith, "RISD Faculty Calls Off Strike upon Settling of Major Issues," *Harvard Crimson,* April 10, 1979, https://www.thecrimson.com/article/1979/4/10/risd-faculty-calls-off-strike-upon/.
4 "Design School Teachers Ratify Pact," UPI Archives, https://www.upi.com/Archives/1982/04/19/Design-school-teachers-ratify-pact/6080388040400/.
5 "History and Tradition: Past Presidents," RISD, https://www.risd.edu/about/history-and-tradition.

them had connections to families that had made their money in the great
Rhode Island industries – textiles, jewelry, machine tool manufacturing, steam
engines – in the century before the Great Depression. (At one time Rhode
Island was the most industrialized state in the country, and Providence was re-
puted to have the highest per capita income of any city.) The ambitions that
the Trustees had for RISD were, I think it fair to say, shaped by this background – in particular, it contributed to their apparent lack of awareness of the
ramifications of efforts to transform RISD by hiring new faculty from prestigious schools.[6] All this would play out in the first two decades of BK's time
there.

Now, with some background established, I can lay out BK's own chronology. I have included in it his RISD milestones and political activism, as well as
some family developments. Overall, I think it shows that in the years between
1962 and 1982 BK was putting out a tremendous amount of principled energy in multiple directions. It also reveals that he sometimes struggled to keep
everything afloat in circumstances where family, institutional, and social and
cultural changes were so interwoven:

1962 BK is appointed to RISD Faculty. Early in his career at RISD,
BK accompanies President Bush-Brown on a fundraising trip to
Philadelphia, suggesting that he was seen as an effective advocate
for liberal arts and for the new direction in which the school was
heading.

1963 BK, Blossom, and their three children move to Providence and
rent a duplex on University Avenue. (There, he gets to know John
Pawlekek and James Drier, two Brown Ph.D. students, who live
around the corner on Lloyd Avenue.)

1965 BK flies, with Drier and Pawlekek, on a Brown University–
chartered Constellation plane (which held seventy-five people or
so), to participate in the third Selma-to-Montgomery civil rights
march.

1965 BK counsels RISD students subject to the draft on
conscientious objector status (Tom Bates, B.F.A. graphic design
1967, later owner of Met Café and the Hot Club,[7] was among
them.)

1966 BK receives his Ph.D. from Harvard.

1967 BK participates in the March on the Pentagon, again with
Drier and Pawlekek, traveling there on a Brown-chartered bus.
BK teaches summer school at St. Augustine's College (an HBCU),
Raleigh, North Carolina, and is Visiting Professor at the University
of Rhode Island.

6 "History and Tradition," RISD, https://www.risd.edu/about/history-and-tradition.
7 "Thomas 'Tom' Bates," obituary, https://www.legacy.com/us/obituaries/providence/
name/thomas-bates-obituary?id=14153970

1967   BK's "Art School Humanities: An Alternative Position" is published in *Art Journal*.

1968   Family buys a house, with help from RISD, located on the northern end of Congdon Street. The house, on the western slope of College Hill, is walking distance to RISD. BK injures his back working on the driveway and is hospitalized. Meanwhile, Providence's desegregation efforts cause turmoil in schools, including in their new neighborhood.

1969–71   Family moves to Rome and lives in an apartment in Campo de' Fiori. BK serves as Director of the European Honors Program at RISD, which had just moved to the Palazzo Cenci. He is selected for this position by RISD faculty member Gil Franklin, the sculptor and Rome Prize winner who founded and ran the program.[8] BK acquired a fine-grained knowledge of the art dispersed in churches and other places throughout the city, and an ability to speak Italian not fluently but with convincing style and accent.

1971   "Primitivism and Impossible Art" is published in *Art Journal*.

1972   Blossom receives her M.A. from Brown.

1973–77   Close friends join the Family of the Mystic Arts commune in Oregon, and through them BK and his family develop connections to the commune, traveling cross-country to visit on multiple occasions. (Some of Mystic Arts' remarkable buildings are still extant – including the centralized gathering place built of logs, with slabs of benching along the walls, facing an open fire pit.)

1975–79   BK serves as chair of the Division of Liberal Arts.

1976   Blossom receives her Ph.D. in English from Brown.

1977   BK's Jan Steen book is published.

1978   The exhibition "Private Parts" opens on May 12 and is raided by police on May 15.[9]

1978?   BK runs afoul of President Lee Hall when he resists her efforts to open a RISD offshoot in New Mexico, to be staffed with faculty from Providence, thus decimating the full-time faculty. Told he will never be promoted, he applies to be provost at Massachusetts College of Art. Although awarded the position, he chooses to stay at RISD after all, in part because he doesn't want to live in Boston.

1979   When the full-time faculty and librarians unionize, BK finds himself caught between activist Liberal Arts faculty members,

---

8   "Artist Biography & Facts: Gilbert Franklin," askART, https://www.askart.com/artist/ Gilbert_A_Franklin/10018589/Gilbert_A_Franklin.aspx.

9   Laurie McDonald, *Private Parts*, video, 1978. https://www.lauriemcdonald.net/private-parts.html. McDonald was a RISD student at time.

who use the division's mimeograph machine for protest flyers,
and the provost, a Lee Hall supporter, who then commandeers
the machine. As a result of these events, BK's position as division
chair becomes untenable, and he resigns.

1980 BK is made full professor (after all).

1981–82 BK and Blossom return to Rome, where BK serves again
as Director of EHP – in part taking the post to get away from
RISD, where his position is still fraught.

1982 RISD faculty go on strike against several Lee Hall policies:
her firing of outspoken faculty; her efforts to remake the school
with a few star faculty, the remainder being part-time; and her
requirement that faculty get permission to have outside work,
which was anathema to studio faculty, many of whom were hired
due to their reputations as active artists and designers.

This chronology reveals quite clearly, I think, that BK was engaged and successful at RISD; that he took part in some of the most important political actions of the time, and not just at RISD; that he had a formidable amount of
energy; and that he continued, after his dissertation, to write, but only inter-
mittently, and now about material more directly related to his teaching. It also
shows how difficult circumstances could be when diverse interests and responsibilities collided.

THE ARTICLE

BK's article "Private Parts and Public Considerations," which was published as
the lead article in (appropriately enough) the photography journal *Exposure* in
1984, might be read as his testament to the Wild West atmosphere at RISD at
the end of the 1970s.[10] Never again, I think I am right in saying, would RISD
students and faculty be able, or willing, to be so unconstrained.

Although he seems at first to be simply reporting on, or even relishing,
this "minor and somewhat frivolous event," in fact, as with "Piss and Light,"
the tone of his writing provides the key to his attitude and depth of engagement (6.1). My discussion below mirrors BK's tripartite structure and section
headings.

1. *The Exhibition and the Raid*

The exhibition "Private Parts" was, BK acknowledges, a provocation. It "contained photographs (mostly) and works in other media which addressed that

---

10 Baruch D. Kirschenbaum, "Private Parts and Public Considerations," *Exposure* 22, no. 3
(Fall 1984): 5–21.

theme. Most, but not all, were explicitly sexual and/or anatomical" (5.1–2). How the exhibition came about, however, suggests a snowballing of incremental decisions: It began as

> a project of students in [RISD's] Photography Department. Intending a show with a thematic basis, two senior students proposed an independent study project to the faculty of the department. They wanted to organize and mount a show that would be a collective effort, involving as many people in the department as cared to be involved. With department support the independent study project turned into a departmental effort. The theme exhibition which became "Private Parts" gradually grew more ambitious, however, when its call for submissions extended beyond the department and even beyond the College. (6.2)

Note how BK's laconic tone suggests that such an ad hoc event was in no way out of the ordinary at RISD. Nor was it, given the artistic and political climate of the times.

In fact, if BK's reporting is to be believed, even the theme of the exhibition seems to have been just a fortuity: "It is not clear, even to the principals involved, how or exactly when they arrived at the theme of private parts for the exhibition. Once suggested however, it was enthusiastically adopted" (6.2). Here his use of an anonymous passive voice amplifies the sense of the ad hoc happening of things.

Then BK goes on to enumerate the appeal of this choice of the theme: "It seemed provocative in subject, open to inventive interpretation, both personal and broadly social; and had the capacity to carry a charge which might elicit response outside the boundaries of the art community" (6.2). Phrased this way, it isn't clear to whom all this was so apparent – the students? the photography department faculty? BK himself?

But it turns out there were major, apparently unforeseen, consequences to this choice of theme:

> Though there was some inkling that in selecting the private-parts theme, the organizers were approaching risky ground, no one anticipated that the show would lead to a police raid and legal action. The exhibition was not mounted to provoke such action nor to challenge the new [state obscenity] legislation, which had been signed into law two days before the show opened and which nobody involved knew about beforehand. (6.2–7.1)

No matter that the exhibition was provocative: the brouhaha over it was more than anyone bargained for.

This, then, is what the article is (mostly) about: how events coalesced that led to reactions so disproportionate to the exhibition itself. To attempt to explain this, BK launches into a report on some key developments, starting with the student advertisement: "Flyers soliciting material presented dictionary definitions of the two words of the title.... At the bottom, this flyer invited submissions of works of 'ANY SIZE ANY MEDIUM ANY THING ANYONE ANY PRIVATE ANY PART', and gave the assurance 'ALL WORK WILL BE SHOWN ANONYMOUSLY'" (7.1–2).

BK acknowledges that the flyer enhanced the riskiness: "Despite the range of possible non-sexual interpretations, most submissions, though by no means all, picked up on the sexual innuendo of the theme and its advertisement. The exhibition's title and the promised freedom of anonymity certainly encouraged that trend and thereby helped to establish the sexual orientation of the show" (7.2-8.1).

He goes on to underscore the implications of the promised anonymity:

> Anonymity, of course, implies that there may be something to hide, some reason for public concealment of identity. Indeed the organizers felt that under cover of anonymity, those submitting works would be freer in their attitudes and in possible self-display.... Like the black strips placed across the eyes of naked figures in anatomical texts, anonymity served to intensify the privacy of the parts revealed. The anonymity principle (if it can be called that) accorded with the exhibitionist/voyeurist appeal of the theme. (8.1)

Having established that the students seemed to get the submissions they anticipated, BK goes on to discuss more specifically the exhibition itself:

> The submissions – there were about 160 of them – were brought to the gallery and the show laid out on the floor in groupings ... derived from the material: the funky/comic, the conceptual, the high aesthetic, the animal theme, the kinky theme, etc.... The result was an uneven show in terms of quality, but one full of the vigor of collective effort. ... [W]ith an emphasis more in indirectness than directness the show fulfilled both its thematic and collaborative intentions. (8.1-2)

The images that illustrate the article bears this out.

BK's tone so far is notably restrained, giving little sense from paragraph to paragraph of where things are going, thus contributing to the suspense, as it were, of his narrative. He reveals that the show actually was not even hung on campus: "Because of sensitive material and late arrangements – it is still not clear which was determinant – 'Private Parts' was not shown in the College gallery. Instead it was hung a short walk away from the College, in a large loft gallery operated by a local video group" (8.2).

The curated works were not the only ones in the show:

> One piece became an analogy of the whole show in both tone and content. Near the entrance to the gallery visitors could enter a Polaroid photo booth. There, for a quarter, they could individually or in concert photograph whatever they considered to be their private parts.

> Results were push-pinned on the wall outside the booth as an on-go-
> ing assemblage. The mode of the Polaroids was a clowning exhibition
> of genitals, buttocks, navels, underarms, ear canals, and so forth. (9.1)

This photo booth would play an outsized role in subsequent developments.

In his discussion of the content of the show BK alludes to the police raid, but still only in passing because he is not done talking about the exhibition: "Near the entrance also were posted blow-ups of the list of contributors; the dictionary definitions of 'private' and 'part' ...; and three other quotations [p]ertinent to the theme of the show" (9.2). He quotes them in full, interestingly without commenting on them. Aside from a fragment from the third of them, I cite here only the works from which they were taken: Charles Albrecht, *You and Your Wonderful House,* 1923; William James, *The Varieties of Religious Experience,* 1902; and Ludwig Wittgenstein, *Philosophical Investigations,* 1953. The Wittgenstein quote is among those pieces of the exhibition, like the photo booth, that will surface later: "'And is there not also the case where we play and – make up the rules as we go along? And there is even one where we alter them – as we go along'" (10.1). Taken together, these quotations, although BK does not say so at this point, seem to have functioned as a lens for looking at the images, one that simultaneously both exonerated the artists and implicated the viewers.

The quotations close BK's discussion of the exhibition per se. When he turns to the initial response to it, his tone changes dramatically: "The *Providence Journal/Bulletin* article which appeared the day following the opening ... was headlines [*sic*] 'RISD show lets you see things you usually don't.' The reporter closed the review by saying 'Unless somebody blows the whistle, the show will continue through Wednesday.... It's open to the public'" (10.1–2). He calls out the *Pro Jo*'s reporting for what it clearly was: "The headline, to use D. H. Lawrence's description of the prurient, tickled the dirty little secret. The final lines of the article suggested adverse reaction and even the possible closing of the exhibition"(10.2).

BK continues: "Thomas Pearlman, a Providence City Councilman, threatened, on the strength of the article alone (for he had not seen the show), to have ... [RISD's] tax-exempt status reviewed and revoked. He called for police action against the show" (10.2). And he quotes Pearlman directly, "'[The show] is definitely not educational. It's prurient in nature and destructive. [The show] was much more serious [in effect] than are adult bookstores. When you have so-called educators mis-directing our youths in that direction, it's much more serious than a guy in the back alley'" (11.1; BK's interpolations).

This is the old town–gown split, and as BK underscores, the school itself was well and truly implicated. It was a question of "who gets away with what and under what conditions of privilege" (11.1). And he nails down the point by quoting Providence police chief Angelo Ricci, who "expressed his antagonism as directly and clearly as Pearlman: 'I think it's wrong. These people

[RISD students and faculty] think they can do whatever they want to, and I don't agree.... If it's obscene, it's obscene. There are no two ways about it'" (11.1; BK's interpolations).

BK reserves his most scathing words for RISD's administrators' response:

> Administrators of the School of Design responded as patly as Pearlman and the police. President Lee Hall, through a spokeswoman, denied all institutional association with the exhibition. She made this disclaimer despite the attack against the students and faculty and despite the unjust impugning of the College's standing in the community and its educational purposes. The denial was a lie. "Private Parts" had emerged from College activities and had received both academic and financial support from the Photography Department, whose head came under threat of arrest once the warrant that led to the raid was issued. (11.1)

This is a blistering denunciation, and reads as if BK had written it in the heat of the moment, even though, by the time of the article, some years had passed, and Lee Hall was no longer president. That he chose not to tone down his outrage, and even doubled down on it, says a lot about his sense of not only the scale of the betrayal but the importance of the issues at stake:

> With Pearlman's outrage, Ricci's condemnation, the School of Design's disclaimer, and the media's attention, all the elements were in place for a raid.... Ironically, on May 16th, the day of the raid, the School of Design's Board of Trustees was meeting. While the trustees lunched up the hill, the police were confiscating the work of students and faculty down the hill. After the raid, trustees and officials at the College seemed unconcerned that the police had acted illegally and selectively, and that the law itself might be unconstitutional, and police operations of this kind could subvert the functions of an art school. (11.1–2)

The exhibition may have been "minor and somewhat frivolous" (6.1), but the fallout from it was anything but. From BK's perspective the response to it had exposed the fecklessness of those entrusted with protecting the intellectual and educational reputation of the school. Most immediately, however, it led to the exhibition being raided by the police under the new state obscenity legislation and works of art in the exhibit being confiscated.[11] The confiscations would, in turn, lead to a class-action suit by some of the exhibitors against the city and police. During this next stage, BK would choose to take an active part.

2. The Legal Action

BK devotes five-plus pages, roughly a third of the whole article, to an account of the legal issues involved. Taken in full, his discussion of the court case reveals

---

11 In McDonald's video (see n. 9), Blossom can be seen engaging one of the policemen.

how immersed he was in the legal strategy of the plaintiffs, and how appalled he was by the defendants' cavalier violation of the exhibitors' rights. It is fascinating enough to cover at length here:

> [E]ight exhibitors joined on behalf of all the exhibitors … to regain seized work, to recover damages, and to test constitutionality of the new law. The case, brought to the Federal Court …, was accepted under that jurisdiction because the plaintiffs claimed infringement of their constitutional rights…. The Providence chapter of the American Civil Liberties Union supplied [an attorney]…. (12.1)

> On the strength of their [the plaintiffs'] arguments, [Judge Raymond] Pettine [on May 22] issued a ten-day order prohibiting further action by police pending a hearing for preliminary injunction, set for June first. The police were ordered to return all seized work within twenty-four hours and to refrain from interfering with the exhibition of either seized or unseized materials. In other words, the show might be re-hung if the plaintiffs desired. The pieces were returned, some in damaged state beyond casual abuse; but the show was not re-hung. (12.1)

On June 1st hearings began for the preliminary injunction:

> Plaintiffs' lawyers presented to the court three main arguments: (1) that the police had violated the terms of the law they were purporting to uphold, and in doing so had denied plaintiffs' constitutional rights of due process; (2) that the material of the exhibition was legitimate art despite its sexual content and therefore not actionable under the obscenity statute; and (3) that if the statute could be construed to apply to the works exhibited it was over-broad and therefore unconstitutional. Only the first two arguments were presented…. (12.1–2)

At this point in his account BK veers to discuss the 1973 Supreme Court decision in *Miller v. California*. This 5–4 decision

> turned over policy on obscenity to local communities…. At the same time the court offered guidelines on obscenity which might be used in the framing local statutes: whether the average person, applying contemporary community standards would find that the work, taken as a whole, appeals to prurient interest; whether the work depicts or describes, in a patently offensive way, sexual conduct specifically defined by state law; whether the work, again taken as a whole, lacks serious artistic, political or scientific value. (12.2–13.1)

In parsing the implications of *Miller* for the plaintiffs, he stresses that "it is not the subject itself which is crucial, but its treatment" (13.1).

BK then goes on at length to enumerate the facts by which the state obscenity law, the warrant issued by the district judge granting the police authority to raid the exhibition, and the actions of the police who closed it down were all found to have violated the plaintiffs' rights to due process. He is particularly incensed by what he takes as police ignorance and bad faith, as shown by police misrepresentation of the photo booth: "In his affidavit in application for the warrant, [Lieutenant Paul] Yacovone stated that 'A charge of twenty-five [*sic*] (25¢) for Polaroid photos were [*sic*] solicited.' The implication was that the charge constituted commercial gain and was therefore grounds for the action" (14.1; all BK's interpolations). As BK sums up their ham-fistedness: "As the hearings demonstrated, the police blundered on just about every procedure the law requires. Thereby they denied the plaintiffs legal protection. It would seem, then, that they enforced not the law but their own prejudice: to close the show" (15.1).

But "to prove artist merit of 'Private Parts'" (15.1) – the second argument, which the plaintiffs needed to win to secure a preliminary injunction – was still to be argued. Here BK, in his explanation, gets to return to home turf, that is, to the works themselves:

> The lawyer for the police … argued that the seized material was meant for sexual arousal and was pornographic; it did not therefore have any serious artistic value and should have been confiscated. The plaintiffs' lawyer argued that the works were by art students, faculty, and independent artists; that the show as a whole had serious artistic and thematic content and should have enjoyed the protection of the law." (15.1)

To make their case, he reports "the plaintiffs individually testified to the artistic intentions of their own works and to the seriousness of the themes in the exhibition as a whole. The quotations mounted with the show were introduced as evidence to indicate philosophical concerns of the organizers and participants" (15.1–2). But BK goes on to say, with unexpected sympathy, "In the drive to establish the show's artistic intention, the Polaroid 'do-it-yourself' photo-booth became a stumbling-block. The judge, in a real dilemma, wanted to know how a bunch of Polaroid snapshots of people exposing themselves, pinned as a collection on the wall, could possibly constitute a work of art" (15.2). Note that BK has not quoted the judge directly but paraphrased him, as if he himself were entering into Judge Pettine's quandary.

His tone is all part of BK's setup: "To answer the question, William Parker, Professor of Art at University of Connecticut, photographer and photo-historian, one of whose photo-paintings of a male nude had been seized and damaged by the police, and who himself was a plaintiff, was introduced and accepted as an expert witness" (15.2). Of course, all this credentialing suggest BK's endorsement of Parker's testimony:

> In defense of the assemblage and the exhibition as a whole he explained to the court the idea behind process art…. He spoke about Duchampian aesthetics and conceptual art, and how they challenge the

idea of set pieces worked over in a traditional artistic manner. In other words, he put the show and its most disturbing inclusion in the context of developments in recent art theory and practice. (15.2)

After Parker's testimony and that of other plaintiffs,

the city indicated it was willing to let matters rest and to accept a preliminary injunction. The plaintiffs, however, insisted that as part of the injunction they and those in the class they represented be free to exhibit the works seized and others like them and to offer them for sale without threat of harassment or prosecution pending the outcome of the actual trial. The city refused those conditions and the hearing continued on that issue. (15.2)

Clearly the plaintiffs had the bit in their teeth, and now, to mix my metaphors, it was BK's turn at the plate.

The thrust of the argument shifted now to demonstrate that sexual content itself, however explicit, could not be used to discredit representations as works of art. As an art historian I was asked by the plaintiffs' lawyers to prepare a series of slides of historically and critically accepted works of art with sexually explicit content. I put together some forty slides, which I reviewed with the lawyers prior to possible courtroom presentation. (15.2–16.1)

In BK's account, what unfolded sounds almost comedic:

However, before I was to present that material, Yacovone was questioned on the stand as to the criteria for his choices of works to be removed. When it emerged from his testimony that he went mostly on the basis of genital exposure whether or not it was close up or could be considered lewd, I was asked to make a briefer presentation of well known works in which genitals were clearly shown. (16.1)

BK's tone is quite blasé at this point: "I chose the usual 'masterpieces' – classical sculpture, Donatello, Michelangelo, Ingres, etc. – and presented the material … to apparent disappointment of Pettine, who indicated that he and everybody else was aware of all that." (16).

At the judge's prompting BK got to show some more provocative examples:

[Pettine] asked whether I didn't have anything else more to the point. On his invitation, then, I elaborated. I showed paleolithic fertility objects; Greek vases with erotic painting; Roman phallic charms; Mochica pottery from Peru; Hindu sculpture; Rembrandt etchings, Boucher paintings; works by Picasso, Bellmer, Klimt, Schiele, and others; and photography works by Samaras, Arbus, Lazorik. At my conclusion, Pettine called some of it 'pretty wild' and more than a little surprising in

> its extent. He was satisfied also [I love the "also"] that all the pieces
> were or had been on display in museums or galleries. (16.1)

But BK was not done on the witness stand: The plaintiffs' lawyer then "posed some questions the general purpose of which was to elicit from me a distinction between art and pornography" (16.1). And now BK recaps the theory that he used to reinforce the plaintiffs' case:

> My argument was based on context. That is, I submitted that the context in which a thing appears can alter purpose and therefore effect. What is base, or ordinary, or common, or even patently offensive, changes when its context invites aesthetic or intellectual contemplation. Context, I argued, with Duchampian logic, transforms function. Art, even when it features explicitly sexual material, transcends its potential prurience by the fact of its identification as art, which implies seriousness of intent if not serious value. (16.1)

BK pointed "especially to the Wittgenstein statement, which raises questions about the rules by which people conduct their lives" (16.1–2).

BK ends his report on his testimony with a paraphrase of Judge Pettine's testing of

> the consistency of my argument. Singling out my premise that context, because it can alter purpose and effect, determines prurience, he asked whether, in my opinion, if some materials from "Private Parts" appeared in a "girlie magazine" (his term), they could be taken as prurient. I answered that that might well be the case…. Pettine seemed satisfied with that position and its rationale. (16.2)

BK then reported the results:

> The hearing lasted most of five days….[Pettine] granted the preliminary injunction as argued for by the plaintiffs, included their continued right to exhibit the works and to offer them for sale even while further legal action was pending. Accepting the argument that content is controlling he added the proviso that pieces could be shown only 'in an art gallery, art show, art festival, art exhibit or art museum.' (16.2–17.1)

BK ends "The Legal Action" section of the article on a triumphant note: "In short, the city's case was a total failure" (17.1).

BK's account of the exhibition and the trial shows the depth and extent of his commitment to the larger issues and intellectual responsibilities that he felt came with teaching at RISD. Nothing had compelled him to become involved in the legal case. The exhibition had nothing to do with the art history department. He did have friends whose work was confiscated. But, more important, he told me he got involved because "the police should not be allowed to get away with confiscating the work. I wanted to help get the works back." Once involved, judging from the article, he was totally engaged and extremely effective as an expert witness.

3. Reconsiderations

If "Private Parts and Public Considerations" had ended with BK's account of the trial, it would stand as a document of a particular moment at RISD, in which he himself, at one point, played a leading role. However, his motivation for writing the article was not only to document the controversial events but to use his account of the exhibition, the raid, and the legal proceedings as a background for a still larger issue.

Although, in fact, BK revealed his motivation for writing the article at its start, I withheld his statement until now. For my purposes, I did not want it to color BK's remarkable discussion about the exhibition and the trial.

The second paragraph of his two-paragraph introduction plainly stated his larger intent:

> Two factors have moved me to write about the "Private Parts" case and my role in it. First, though a minor and somewhat frivolous event in itself, the show and case that followed raised disturbing questions about relationships among art and prurience and law. Second, while my testimony seemed effective enough in court, it left me feeling ill at ease with the position I had taken and with my arguments in support of that position. (6.1)

What discomfited him about his testimony, it turns out, was that he had ducked the issue of prurience. In his words, "What nagged at me was the suspicion that in assessing the show the cops in some way might have been right. 'Private Parts' had in fact based its appeal upon prurience – whether or not that prurience was actionable under law" (17.1).

The rest of the article then is BK's remarkable refutation of the very argument he had made to such effect before Judge Pettine: "The main premise of the argument on context is that context can change both the purpose and effect of what is presented" (17.1). The problem with that argument, he states, is that it "implies that the nature of an object is not fixed, but can sometimes be (or mean) one thing and under different circumstances something else entirely" (17.1).

For BK this question is not simply an abstract philosophical issue but one that has major implications for the very definition of art:

> An attendant argument is that art, by force of seriousness of intent and its concern with form, redeems or transcends its own content.... It would follow, as suggested in the law itself and in the Supreme Court decisions upon which it is based, that there are two mutually exclusive

categories of things, one of which we call art, the other pornography. (17.1–2)

Note his use of the phrase "we call art." He then states the obvious more directly: "Through such an intellectual and legalistic construct we defend art from possible profanation and restriction, and pornography from elevation above its usually accepted station in life" (17.2).

BK then goes on to argue against such easy binaries, paraphrasing the scholar Morse Peckham to note that "the categories of art and pornography are not mutually exclusive; they are independent categories. Therefore, as Peckham says, that the attributes of one apply does not mean that the attributes of the other cannot also apply" (17.2–18.1).[12] BK restates this even more bluntly: "Art then can be pornographic, and pornography can be artistic" (18.1).

Having laid out his position, BK then reinforces it with a discussion of various works of art with sexually explicit content. He then asserts that responses to such content are based not only on context but on circumstance:

Response to sexual description or representation varies from person to person, from mood to mood, and from place to place. Some situations, or contexts, may inspire direct sexual responses; others may inhibit them.... Differences in response do not, however, change the nature of the material or its capacity to excite. No more does the context in which the material appears or the seriousness of its associated themes. (18.1)

Thus the real issue for BK is not prurience per se but the categories of pornography and obscenity.

In this I now seem to side with Yacovone, who maintained that after thirty years as a cop he knew perfectly well what was and wasn't obscene.... Unlike ... Yacovone, however, I do not oppose prurient content in art. Nor do I equate pornography with obscenity, ... as is often done by those who claim to uphold public morals. I take "pornography" as a descriptive term and "obscenity" as judgmental. (18.1–2)

BK then tries out different descriptive terms, "erotica" and "soft-core and hard-core," as if to allow for more nuanced labels (19.1). But he acknowledges these also fail to make the problem go away. And now he gets to the heart of his position:

The main reason for problems over the relationship between art and pornography is that art, even modern art with its questionable reputation, has been elevated as an absolute good in society.... We are urged

---

12 BK cites Morse Peckham, *Art and Pornography* (New York: Basic Books, 1969) in a number of footnotes. Taken together, it is clear that BK is not writing off the cuff but has reached his positions through research on the most recent literature on art, obscenity, pornography, and the law.

> to venerate it – sometimes idolatrously…. Pornography, on the other hand, gets only private support and is considered, in public dictum, if not an absolute evil then certainly a serious social problem…. Since it is impossible to suppress pornography because it is in continual demand, … it is most often controlled through negation. Pornography becomes taboo. (19.1–2)

Notice the tone he uses to distance himself from both positions.

BK then asserts that art must be allowed to have prurient content if it is to use its power to counter society's hypocrisies: "When art adopts prurient iconography usually linked with pornography, it takes that iconography out of its assigned frame. It presents it as respectable…. [I]t challenges that taboo with the power, the endorsement, of its own legitimacy as art" (20.1).

BK, after laying out his position, turns the lens of this argument back on his testimony at the "Private Parts" hearing:

> The main residual meaning of "Private Parts" inheres precisely in its prurience. To neutralize that prurience, as I did in court by an argument on context … is to destroy that potential meaning. It is, so to speak, when things get tough, one can hide behind the protective skirts of art as an inviolate, autonomous, and self-justifying activity…. The thrust of "Private Parts" was to challenge artistic loftiness through engagement with a charged theme based upon common experience. The show flaunted exposure, teased conventional distinctions between image and actuality, and invited redefinitions of what should be called decent and respectable. But its good humor was not appreciated by those who are already quite sure of … their own standards of decency and respectability – and who do not wish the question reopened. (20.2–21.1)

BK, speaking once of his teaching, said to me, "I try to present the material as honestly and openly as possible." This article is an exemplary manifestation of his intellectual integrity. And his closing paragraph is a final exercise in self-examination:

> Reconsideration of my role in the "Private Parts" case leaves this quandary. I now consider my testimony fallacious, mistaken; but the outcome of the case I consider right. "Private Parts" should never have been raided and indeed was protected under the law used to attack it. … There was no reason to argue that its status as art altered its content or possible effects of that content. Were I asked again to testify in such a case, I would have to take the position that to deny prurience on the basis of context would be to deny the nature of the particular material. (21.1)

Why is this so important to him? The answer is predictable: "Such testimony might not help the plaintiff, but it would help focus concern where it belongs. And where it belongs, in my estimation, is on the actual life-content of works of art whatever that might be, unprotected by special status or the circumlocutions of criticism and defense. Without such awareness art loses its effective power" (21.1).

"Private Parts and Public Considerations" was, then, never really about the events surrounding the exhibition, or his part in them; it was always already about the power of art. The article is of a piece with his earlier rehabilitation of Jan Steen's history paintings and foretells his piece about Serrano's "Piss Christ." BK is steadfast in his commitment to this idea: Art is never separate from life but revelatory of it; that is its power — and that is so even for the art made for the "minor and somewhat frivolous" exhibition "Private Parts."

IV

A DIVERGENT VIEW ON ART SCHOOL
HUMANITIES (1967)

Lᴵᴷᴱ ʜɪꜱ ᴀʀᴛɪᴄʟᴇ ᴏɴ ᴛʜᴇ "Private Parts" exhibition, this one, on art school pedagogy, is directly related to BK's experience working at RISD. However, here his concerns address a matter that was not, as it were, thrust upon him, but that had engaged him from the moment he came to teach at RISD.

His article "A Divergent View on Art School Humanities," published in the *Art Journal* in 1967, is his declaration about what the role of the liberal arts in an art school should be. When I first glanced at the title, I thought this three-page piece might have been "commissioned" by RISD's administration to make a case for the uniqueness of its curriculum. However, it is not that at all. "A Divergent View" does not challenge an established approach to teaching humanities in art schools. Rather, it is a direct response to an article published in *Art Journal* just two issues earlier. The claims made in that article, "A New Approach to Teaching Humanities in an Art School" by Kenneth Lash, chair of the Humanities Program at the San Francisco Art Institute (SFIA), are what BK aggressively takes on in "A Divergent View."[1]

BK's purpose in the article is to make the case that RISD's humanities program is a more useful model than the new one of SFIA touted by Lash. It thus might seem that BK would be under distinct constraints here, hemmed in, as he is, by having to respond to both Lash's text and RISD's program. Yet somehow he manages to write an article that reveals a lot about his own approach both to the material and to the students he taught at RISD.

BK appears, at first, quite deferential to Kenneth Lash, which would seem appropriate given that BK was only an assistant professor at the time, while Lash was not only considerably older, having been born in 1918, but also head of the SFIA humanities department. He begins by introducing himself to readers:

---

1 Baruch D. Kirschenbaum, "A Divergent View on Art School Humanities," *Art Journal* 27.2 (1967): 166-67, 175, is his rejoinder to Kenneth Lash, "A New Approach to Teaching Humanities in an Art School," *Art Journal* 26.3 (1967): 252–56. Quotations for each are identified by both page and column number.

"For five years I have taught in and helped shape the humanities program at Rhode Island School of Design" (166.1). He does not mention his Harvard Ph.D. (which he was awarded just the year before) and which would have boosted his credentials vis à vis Lash, who had only an M.A. He also doesn't say that he was hired by RISD to help remake the humanities curriculum, or that he is an art historian. (Lash was a professor of literature.) Even at the start of his career, BK seems to have assumed that it was his ideas and work ethic that gave him value, not his credentials per se. (In my experience, it was only when he wore his crimson robe and Ph.D. hood in academic processions, or when he quipped, in some unlikely context, that he had "a Harvard-trained eye," that BK might reveal his Harvard connection.)

At the start, and scattered throughout the article, BK seems at some pains to state his areas of agreement with Lash. He seconds Lash's view that at art schools, as compared with liberal arts colleges, "the amount of time devoted to the humanities ... is fractional." He states also that "art school students, as Mr. Lash recognizes, often demand a personal significance in what is required of them" (166.1).

But his points of agreement more often are launching pads for BK's quite strident objections to the SFIA program, as in this early passage: "In short [in Lash's words] 'little less than a cultural history of the world' is to be given in a four-year sequence of courses taught in concert by several instructors and visiting lecturers. He presents this program as experimental. The goal might be called total education" (166.1). BK's skepticism about these claims is palpable.

He goes on to give an extended quotation from Lash's description of the teaching of Homer:

> [I]nstead of studying Homer in a course called Western Literature, the student will come upon him in the midst of a series of interrelated lectures on early Greek history, society, religion and mythology, art, ancient science. Furthermore he will have worked his way to this point through a [*sic*] study of prehistory and of whatever major civilization [*sic*] predate the Greek. Thus the linear effect of cumulated learning is given full scope, yet this learning is at each moment being achieved by study in depth, by organic examination of cultural objects and events in context. (166.1 [Lash 253.1])

BK is having none of it: "[W]hat we have here, though Mr. Lash understandably avoids the term, is a cross-disciplinary survey. Such a course, I protest, has to be only a collection of necessary generalizations with glimpses of a rapid scattering of items and data: a cultural patchwork stitched together into the pattern of classical civilization. Claims for study in depth cannot be convincingly defended" (166.2).

BK then directly accuses Lash of obfuscating the real nature of the SFIA program: "'The linear effect of cumulated learning' is just another way of noting the traditional chronological development" (166.2). He seems particularly exasperated by Lash's refusal to call the curriculum a survey: "The whole program, it seems to me, is a sequence of surveys strung together chronologically. Surveys are surveys by any name. When cross-disciplinary they are likely to suffer even more from the shortcomings of condensation" (166.2).

BK is troubled not by surveys per se; in fact, he declares, "I have no argument here with such courses" (166.2). Further along in the article he even uses the term "survey" to describe the foundation courses of RISD's own liberal arts program – which was revised in 1962, the year that he came to RISD: "In recognition of the need for a general cultural background, freshmen and sophomores are required to take a cultural survey similar to that described by Mr. Lash. Given in two years rather than in four, the program has a coverage less ambitious. Deliberately the emphasis is placed on art history, literature, and philosophical ideas" (167.2).

His characterization of SFIA's four-year program as "a rapid scattering of items and data" was not just flip; it reveals BK's aversion to the very idea of a college liberal arts program constructed as just one long survey. In his view, survey courses might be necessary as a foundation for a liberal arts program in an art school, but they were hardly sufficient.

BK makes very clear what he thinks the SFIA program that Lash touts is lacking: "Specialized courses are my concern here" (166.2). And I think "here" should be taken not merely in the context of this article but as *here,* where he stands as a teacher:

> Whether taught to art students or anyone else, they are not *ipso facto* irrelevant, dull, or useless. They serve notice that things can be studied critically in depth for themselves, and that most areas have internal histories which can be separated from broader considerations, and that men [*sic*] of spirit and intelligence have sometimes spent their lives in pursuit of what might appear to be minor considerations, especially when viewed from the panoramic perspective of human culture. Cumulative knowledge [BK will have nothing to do with "cumulated" used as an adjective] originates in meticulous endeavor. The seven-league-boots approach[, which in contrast covers too much territory too fast,] ignores all that; and I feel that it is important and even exciting to learn some new things in detail, to acquire some more specialized knowledge, and to grapple with the intricacies of a subject. (166.2)

This statement suggests one of the reasons that made BK such an effective teacher and advocate for liberal arts at RISD: he believed unequivocally that specialized liberal arts courses could engage art and design students, and he designed courses to do just that. (I discuss his courses more directly when I consider his article "Primitivism and Impossible Art" in Chapter V.)

But "specialized courses" are not, for BK, only goods in themselves. He values them as an antidote against the lure of "total education," which is what he sees Lash as offering: "It is disheartening after a while to see things always in the context of broader themes, always in terms of other things, always nicely syllabized for their place in the overall picture and in total education" (167.1). He considers this trend as bad pedagogically because it tends "to give students a false sense of security about the nature of historical reality" (167.1). More significant, he views it as intellectually suspect, if not dangerous: "Some things just don't connect. For the most part we simply leave them out, but sometimes in our eagerness for order we give them Procrustean treatment and come out with mutilated truth. History is an immense tangle, and it is presumptuous and misleading to give the impression that we can untangle it by the coherence of our survey syllabi" (167.1).

It becomes clear later on that BK objects to total education in part because he sees it as symptomatic of trends in the larger culture: "I know that in this age of totalism (total thought, total nourishment, total entertainment) and the big experience (the car ride that's more than a car ride, the insight that's more than an insight) – in this age of totalism, diversity and complexity are frowned upon. That may be reason enough to pursue and conserve them." (167.2) BK's capacity to see the big picture and his predilection for resisting the intellectual moment made him, at once, a disruptive force in the academy and a particularly compelling teacher for art school students.

But before he gets to totalism, BK first bluntly sums up his objections to Lash's claims for the SFIA curriculum:

> My objection, then, to the program as described by Mr. Lash, is that it pretends to accomplish more than it can, and to be more than it is, and that in its broadness it necessarily ignores much of the depth required for advanced learning. The use of the word "experimental" will just not alter survey education into thorough education – if such can be said to exist. On that score also much of what Mr. Lash describes as experimental is really quite common. Cross-disciplinary humanities is an old idea; the chronological organization by semester is as traditional as you can get.... The only thing that is new perhaps is the extension of a usually shorter introductory program into a four-year sequence and the attempt to make it an all-in-one educational package. (167.1)

BK is still not done with his attack on Lash's claims. After a three-paragraph interval in which he summarizes the structure of RISD's liberal arts program, listing a few titles of the specialized courses (none of which are his), he shifts his focus to Lash's attitude toward the students themselves. Again he starts out agreeing with Lash:

> In his article Mr. Lash is also at some pains to describe the art students at San Francisco. His description fits those in Providence as well. He sees them as a new breed of disaffected, alienated young, mistrustful of their culture and their elders, but eager to grab what "gets" to them. Often, ... they are antagonistic to required liberal studies, feeling that

they interfere with their deep studio involvement, and that these studies furthermore tend to be overly analytical. (167.2)

BK grants the accuracy of this characterization:"The description is a good one,
and it is refreshing to hear some praise for these students' directness, their energy, and their willingness to engage in what is relevant to them" (167.2, 175.1).

And yet, once again, BK agrees only to set up a strenuous objection:

> For all that I agree here with Mr. Lash and share his enthusiasms, there
> is another side of the matter which also needs mentioning. Often in
> their freedom these students are pitifully lost without discipline in a sar-
> gasso of dripping subjectivity. They mistake their own instantaneous re-
> actions for "vital" (a student word) responses, as though the less thought
> one gave, the better and more genuine the result. Intense, immediate,
> and sometimes humorously outrageous, they are too often narrow-
> minded and ungenerous in their judgments. The classroom revelation,
> which Mr. Lash admiringly calls "epiphany-on-the-spot" learning, may
> be very inspiring and exciting. However I find it frequently accompa-
> nied by a nihilism towards all except what scores, what grabs. It is part
> of the current instantness [*sic*] cult — instant coffee, instant communi-
> cation, instant intimacy. I mistrust its substantiality and its staying power.
> (175.1–2)

BK ends his article with an ad hominem attack that surpasses, in its bluntness, all his earlier criticisms of Lash's claims:

> In his method as well in his style of writing Mr. Lash seems to be align-
> ing himself with the new breed of student in a kind of bread-and-
> circuses desire to please – make it relevant man, or humanities turned
> on. It may be, as a friend of mine suggests, that he has been touched
> by the "over-30 paranoia syndrome" with the attendant fear of being
> square. (175.2)

After this salvo, BK's final sentences seem more patronizing than collegial:
"Much of the criticism leveled against the liberal arts is justifiable and I admire
Mr. Lash's energetic response to it. I do suggest only that his program for total
education needs some tempering in depth and diversity, even if that means it
will not be so immediately attractive" (175.2).

This final paragraph exposes, if there could be any doubt remaining, just
how personally invested BK was in the issue of art school liberal arts. In his
indictment of total education and the cult of instant gratification, he underscores his distaste for anything identified as intellectual fashion or that devalued
the work, and thus the rewards, of learning.

BK used to say, "My responsibility is to the material not the students." That
may seem harsh, but it may be why the students admired him: BK didn't pan-
der to them by oversimplifying things or providing answers. Rather, he assumed

that students were as open to learning as he was, and to thinking about how to live within a reality fraught with ambiguity, complexity, and fragmentary understanding. That was his BK's strength as a person and as a teacher – which, of course, were one and the same. And that is why he took such offense to Lash's claims for the SFIA curriculum as "little less than a cultural history of the world" in four years of college. It demeaned liberal arts, trivialized learning, and undervalued the students. BK would spend his thirty-nine years at RISD trying to do just the opposite.

Coda

I perused Lash's article, in light of what I had written about BK's response to it, to see if I agreed with BK's criticisms.[2] I came away thinking that BK had been generous. I found the combination of Lash's puffery, his flowery claims for the program coupled with his laments about the difficulties of teaching humanities to SFIA students, quite unpalatable.

More significant, I realized that Lash was enamored with the idea of education's relation to world power. He espoused this by suggesting the SFIA program had the endorsement of the Carnegie Corporation and of a report issued by the Committee on College World Affairs published in 1964.[3] Lash's paraphrasing from the report suggests that he had quite a teleological view of education, and admitted of no reservations to the idea that education and American power should be joined at the hip:

> the [Carnegie] report goes on to point out what we all know and admit: that the United States is at the center of a new world, a world of new complexities, but is not prepared for its role, that we are not in fact educated for it. That one of the major reasons for our disabilities lies in the present provincialism of our learning, that we must somehow divest it of its preoccupation with the western heritage, for example. That in order to understand the meaning of culture we must be able to compare cultures, find out how different cultures solve the same problem, know other cultures well enough to truly understand our own, and in the process come to know the value of diversity as against standardization. (252.2)

Lash equated the report's call for "'a reformulation of purpose'" that "demands the application of new strategies of learning" with the SFIA program

> [The program] constitutes, we believe, a practical recognition of what has come to be held as a major belief of the twentieth century: that all

---

2 Quotations in the Coda are taken directly from Lash's "A New Approach to Teaching Humanities in an Art School," except as noted.
3 See Lash, "A New Approach," 252.1.

things are part of each other, and can be truly comprehended only insofar as the terms of their interrelatedness are discovered. An integrated Humanities Program would seem to make such discoveries by the student more likely. At the least it removes obstacles, foregoes the habit of "compartmenting" knowledge. (253.2)

Viewing BK's article again in light of the above, I am struck by the fact that he did not address the Carnegie connection directly. He did, however, object strongly to Lash's claim that an emphasis on Western studies was tantamount to provincialism:

> While I salute his far-eastern inclusions and agree that our shrinking world demands a new internationalism in learning, I don't know why he thinks we should divest ourselves of the just preoccupation with our own past…. How else shall we know what we look like? How else shall we recognize our unique contributions to the whole culture of the world? I accept the idea of cultural comparison for increased richness, as well as for other values. I wish only to correct what might be called a misplaced globalism. (BK, 167.1)

If the wording here of BK's argument (if it can even be called that) seems rather underconsidered, it may be because he is not terribly interested in the issue of Western studies per se. Rather, I think, BK is offended by Lash's efforts, under the flag of globalism, to harness art school humanities for a U.S.-power agenda. Given BK's activism at this time against the Vietnam War, this seems more than probable.

V

PRIMITIVISM AND IMPOSSIBLE ART

(1971)

MY ANALYSIS OF BK's "Primitivism and Impossible Art," unlike my other analyses of his writings, places the article in the context of the courses he taught at RISD, particularly his "Primitivism in Art." Thus my discussion of the article is interwoven with other material: his lecture notes, book annotations, and so on. There are also more explanatory footnotes herein than usual.

To set the tone, this essay begins with three discontinuous quotations from his article:[1]

> In terms of work, the world's work – not simply labor or employment, though that too – the prognosis for the future is grim. Thus we have tribes of young wanderers, the nomads of advanced technological society, seeking grazing grounds for their own spirits – another Woodstock, a gathering of tribes (Abbie Hoffman), a new or any rate relived archetypal event that will connect up the future with the past, and avoid revolution.... Intensity of vocation leads to grace; vocation being denied, there results a hatred of work in the traditional sense. (172.1)

> This aspect of the new primitivism, if I am not being overly dramatic, is part of an impassioned and confused search for some possible place within the total structure, and for continuity where all signs suggest that no continuity exists. It is not that life is too organized, but that it is too arbitrary, too haphazard.... The alternative image is that of a primitivized life in which all labor is needed and in which each individual finds place within the continuous round of activity upon which life depends. The inaccuracy of this image of primitive life matters little. (172.1)

> Still, underneath, the problem of loss of place and ultimate boredom remains. One possible escape from that hell is to transform activity and being into art. If ordinary acts can be elevated to the level of expression

---

1 Baruch D. Kirschenbaum, "Primitivism and Impossible Art," *Art Journal* 31.2 (1971–2): 168–72.

just by their doing, if people can in themselves become art, then a life of meaningful existence can be conceived….Art as labor – the producing of objects – is measured in terms of critical and hopefully financial recognition. Art as behavior is invested with meaning for the participants through the quality and shape of time created. It is primitive-ritualistic. (172.2)

With their mixture of hope and alienation, and of exhilaration and righteous anger, these quotations, the penultimate paragraphs of BK's "Primitivism and Impossible Art" may seem alien and even impossible to fathom. Today, writing of this sort, fueled as it was by the social and cultural radicalism of the late 1960s, would likely never get accepted by a mainstream publication like *Art Journal,* the leading professional journal for artists, critics, and art historians. Written in 1971 when BK was in Rome with RISD's European Honors Program, his statement is too raw, too intimate, too immersed in the moment to qualify as "scholarship." Yet for these very reasons, this article turns out to be the most revelatory and also the most abstruse of all BK's publications.

I was not expecting it to be so. I wondered, before I read it, whether I might position it as pendant to his discussion of curriculum in his earlier *Art Journal* article, "A Divergent View" (see Chapter IV). I expected it to be about his specialized RISD course "Primitivism in Art," which he had launched in 1968 – the year before he left for his three-year stint in Rome – and was still offering in 1994. Some of his notes from the course, as well as from his other courses, are stored in our basement with their titles scrawled on the boxes in thick black ink: "Primitivism and Baroque," "The Human Figure in Art," "Baroque and Portraiture," and "Iconoclasm Functionality."

The article "Primitivism and Impossible Art" turns out to make no reference to the course itself. It does provide, though, the ground to understand *why* BK came to create his "Primitivism in Art" course. His boxed lecture notes, exam questions, and so on for that course date back only to the late 1970s.[2] The article, in contrast, reveals BK's intellectual stance at age forty, after his involvement in the civil rights and antiwar protests of the 1960s, when he was on the cusp of being promoted from assistant to associate professor.

Although the existing lecture notes for "Primitivism in Art" postdate the article, they are not irrelevant to it. They contain extensive references to, and quotations from, specific pages in the books he assigned to students, providing a substantive exegesis for the article. Happily, BK's library of art history and theory books remains pretty much intact. The marginalia and underlining in these volumes allow identification of works referenced in the article as well as those assigned in the course.

---

2 Their box is labeled "Primitivism and Baroque." I have numbered the file folders containing his notes for the course in the order in which I found them in the box, although, as I note in the text, that order seems random.

The course notes in the box are collected in file folders, grouped roughly by topic. And although those topics cannot be mapped directly onto the article, they do confirm that categories are key to BK's way of constructing his argument. His lecture notes are handwritten, usually on lined yellow paper, with page numbers (always) and years (usually, at least after 1981), with images listed in the margin. What he wants to say is written out fully enough that we get what he would actually say to the students. Any given lecture topic incorporates notes from previous years, so it is possible to see what he has added and also what he decided to eliminate. The notes convey not only ideas and information but also BK's take on the material. Their organization suggests an openness to discussion that was not bound by the limitations of a class period. (In fact, by the time BK was to be, according to the syllabus, two-thirds of the way through the course, he was usually behind.) This openness is also part of the construction of the article, though there it manifests as an unsettling of conclusions.

BK, as I've suggested, was always revising and editing his courses. They were, in that way, living things that afford a remarkable and intimate glimpse of BK the teacher. The notes, one could say, are documents of both his private and public personae. Perhaps that explains, in part, why he has kept them – and wants them burned rather than just tossed out.[3]

The Article

Interestingly, in contrast to the lecture notes, BK apparently kept no copy of the article – not as a photocopy, nor an offprint, nor in the journal itself. I could not find it in his library or in the boxed "Primitivism" material. That seems in keeping with his general attitude toward his published writings. They were just not that important to him.

As I have indicated, the article itself is not easy reading, at least not from the distance of fifty years on: It is so condensed in its argument, so wide-ranging in its coverage, and so embedded in the social, cultural, and artistic moment that in parts it is arcane to the point of impenetrability. Most of the artists he mentions in the second half of the article were just starting their careers in the 1960s; not all of them gained lasting prominence, making them hard to place.

It doesn't help that the article has no footnotes and no bibliography. The most BK provides in the way of citations are names, sometimes in parentheses, sometimes not, scattered throughout the text. In order of appearance, these are Mircea Eliade, Thomas Hobbes, Robert Ardrey, Rousseau, Robert Goldwater, Vlaminck, Kirchner, Matisse, Picasso, Gauguin, Darwin, Frazer, Freud, Klee, Henry Moore, Miró, Albers, Dubuffet. These are just the names from the first two pages. With the exception of Goldwater and Ardrey, and possibly Eliade,

3 I will have more to say about the notes at the end of my discussion of the article.

they are all probably familiar today to someone with a humanities background, especially to those who are museumgoers.[4]

But as BK gets further into the article and closer to 1971 the names, with only a few exceptions, become more obscure: Rafael Ferrer, Jill Johnson, Robert Morris, Dan Graham, Hanna Wiener, Christo Javacheff, Richard Long, Jannis Kounellis, Robert Scull, Michael Heizer, Dennis Oppenheim, Douglas Davis, Gregory Battcock, Jan Dibbets, Forrest Myers, Leary, John Perreault, McLuhan, Abbie Hoffman, Wordsworth.[5]

It goes without saying that BK's ability to deploy all these artists, activists, and intellectuals in order to make an argument about primitivism in art in a five-page, double-columned article is remarkable, especially for someone who was, after all, a specialist in seventeenth-century northern baroque art. At one level, "Primitivism and Impossible Art" reads as a testament to the conversation about art making that BK chose to join when he came to RISD. At the same time, the article turns out to be a logical extension of BK's interest in religious ideas, as well as yet another manifestation of his skepticism about too-simple explanations and solutions. At the least, it is a demonstration of his intellectual firepower, and that alone makes it worth trying to parse despite its difficulty.

The article begins with a rather inscrutable epigraph, quoted from Herbert Marcuse's 1955 *Eros and Civilization*: "If the guilt accumulated in the civilized domination of man by man can ever be redeemed by freedom, then the 'original sin' must be committed again…." (168.1)[6] BK then plunges into a dense, paragraph-long explanation of what he means by the term "primitivism." I quote it here in full, though interspersed with my comments: "Primitivism refers to an attitude of mind working from a cultural state to an imagined pre-cultural state uncontaminated by the ills of civilization. It arises out of the suspicion (even conviction, depending on how bad things appear) that civilization has brought with it a progressive deterioration of the true state of being" (168.1). Two points might be noted here at the start – that the Marcuse quote established a biblical resonance and that the phrase "attitude of mind" implies BK's skepticism, rather than his embrace, of the idea of primitivism.

Having thus launched the topic, he continues:

> It then becomes necessary to return to an exemplary pre-civilized (primitive) state in order to rediscover the fundamental realities of life, which will obviate the ills and restore modern fragmentation to wholeness. Within such thought, the essential human condition always precedes the actual; this idea shapes our location within the infinity of

---

4 The following books by the authors in this list are identified in his 1968 syllabus for the "Primitivism in Art" course: Mircea Eliade, *Myths, Dreams and Mysteries* (1957, trans. 1960) and *The Myth of Eternal Return; or, Cosmos and History* (1949, trans. 1954); Robert Audrey, *African Genesis* (1961); Robert Goldwater, *Primitivism in Modern Art* (1938/1966).

5 In 1968 syllabus: Marshall McLuhan, *Understanding Media* (1965). The 1968 syllabus is in File 12, as are all the syllabi for the course except 1994.

6 In 1968 syllabus: Herbert Marcuse, *Eros and Civilization* (1955).

time, for we move continually forward to an ultimate return (Mircea Eliade). More abstractly the Millennium always achieves the past – a perfected, mythologized past. (168.1)

There are a variety of points to be made here related to the cultural and intellectual background to the article:

First, his pointing to the contrast between modern fragmentation and wholeness might recall not only the second quotation at the start of this chapter, but also a similar contrast BK made when calling out the cult of totalism in the article "A Divergent View" (see Chapter IV).

Second, BK did not identify to which of Eliade's books he is referring. He owned two of them. However, given the annotations and the fact he wrote his name on the flyleaf, it was likely Eliade's *Myths, Dreams and Mysteries,* first published in French in 1957 and translated into English in 1960. BK owned the 1967 paperback edition. It is in his list of readings for the 1968 syllabus.[7]

Third, some readers of his article at the time, if they noted BK's reference to the Millennium in the last sentence of the opening paragraph, might have connected it to Norman Cohn's *The Pursuit of the Millennium,* first published in 1957 and reissued in 1970. BK owned the 1970 paperback edition and he heavily annotated portions of it.

Fourth, on page 27 of his Eliade book, where Eliade discusses Germany's National Socialists, BK has written – taking issue with a point about the Third Reich's grounding in German myth – "See Cohn" and "There was a Christian Armageddon." I cannot, however, be certain BK had read Cohn's book prior to writing the article: unlike Eliade's, it was not listed in the 1968 syllabus.[8]

Fifth, BK's systematic study of religious beliefs, which supported his work on Steen, gave him a particular expertise with which to engage the ideas of Eliade (and Cohn).

Sixth, the 1960s were a time of the back-to-nature movement; Woodstock, billed as "an Aquarian Exposition, 3 Days of Peace and Music," was held in 1969. In short, millennialism was in the air.[9] When he comes to discuss the art of the 1960s BK will associate it with the new types of that decade: "Indians of the city, frontier types, astrological romantics, Myshkin-like holy idiots, narcotized and progressively anarchistic…. Some would even drop back (or out – Leary is one of the high priests of the new primitivism) into a state of insouciant stupidity … in order to come in touch with a truer sense of their own being" (171.1). His awareness of these 1960s social phenomena, as much

---

7 Mircea Eliade, *Myths, Dreams and Mysteries: The Encounter between Contemporary Faiths and Archaic Realities,* trans. Philip Mairet (New York: Harper & Row, 1967).

8 Norman Cohn, *The Pursuit of the Millennium: Revolutionary Millenarians and Mystical Anarchists of the Middle Ages,* 3rd ed. (London: Paladin, 1970); also, rev. and exp. ed. (Oxford: Oxford University Press, 1970). BK had marked copies of both editions.

9 As noted in Chapter III, the Family of the Mystic Arts formed in Oregon in 1968. For Woodstock see the poster: https://www.hudsonvalleyjewishheritagetrail.org/woodstock. The opening song of the 1967 musical *Hair* heralds "the dawning of the Age of Aquarius."

as his familiarity with the ideas of Eliade (and Cohn), undergirds his analysis of contemporary art.

Seventh, like Eliade (and Cohn), BK was well aware of the dangers that millennialism posed. On page 182 of Cohn, above a passage having to do with a particular medieval religious cult, BK has scrawled "Manson," referring to the Manson Family cult, whose followers believed Charles Manson was a manifestation of Jesus Christ.[10]

Having defined the concept of primitivism in the first paragraph of the article, BK goes on to divide primitivism into two categories: The "'hard' view … sees the beginnings as bestial and therefore unenviable in any way.… In this hard-headedly practical view civilization, for all that may be wrong with it, is the only salvation … from barbarism" (168.1). He associates Hobbes and the anthropologist Ardrey with this view. However, he says, it is rather the "'soft' view …. with its millennial tendencies, [that] has dominated imagination. Perhaps this is because it supplies some relief from the responsibilities of civilization and a comforting sense that things will fulfill themselves" (168.1).

It is "soft" primitivism that is the focus of his article. His characterizations of it suggest the BK is susceptible to its allure even as he recognizes its dangers: Virgil's invention of the "mythical sweetly-sad world of Arcady where the honey and wine of eternal evening would relieve them of the burden of their own crass culture" (168.2). The Renaissance took up this idyll, as "an antidote to the sado-masochistic compulsions of medieval Christianity" with its "retributive holocaust of judgment" (168.2). Later in the eighteenth century, "Rousseau constructed the concept of the Noble Savage.… Even as they were slaughtered as heathen, the Indians of America were idealized as dwellers in innocence close to paradise" (168.2).

BK concludes his definition of "soft" primitivism with an observation about modern times:

> At one time it might have been possible to look at modern primitivism as an extension of a wayward romanticism. But as the problems of modern society deepen, the desperation of reaching out for the "primal sanities" becomes more and more intense. Always the desire has been for a freedom that seems denied the individual in the structure of things as they exist. In this most free of times, always that freedom evades us. (168.2)

It seems that BK, in the famous words of Yogi Berra, views the present fascination with primitivism as "déjà vu all over again."

Having established the intellectual framework for understanding "soft" primitivism, BK is ready to proceed to the crux of the article, which is the

---

10 See Vincent Bugliosi, with Curt Gentry, *Helter Skelter: The True Story of the Manson Murders* (New York: W. W. Norton, [1974] 1994) for details of the cult, which dated from c. 1967 until Manson's murder trial in 1970. At his trial Manson testified that "the music is telling the youth to rise up against the establishment" (391).

importance of primitivism for understanding modern and contemporary art. First, he proposes two subcategories of "soft" primitivistic art:

> one (the earlier) leading to expressive freedom through primitivized form, a kind of millennium of artistic language; and the other leading to rediscovery of creative capacity through primitivized behavior, perhaps a millennium of self. In the loss of religious consciousness, art and its practice have become the means to spiritual awareness and accomplishment. If art could be free then we could be free and the millennium would be achieved. (168.2)

Only someone educated in religious thought, as well as fluent both in the literature on the concept of primitivism and in the history and contemporary theory of art making, could have proposed these categories and understood their implications. They are evidence of how immersed BK had become in the studio culture of RISD, while also achieving an intellectual distance from it.

BK's discussion of both formal and behavioral primitivism is quite dense, involving references to individual artists, art movements, and occasional works of art, which he sorts into still smaller subcategories of primitivism. He credits Robert Goldwater with having written about the earlier primitivism.[11] It is the more straightforward of BK's two art categories, perhaps because the art he discusses is more familiar. BK begins by dismissing as unimportant the question of which artist, and when, "first discovered primitive sculpture"; but he gives the credit to Gauguin, who, in BK's words, "insisted that art could find its 'nourishing milk' only in the mysterious anti-naturalism of its own primitive (for him barbaric) beginnings, which he struggled to re-invent" (169.1). But whether Gauguin, or Vlaminck or Matisse or Picasso, or whether the inspiration was archaic art or West African sculpture, the result was "the creation, simultaneously, of a new primitivized imagery and a new sense of the inventive possibilities of form" (169.1).

BK argues that in fauvism, cubism, German expression, surrealism, and the work of Matisse, Klee, and Henry Moore, "the struggle in art became one of directness, immediacy, and economy of means. It seemed necessary to break through whatever stood between the artist and his [*sic*] work, whether preconception of rendering and color, or self-consciousness of intent, or the responsibilities to tradition" (169.1).

He relates "[t]hese transformations in form" not only to the artists' interests in archaic and ethnographic sculpture, but to "a general primitivizing trend" in the first half of the twentieth century that affected biology, anthropology, psychology, and politics (169.1). This trend, he says, "directed attention to the origin of things as the source of their true explanation. Revelation of origins

---

11 Robert Goldwater, *Primitivism in Modern Art* (1938/1967). BK assigned this book in his 1968 syllabus.

would strip away the layers of civilization and restraint which have kept us from our truer, more fundamental selves" (169.1).

BK sums up the import for art: "Whatever the source and whatever the particular need, primitive images and primitivizing ideas were used to instruct art to new possibilities. This was a primitivism of form or formal primitivism that would ... bring about the millennium of artistic language" (169.2). Having just made the case for the importance of formal primitivism for the development of twentieth-century art, he then begins to challenge its primitivizing claims:

> In the drive for formalistic autonomy or pure form primitive affinities were left behind or, perhaps better, outrun; and there emerges a highly sophisticated art and criticism bereft of earlier primitive sensitivities and purpose. Minimalism is a direct line from economy of means. Even what could be thought of as the latter-day primitivism of abstract expressionism ... ends in provocative patterning. Only Dubuffet manages an insistent primitive vision. (169.2)

Formal primitivism, he suggests, has reached a dead end. (His critique here might call to mind his objection to formalist criticism in his book on Jan Steen.)

The problem BK identifies is the gap between artistic primitivizing efforts and the achievement of primitivistic ends:

> Within the context of primitivism, the predominance of formalistic or stylistic thinking makes for a certain conflict. In argument the desire may have been for release from self-conscious intent, but style is the result of analytical and critical processes. These processes assure preconsideration of intent. That is, art cannot be accidental; accident must be transformed into discovery; and someplace along the line the artist becomes the critical respondent to his [sic] own work. (169.2)

The making of the art thus seems to be inherently at odds with primitivistic ends.

BK's reason for insisting on this contradiction is not just because he believes primitivism itself cannot be achieved, but because, as he insists, of the nature of art itself: "From here follows (within the concept of style) the self-evident distinction between art and life. [Note the parenthetical phrase here.] Art is purposeful (criticism will make it so), life is fortuitous. The whole critical and commercial apparatus of artists and appreciators, creators and consumers (collectors) which supports the art world as we know it, stems from that distinction" (170.1). In short, however powerful the art was that was inspired by the dream of a return to beginnings, it could not free itself from being art. It is not surprising, of course, that BK would confront us with this reality. Just as he admitted to the allure of primitivism and recognized its fruitfulness in the production of art, his intellectual honesty compelled him to acknowledge that its apparent simplicity was, in fact, evidence of its sophistication.

This dichotomy between art and life, however, seems not to be a dead end. In fact, it is the bridge BK has constructed for discussing the primitivized art of the 1960s: "A possible way to break the distinction between art and life, assuming that one should purpose to do so, is to turn from style to behavior as the essential means to expression" (170.1). In the rest of the article, BK makes the case for the value of the connection between behavioral primitivism and contemporary art.

He explains some salient aspects of this connection as follows: "If earlier the means to expression were equated with expression itself, now the tendency is to equate behavior with expression. The important thing is *to do art*. Any resultant thing or object becomes a by-product of that activity to be more or less valued as a document of something that happened, rather than as anything of intrinsic worth or as an end in itself" (170.1). He gives a couple examples: "the ice-man's bill which Rafael Ferrer suggested might do for a collector's drawing for his ice-blocks melting on leaves at Whitney. It is enough, as [artist] Jill Johnson put it, back in 1965, to stake out a claim (through behavior) to be an artist. In this case, lying on one's back and criticizing the constellations" (170.1).

BK clearly selected these works, if I can use that term, to illustrate a central aspect of this behavioral primitivism:

> Almost always the results of art behavior (activity, action, event – any of these terms apply) are, like the melting ice-blocks, ephemeral. The best one can do is subject the behavior to recall…. All that exists is an encapsulated period of time during which something took place, and other things did not take place, and in which energy was expended in the way of gratuitous activity. (170.1)

However, it turns out that this ephemerality is itself a problem, not because BK thinks that art cannot be art and also be ephemeral, but because the artists don't seem to have the courage of their convictions:

> It would be nice to let it go simply at that, but either because the truly ephemeral is difficult to accept, or because of outrageous narcissism, the whole enterprise is filmed and photographed (slides no doubt for some pocket-portfolio). There follows the inexplicable but happy assumption that the cameras have recorded things as they are. The celluloid … becomes the non-object object, the non-image image, a spur to total recall (document) of a primary and now mythologized event. (170.1).

BK is making a devastating critique of the contemporary art scene, exposing its pretensions, the weakness of its claims to radicality, and its dependence (still) on the establishment institutions of art.

This critique in part explains why he has titled the article "Primitivism and Impossible Art":

> The more "impossible" art becomes, the more its meaning is resident only in its own activity. The exhibition of such activities or their results in galleries or museums either in process or, as more often, in photograph would, when pushed to extreme, have to be seen as an absurd leftover of another orientation and involves everybody in cross-purposes. … It is still, like it or not, for sale in one way or another. (170.2)

However, while critical of the artists' claims to ephemera, he allows that they may have found an escape from the art system: "The experience of seeing the films and slides becomes a kind of post-ritual reliving. With video-tape the event and its external consideration can exist simultaneously, creating the *ne plus ultra* of self-consciousness hiding under the cover of extreme spontaneity" (170.1–2).

His choice of the phrase "post-ritual reliving" is not incidental: "Either in recall or in event itself, the new art exists for those involved in it. The experiences (like the expension [*sic*] of energy is theirs) and not that of some imagined audience responding to what passes before them" (170.2). It would seem that if the actions are rituals, then by extension, the actors are believers. BK makes precisely this connection explicit with his next examples: "The piling up of earth and the remains of excavation (Robert Morris), the burial of a steel cube (Sol Lewitt), the dissolving of detergent-soaked sugar cubes in the sea (Dan Graham), the distribution of hot-dogs on a Manhattan street (Hanna Wiener), are the rites of initiates engaged in ritual activity" (170.2).

The enumeration of these examples, and of others by Richard Long and Christo, allows BK to grant that this art of behavior might not be so impossible after all. Instead, it may presage the end of the art system that has separated art from life. The location of this art is what makes its claims convincing:

> Outside of the gallery or the publication, art as participatory ritual is at once more public in that it takes place in the context of life (Dennis Oppenheim convinced a farmer to let him plot a harvester's course) and more private in that it truly absorbs only those actively engaged in its doing. Ultimately, in a world crammed full of things almost to saturation, *to do art* may be far more satisfactory than *to make objects*. (170.2)

He seems to offer even further endorsement:

> Whichever way one looks at these new tendencies, the result is the blurring of the line between art and life. To accept the life situations as art itself rather than the subject of art (Douglas Davis), – to think of life as a qualitative event at the expense of art (Gregory Battcock), – derives from a desire to find a new integration of meaning and activity in our lives.[12] (171.1)

12 I am not familiar with Douglas Davis, nor could I find online any links to works by him that predate BK's article. However, two years after the article, Davis published the book *Art and the Future: A History/Prophecy of the Collaboration between Science, Technology and Art*

This linking of art and life is for BK the key to behavioral primitivism: "Art becomes more mundane, less intellectually and commercially sacred, and life hopefully becomes more filled with significance. The new integration of creative activity with life will bring about the rediscovery of center and a return to an imagined primitive wholeness in which all things are part of all other things, and one need not worry too much about definitions" (171.1). Of course that phrase, "one need not worry too much about definitions," is, one might say, the worm in the apple.

He then goes on to give more cosmic examples of this art "[r]eleased from image" (171.1). On one hand, such art

> can reach out to encompass the elemental forces of the earth: the action of the sea (Jan Dibbets), the contours of the land (Dennis Oppenheim), the sky (Forrest Myers), and by extension our own place within it all. Nature becomes a norm – a space-age nature in which for the first time we can experience the earth as a shared whole.... The sophistication of our technology has brought us back to a primitive recognition of the center of the universe which we occupy. (171.1)

On the other hand, at the opposite end of the behavioral art scale, are urban street works:

> While technology thrusts us willingly or unwillingly into a terracentric primitivism, its white-sleeve impersonality and brave-new-world potentials are challenged by a growing band of primitivized street people who antithesize technological values.... Street people like street works are made simply by identifying them as such (John Perreault).[13] Anything, anyone can be a street work. Without manifestos, without theory, but only through declaration it is possible to turn oneself and whatever else one wishes into art.... Behavior becomes expression not only through doing but simply through being. (171.1–2)

Yet, in the end, BK rejects the premises of all these behavioral art approaches:

> The art/life, life/art equation could conceivably be a way out from these dilemmas except for one glaring mis-conception. Art, modern no less

(cont.)
(New York: Praeger, 1973). Perhaps it was Davis's work related to this possibility that drew BK. Gregory Battcock was famous (or notorious) in the 1960s for his advance of Marcuse's theory of anti-art and the disruptive connection between art and male eroticism. In 1970 Battcock appeared on the cover of *Arts Magazine* in his underwear: https://www.artforum.com/print/201207/transformer-gregory-battcock-31960.

13 For John Perreault and street works: https://www.granarybooks.com/pages/books/2999/john-perreault-judy-collischan/in-plain-sight-street-works-and-performances-1968-1971?soldItem=true. I read somewhere online (but cannot find now) that art occurred whenever a stranger on the street acknowledged him.

than primitive, has always served to delineate areas of sacredness and significance from the rest of life. This had been its force and its importance. Its elevating and even revolutionary power derives from intensification. We need that separating-out of the sacred to relieve the leveling power of the ordinary, and to bring us beyond ourselves in thought and sensitivity.... The distinction between art and life is what sustains us, and what sustains art. (171.2)

Note that BK is not denying that these activities are art, nor is he advocating for a formalism that makes art only about art. Rather he is resisting the siren call of primitivism, and thus the contemporary discourse about art, a discourse that he himself could not avoid being part of, given that he worked at RISD.

Yet even as BK insists on that art cannot also be life, he seems to yearn that it were otherwise:

> Still the new primitivism is deeply impressive, perhaps because, even in its chaos, it focuses on life itself (the art I think is sometimes an excuse), and not simply on poetic or intellectual yearnings, or formal problems. If earlier, primitive examples were used to instruct art, primitivizing ideas are now used to instruct life, and have run over into a politics of confrontation … with the civilization which has spawned them. The millennium will be one of rediscovered creative capacity of being – a millennium of self located in wholeness. If impressive, these visions are also deeply saddening as all reachings-out for the Edenic dream must inevitably be. (171.2)

Had BK just ended the article here, he would have written an insightful and deeply sympathetic portrait of the contemporary art scene. However, he clearly wasn't satisfied: "Perhaps there remains no more to say.... Still some left-over thoughts fit in here somewhere" (171.2). The quotations at the very start of this chapter follow here, exposing the reasons for his discomfiture: BK is profoundly concerned with the state of contemporary society.

The lens of primitivism had allowed him an exegesis of the contemporary art scene; it had also, however, led him to identify the art–life issue as the central problem confronting artists. Yet by the end of the article it seems he concluded that the art–life dichotomy was not the real issue after all:

> If I were to be most harsh in my estimation, such art constitutes the playtime/work-fun activities of the superfluous child/adults of our age. If I were to be most open and accepting in my judgment, it is the primitivized beginning of a liberation from old forms and concepts – the first step in breaking the work/labor/success syndrome which has enslaved our spirits and lives and has set us as individuals in counterstance to society. The latter sounds too grand, the former too dismal. Meanwhile, we remain desperately in need of new structures for our creative energies. (172.2)

BK, for all his insistence on a distinction between art and life, at least in this article made no distinction between his work as an art historian and professor at RISD, and his activism.[14] Instead, like the contemporary artists whose works he had just analyzed, BK clearly positioned himself as having to rethink the institutions of art, institutions in which he was now himself deeply embedded, or, as he might say, implicated. In my view, that is why he had, in the end, to call for "new structures." They were where the possibilities for effecting change lay. The article is, in the end, a call to do the work on the institutions that might make art possible again.

Coda: BK's Lecture Notes for "Primitivism in Art"

I found five syllabi for BK's "Primitivism in Art" course, dating from 1968 to 1994.[15] They are fascinating documents of how his thinking about the subject evolved over time, and provide important insights for the way he taught his courses. Therefore I am going to describe the notes at length here, starting with the syllabi, to provide more in-depth evidence of his teaching and perhaps insight into the article itself.

The 1968 syllabus for "Primitivism in Art" is the only one extant that predates the article. It is organized as a list of weekly readings with chapter titles from the books he assigned serving as the topic headings. These make it possible, however, to get some sense of the ideas BK covered the first time he offered the course.

Goldwater's book *Primitivism in Modern Art* dominates these readings. From it BK assigned "A Definition of Primitivism," which appears late in the book, and the earlier "Romantic Primitivism," "Emotional Primitivism," "Intellectual Primitivism," and "The Primitivism of the Subconscious." In addition, he had students read the "Myth of the Noble Savage" from Eliade's *Myths, Dreams and Mysteries,* and recommended they read McLuhan's *Understanding Media* and Marcuse's *Eros and Civilization* for the final two weeks of the course. The syllabus format leaves him a lot of leeway, which suggests that he was going to decide what to teach as he went along. By contrast, the article – written after he had taught the course – showed BK fully in command of the material.

In contrast to that first syllabus, the one for 1978, ten years later, is both more detailed and more expansive in scope. This syllabus is divided into seven topics, each with multiple subtopics, with the art ranging from medieval to contemporary, though chronology is not the point For example, the title of Topic II is "Edenic Primitivism," and its subtopics are "The Messianic Tradition," "Eden and the *Garden of [Earthly] Delights* (Bosch)," and "The Holy Idiot." The last topic of the syllabus is "Behavioral Primitivism," echoing his article. He

14 See Chapter III for BK's involvement in protest movements.
15 All but the last one are in File 12 of the box; for 1994, see note 19.

divided this topic into "The New Tribalism and the Death of Art," "The Self and Elemental Forces," and "The WEC and Geocentrism."[16]

By 1978 BK has also diversified the readings. He required all of Goldwater, but assigned it only for his first topic – that is, the introduction to the course (for which he also assigned two chapters from Eliade) – and for the topic of "Formal Primitivism." For the "Edenic Primitivism" topic he assigned Cohn's *In Pursuit of the Millennium* and advised the students, "Would recommend the whole book but Foreword, Introduction and chapters 3, 7, 8, 9, 10, and 13 will do."[17] BK required a tremendous amount of really challenging reading, and clearly assumed students would do it.

In 1982, the syllabus is almost the same as that for 1978, the most notable changes being to the last topic. Though it is still called "Behavioral Primitivism," he has retitled the subtopics as "The New Tribalism," "Art and Elementary Forces," and, inscrutably, "The new wane and the 'high-dumb.'"[18] Finally, more than ten years after it was first published, he assigned as reading for this topic his own "Primitivism and Impossible Art."

The syllabus for 1984 is identical to that for 1982, but by 1994 (the last year of the syllabi) BK has made substantive changes:[19] The assignments from Goldwater are far fewer. Instead he has incorporated new readings from the 1980s and '90s, influenced by postcolonial theory. The bellwether last topic has changed to "The New Primitivism," with four subtopics: "Behavioral Primitivism," "Icons and Totems," "Art and Elemental Forces," and "The New Wave – 'The re-enchantment of art.'" For this he assigned (among others) readings by Kirk Varnedoe from the catalog for the 1984 MoMA exhibit "'Primitivism' in 20th Century Art: Affinity of the Tribal and the Modern" and by Lucy Lippard on the connections between contemporary and prehistoric art.[20]

In addition to the syllabi for "Primitivism in Art," BK saved the exams for the 1982 version of the course, which show how high were his expectations for the students. For the midterm, he gave two essay questions. The first was to explain the Eliade statement "'The essential human condition precedes the actual' as a central idea in primitivism." They were to do so utilizing six terms taken from Eliade and Cohn: "edenic, messianic, utopia, *illo tempore,* paradise, millennium." The second exam question, a slide essay, was equally demanding.

16 I am not certain what WEC stands for, but I suspect it is *The Whole Earth Catalog,* published during 1968–71.

17 File 5 in the "Primitivism and Baroque" box.

18 BK does not recall what he had in mind with these labels. It is likely the "wane" is a typo, and BK meant New Wave, a phrase he uses in the 1994 syllabus. The "high-dumb" may have been part of what came to be labeled "Bad Art": https://blog.artsper.com/en/a-closer-look/good-to-know-the-bad-painting/.

19 This syllabus was found stuck between the pages of his copy of Cohn's *Pursuit of the Millennium.*

20 Lucy Lippard, "Introduction" and "Homes and Graves and Gardens," in *Overlay: Contemporary Art and the Art of Prehistory* (New York: Pantheon, 1983).

Students were to analysis Bosch's *The Garden of Earthly Delights* in terms of "a connection with the doctrines of 'mystical anarchism' preached by the adepts of the Free Spirit (Adamites) and other radical religious groups at the end of the Middle Ages." They were advised that they would "want to consider Bosch's *Haywain* triptych" and relate both to "what the controversy over the meaning of the *Garden* has to do with Primitivism."

One way that BK succeeded in getting RISD students to care about such arcane issues was to make them pertinent. How he did so is suggested by the first question of the 1982 final exam, which reads as follows: "I. Essay (20 minutes). Listen to the song (Joni Mitchell's 'Woodstock' as sung by Crosby, Stills and Nash [and Young]) and read the words." [He then gives all three verses of the lyrics, starting with "I came upon a child of God / He was walking along the road," and ending with the famous chorus, "We are stardust / We are golden / And we've got to get ourselves / Back to the garden."] The students were then directed, "in an essay pick out the primitivizing elements in the song and relate them in [*sic*] the themes of primitivism developed during the course of the semester."

I find it amazing that he thought the students could not only do this in twenty minutes, but then go on to write two slide essays, each of which was as challenging as those he had set in the midterm. Expecting RISD students to be able to write even acceptable responses to such questions suggests how high BK's standards were – and also how much faith he had in his own ability to explain such difficult material in a manner they could not only grasp but deploy themselves.

Reading over his lecture notes suggests how he accomplished this. Here, with little comment and as he wrote them – emphases and all, but with spellings adjusted – are a few quotes from his lecture notes:

[On lined yellow paper in blue ballpoint:][21]

<u>Edenic Primitivism</u>
Already introduced the notion of the idyllic beginning in Eden – and the <u>subsequent fall</u>. When you read Cohn's The Pursuit of the Millenium you will see that in Christian Thought the notion of the fall from grace accompanied by a promise of <u>salvation</u>

[And scrawled across the verso of this page:]

---

21 The excerpts below are identified using BK's identification system. Each footnote is for a new piece of paper. File 5 Clark, 1981.1 (i.e., these notes are in File 5 of the "Primitivism and Baroque" box, for the version of the course that he taught at Clark in 1981; 1 is the page in that version of the course). As I've already described, BK wrote and rewrote this course, putting together pages from various versions and amending them with additions and deletions. In some instances there is a second page number crossed out, indicating where the page fell in a previous course.

On reading Cohn – don't get scared by the formidable scholarship – lots of names, dates, doctrines etc. – but basically his argument is simple – that the Messianic trad. of Millennial thinking lays the groundwork for an <u>egalitarian concept of salvation</u> – and therefore carries a <u>revolutionary impact</u>.

[Then in red ink below with an arrow, so rewritten for another version of the course:]

The Messianic impulse – is to prepare the world for the coming in [of] the Messiah.

[On RISD Memorandum paper in pencil:][22]

When you read the book you'll see how extreme some of the sects were both in behavior and belief. James [i.e., Jim] Jones in Guyana is a contemporary version of dictatorial <u>millenarianism</u>.

[In the margin opposite the reference to Jones is written "hold off on Jones."]

And it's Cohn's belief which he tempered in a new conclusion [that] the same can be said for earlier revolutionary movements of the century – particularly the rise of the Nazi movement in the 30's – the <u>third Reich</u> – means the third age which would follow – the age of law (The Father), the age of the gospel (Son).

[Beneath this he wrote "the Millennium" in blue ink, with a line curving upward into a circle around "third Reich."]

Now, many of these Messianic cults like Jones' believed it was possible to find through certain practices the millennium here and now on earth or if not that then to anticipate it though certain activities – some of them quite extreme – there is one great painting which has been interpreted as revealing such ideas – Bosch

[On lined yellow paper in black ink:][23]

<u>Review Syllabus</u>
– First – not a course in <u>Primitive Art</u>, but a course which traces the influence of primitivizing ideas on the production of Art on a number of different circumstances – So if any one has that mistaken impression perhaps they should reconsider the course.
In fact you might say that though this course carries Art History credit it is not strictly speaking an art history course but a course in intellectual history

22 File 5 Clark 1981.3.~~18~~.
23 File 5 Primitivism 1985.1,3.

[On lined yellow paper in black ink:][24]

2. Before I continue with line of thought let me introduce this note of caution: The Terms Primitive/Primitivizing/Primitivism as used in this course do not refer to any <u>reality of early human life</u> or experience, but myths of beginnings such as Eliade addresses in the two essays assigned. These myths arise out of a longing for a dream of perfect origins. That at certain times (18th-early 20th c) these beginnings were thought to have actual existence among the "simpler" people of the world does not change mythic to historical reality.

[Folded lined tan paper in red ink:][25]

It is my estimation that the whole pastoral tradition is a kind of soft primitivism – and this [is] what I want to talk about next week – let me just say by way of introduction that if Christian soft primitivism is a obscure business which leads it in the occult showdown of Christian thought the Pastoral tradition is absolutely central to European concerns.

These few quotations show how clear BK was in his thinking and how skilled he was in distilling arcane and complex ideas for students who had no prior knowledge of them. These passages also underscore his concern that students do the readings and not be intimidated by them. Perhaps most important, his notes show that BK spoke as one person to another, using the first person, making it clear that this material was something he was actively thinking about himself. That he believed deeply in the importance of what he was teaching was his gift to the students, an act of generosity for which he expected in return that they take the material seriously. That was, I think, the foundation of his authority and success as a teacher.

But beyond all the examples I have given from his lecture notes is the sheer creation of his course on primitivism in art. BK came to RISD as a Harvard-trained specialist in the northern baroque, and throughout his career he continued to teach courses on seventeenth-century art. However, he also introduced courses on portraiture, the human figure in art, and aniconism that were not based on traditional periodization. I think it fair to say that BK created these courses not so much to serve the students' interests, but to expand their historical horizons and challenge their too-easy intellectual assumptions. He wanted them to work as artists and designers, not from a state of innocence or ignorance, but with an appreciation, even passion, for learning and for the benefits of knowledge.

24 File 5 Class Notes Primitivism 1985.1–2.
25 File 5 Clark 18 ~~26~~.

VI

TWO REVIEWS OF BOOKS ON MUSEUMS IN *WINTERTHUR PORTFOLIO* (1980)

O NE OF THE UNSTATED RESPONSIBILITIES of academics to their profession is to review publications of other academics who share roughly the same specialty. There is only one book review listed on BK's CV, and it is not on a subject in which he was in any way an expert. It is a review of two books on art museums: one by Karl E. Meyer and the other by Artists Meeting for Cultural Change.

Presumably, as is the usual practice, *Winterthur Portfolio,* which published this review, invited BK to review these particular books.[1] Assuming that is the case, then the offer seems serendipitous, for it gave BK just the forum he needed to attack the position of museums within the contemporary art scene.

The standard format for reviews is for the reviewer to give a brief account of where the book fits in the literature on a subject, and to analyze dispassionately and in some detail what the book covers, usually saving any criticisms and reservations for the end. BK from the start departs from this paradigm, first by the bluntness and personal characterization of Meyer's book. He begins:

> Karl Meyer's study of the American art museum and its current problems carries the subtitle *Power, Money, Ethics.* My reaction is that while the book makes abundantly clear the role of money and power in museums (their order is better reversed), it reveals little of the ethics. The story of burgeoning art museums since World War II, which Meyer documents with an array of impressive and convincing statistics, turns out to be one of self-serving cupidity, conflict of interests, influence mongering, competitive status seeking, overkill commercialism, and simple greed. (173.2)

---

1 Baruch D. Kirschenbaum, review of Karl E. Meyer, *The Art Museum: Power, Money, Ethics — A Twentieth Century Fund Report* (New York: William Morrow, 1979), and Artists Meeting for Cultural Change, *An* Anti-*Catalog* (New York: Catalog Committee of Artists Meeting for Cultural Change, 1977), *Winterthur Portfolio* 15.3 (1980): 273–76. This journal is the publication of the Winterthur Museum, Garden and Library.

BK then lists some of Meyer's examples as proof of all these. The accusations that BK lobs at museum practices are the more raw because they are not given as quotations from Meyer. In fact, nowhere does BK make clear whether such inflammatory language appeared in the book, or whether this language is his own, based on information he gleaned from reading the book.

Certainly BK seems not so much interested in Meyer's account of art museum corruption as he is in Meyer's personal attitude toward what he documents:

> Given the ethical abuses and attitudes of those in power (particularly trustees), one might expect an angry book or a least one derived in part from a deep anger carefully controlled. Meyer's is no such book. In place of what would be justifiable moral outrage, he offers sweet reasonableness based upon historical explanation. He admonishes and cautions; but on issue after issue he refuses to take a stand. The result is a book more apologetic than demanding, one which smacks of the complicity of understanding. But to understand is not necessarily to forgive.[2] (274.1)

And then BK nails his indictment: "The point here is not that Meyer's book is weak because he does not get angry but that in it he avoids the moral, intellectual, and aesthetic issues that shriek from his own pages. While proposing governmental control to soften abuses, he upholds the status quo of a system shot through with corruption" (274.1).

BK then goes on to consider one of the particulars of the report: "Meyer deals at some length with the question of acquisition policies. He cautions against the continuing competitive chase after prestigious works, which has led to enormously inflated prices, to collusion between dealers and museum officials, and, I believe, to the idea that artistic value is established by price" (274.1).

BK clearly agrees that Meyer has identified a major problem. What he cannot accept, however, is the solution that Meyer proposes:

> He accedes, however, to the argument that a museum's lifeblood depends upon the continued building of collections through purchases as well as through gifts. Only a moratorium on market acquisitions could clean out that mess, but Meyer does not recommend it or even suggest it as a possibility, perhaps because such a recommendation would go unheeded. Yet the great museums of Europe do not purchase and have hardly become moribund. (274.1)

What really incenses BK is that "Cataloguing ethical abuses is neither the purpose nor the central theme of Meyer's book. He cites them in various sections of his study only as examples of the practices of museum directors, cu-

---

2 Until I tried to find the author of the phrase about understanding and forgiveness, which is one of BK's mantras (and most often attributed to Madame de Staëhl), I did not realize that the usual English version is "To understand is to forgive." *Bartlett's Familar Quotations,* 15th ed., revd. and enl., ed. Emily Morison Beck (Boston: Little, Brown, 1980), 417:15 and n. 5.

rators, and trustees that have contributed to the present difficulties. It is those difficulties themselves on which Meyer focuses."[3]

And Meyer's solution to those difficulties clearly troubles BK. "American art museums are in serious financial trouble. While there is a lot of money for sensational acquisitions, … there is not enough to maintain buildings, keep the lights on, and in some cases even keep the doors open. As might be expected, the cry for help has been directed to the federal government" (274.1–2).

Although BK first offers multiple pragmatic reasons for rejecting the idea of a government bailout for museums, his real objection is a moral one.

> There is a great irony in concluding that direct governmental support for art museums in necessary to save them from final ruin. Art museums, as Meyer shows so well, have always been the cultural precinct of the superrich…. There are those who feel strongly that the association of art with capitalistic wealth has resulted in the loss of art's political and cultural meaning; thus museums have become repositories of the art of those in power: art officially defined and interpreted. (274.2–275.1)

BK clearly thinks that if museums are in trouble of their own making, and are creatures of the wealthy, it should not fall to the taxpayers of the country to bail them out. Furthermore, he seems to endorse the idea that wealth has corrupted their collection policies

I wish to stress here what I think is the most notable characteristic of BK's review of Meyer's book. It is not the bluntness of his criticism per se. Rather it is the fact that most reviewers, even if they held the same opinion of Meyer's book as BK, would have couched their criticism in terms of the book's shortcomings. BK has no use for such reification. By his ethics, the problem lies not with the book but with the person who wrote it. BK, by writing in the first person and the active voice, not only makes his prose more vivid but also declares that he owns what he writes. It is this ownership that, in turn, gives him standing to attack Meyer for what Meyer has written, calling him out for what BK sees as Meyer's complicity with museum corruption.

For BK, no matter what the subject, the issue was always, fundamentally, how to address it with ethical as well as intellectual integrity. In fact, the two, for him were the same.

BK ended his review of Meyer's book by identifying the connection among art museums, wealth, and the definition and interpretation of art. He then says:

---

3 In his article about the 1978 RISD-associated "Private Parts" exhibition (see Chapter III), BK's negative tone about the Trustees in part reflected general RISD faculty disaffection: from this point of view the Trustees were more interested in the Museum of Art, RISD, and its collections than they were in supporting the work of its faculty and students. RISD's original purpose of acquiring works of art and design had been to further the mission of educating its students. However, by BK's time, as the museum's mission expanded, and likewise its independence, faculty had come to perceive the museum as the favored beneficiary of Trustee philanthropy. RISD's culture thus fed BK's view of art museums as creatures of "capitalistic wealth" and "repositories of the art of those in power."

"For those who share this view the museum becomes an arena for ideological confrontation" (275.1). This sentence serves as the lead-in to the second book he is reviewing, *An* Anti-*Catalog* by Artists Meeting for Cultural Change.

An Anti-*Catalog*, published in 1977, is, like the famous Salon des Refusés in Paris of 1863, a work of artist protest. According to BK's review, it was "[w]ritten by a committee of artists associated in a group called Artists Meeting for Cultural Change" as part of a movement of boycotts and street demonstrations that were held to protest the Whitney Museum decision "to show as part of its bicentennial fare the collection of American art formed by Mr. and Mrs. John D. Rockefeller III" (275.1). *An* Anti-*Catalog* was a counter to the catalog of the Whitney exhibition of the Rockefeller collection.

BK compares *An* Anti-*Catalog* directly to Meyer's book: "*An* Anti-*Catalog*, like Meyer's book, addresses power, money, and ethics in museum practices. Unlike Meyer, however, the writers of *An* Anti-*Catalog* take an emphatic stand against the ethical and intellectual abuses arising from the association of art and wealth" (275.1).

An Anti-*Catalog*, in BK's view, is a decidedly antiestablishment work and he acknowledges its strident tone: "At first glance *An* Anti-*Catalog* may seem merely a diatribe against the entire concept of the fine arts and its supporting class structure" (275.1). Yet he immediately deflects such a reading. His characterization is worth quoting at length:

> It is, however, much more than that. The issues it raises are important. The main contention is that by showing the Rockefeller collection as American art, the Whitney Museum legitimized it as an adequate sampling of the art of this country and thereby supported the interpretation of American history explicit in that selection. The committee also charges that the exhibition and catalogue pretend political and cultural neutrality although just the opposite is true. The Rockefeller collection, the authors … maintain, ignores minority artists, including women, and offers a vision of America in which the poor are sentimentalized, the land is romanticized, and the rich and powerful are celebrated for their beauty and gentility. (275.1)

(It is hard to believe, and very sobering, that today, more than forty years later, artists and their supporters are still having to fight these battles.)

BK, however much he may support the views of the writers of *An* Anti-*Catalog*, does have reservations about their view of the function of art in society: "With heavy reliance on English critic John Berger's *Ways of Seeing* [a book BK used in his classes], the writers … maintain that the emphasis on formal appreciation in … [the Whitney] catalogue leads to mystification of art (Berger's term) and deprives it of other meaning. The object becomes more important than its both past and present meaning" (275.1–2).

BK gives some examples to clarify what is meant by "formal appreciation," such as focusing on Copley's and Sargent's paint handling, then continues: "With such an approach (and *An* Anti-*Catalog* is very insistent on this point), value inheres in the thing itself rather than in what the object may reveal, and art becomes simply the precious object" (275.2). BK's objection is not to this point of view per se but to the all-or-nothing view of the writers of *An* Anti-*Catalog,* who put

> an over-emphasis on social and cultural meaning as opposed to artistic accomplishment and purpose. It is possible to react to Copley's and Sargent's brilliance as painters without losing sight of the broader historical implications of their painting. The purpose of the patron need not be the purpose of the artist. The converse is true as well. The use to which art is put often separates the intention of the artist from that of both owner and interpreter. (275.2)

Here is BK standing, yet again, against simplification, calling instead for a full valuing of the complexity of art.

Then, as if he feels that he has left readers with a too jaundiced view of art museums, BK rounds into his conclusion of the review by raising the subject of MoMA:

> Last year was the fiftieth anniversary of the founding of the Museum of Modern Art. It was established with Rockefeller money and support at a time when "modern art" was not exactly popular in this country. No one, not even the writers of *An* Anti-*Catalog,* despite their disagreement with museum policy, could hold that the effect of that institution has been detrimental to American artistic consciousness. (276.1)

Having cited a positive example, he feels free to allow that "[f]or the most part American art museums have served well, if not brilliantly, in bringing art and knowledge of it to a broad audience" (276.1).

BK is not conceding much, however: "What is at issue, and what is brought into focus by these two books, is that success has often been accompanied by intellectual and moral failure. And it looks as if the situation is getting worse rather than better as museums compete for greater attendance and increased revenues" (276.1).

BK ends with what can be called, with only slight exaggeration, a fire bell in the night:[4]

> What is needed is leadership willing to forego [*sic*] the attractions of power and the hierarchy of taste for the sake of transcendent ideals of what is right and what is wrong in the world. Art has often been considered, along with religion, as a means to spiritual revelation. For many who could not stand the corruption of the earthly church, it was the

---

4 The phrase is from Thomas Jefferson, writing to John Holmes regarding the 1820 Compromise Line drawn to balance free and slave states when admitting Maine and Missouri to the Union.

only means to such knowledge. If that collapses, we are left only vast collections of overvalued stuff, mass idolatry, and the reactive threat of violent iconoclasm. (276.1)

BK's review is hardly what readers of *Winterthur Portfolio* would likely expect to find in the journal. He had raised the alarm already in "Primitivism and Impossible Art." Now, nine years later, he does so again, and with even greater urgency. BK has written not a review, but a manifesto, and an exultation of art.

VII

THE SCULL AUCTION AND
THE SCULL FILM (1979)

A YEAR BEFORE THE PUBLICATION of BK's review of the two books on art museums, his article about a different aspect of the art scene was published in *Art Journal*. This time the subject was the auction of art from a private collection. Titled "The Scull Auction and the Scull Film," BK's review is interesting for a number of reasons, not incidentally because it demonstrates that he had acquired enough knowledge of filmmaking to be able to offer a compelling analysis of the film and its message.[1]

I was able to watch an admittedly much degraded streamed copy of the film on a TV monitor. Even allowing for better-quality sound and visuals, I imagine that it must have taken BK many hours of watching and rewatching the film to write his review. The filmmaking is complex: The visual and aural structure of the film, as BK makes clear, is both chronological and dialectical, transparent and layered, clear and ambiguous, with lots of changeups of pace and focus that exploit the potentials of this time-based medium. The same complexity of structure, I think, can be attributed to BK's review. The assuredness of BK's visual and technical analysis, the precision of his points, and the sophistication of the article's structure are all noteworthy.

BK opens the article with a rather laconic description of the event that he labeled the "Scull auction," although it soon becomes clear that his opening is a bit of a shorthand. "On the evening of October 18, 1973, at Sotheby Parke Bernet [SPB], taxi-fleet owner Robert C. Scull sold 50 works from his well-known collection of contemporary American painting and sculpture" (50.1). That is the first sentence – when, where, who, what – as in a good newspaper story, though one could quibble with the editorializing "well-known." BK continues in the same reportorial style: "The sale brought record prices for works by living artists and earned a total of $2,242,900. Jasper Johns' *Double White Map,* which Scull bought around 1965 for $10,200, brought the highest

1 Baruch D. Kirschenbaum, "The Scull Auction and the Scull Film," *Art Journal* 39.1 (1979): 50–54.

price of the evening, $240,000 from dealer Ben Heller, who that summer had sold Jackson Pollock's *Blue Poles* to the Australian National Gallery for $2,000,000" (50.1). BK's tone is pitch-perfect, allowing the facts to say it all about the astronomical prices, who benefits from them (i.e., not the artists), the dealer–museum connection, and nothing about the art itself except artist, title, price. BK ends this opening paragraph with a final piece of information: "Outraged by the implications of the sale, Barbara Rose titled her stinging report of the auction in *New York Magazine* "Profit Without Honor"(50.1).

BK's article, however, is not about the auction itself. It is actually a review of a film that was made about the auction, as becomes clear in his next paragraph:

> The auction itself, the pre-sale activities and preparations, and the protests and confrontations are all documented in a remarkable film originated and produced by E. J. Vaughn in collaboration with John Schott. The identification of this film, *America's Pop Collector: Robert C. Scull – Contemporary Art at Auction,* as an important, indeed irreplaceable art historical document is the direct subject of this paper.[2]

BK then goes on to discuss why he considers the film so important:

> The film does more than simply document the sale. It offers an idea of the broader social, cultural, and economic context in which the events of that evening took place. In doing so it suggests the complex interconnections of the "art world," which reach far beyond the making and even the exchange of art itself. It also integrates within the action a series of cinematic portraits of the principals involved, particularly Robert and Ethel Scull. The study of the individuals raises the question of personal motivation and introduces a psychological dimension to the description of what took place. (50.1)

From the start BK leaves no doubt that, as well as valuing the film as a document of the contemporary art world, he admires the film deeply for its range and depth.

To make the case for the value of the film, BK first has to analyze it. He gives credibility to his analysis by putting the film in context of film history.

> The film was conceived and directed by E. J. Vaughn and John Schott and filmed by Susan and Alan Raymond along with Ron Dorfman. It was edited by John Schott and Leah Siegal. The cinematic philosophy followed by the group has been called "direct cinema" and sometimes referred to as "reality filmmaking." It is based on the ideas of Richard

---

2 The film was released, almost a year later to the day, on October 16, 1974, according to the online AFI Catalog of Feature Films (https://aficatalog.afi.com/). It is not clear when BK actually wrote the article, only that the article was published about five years after the film was released.

> Leacock, who with others in the late '50s and early '60s pioneered the use of portable, hand-held and synchronous sound equipment in the making of documentaries. (50.1)

(This, by the way, was the same sort of equipment that BK talked about when discussing the documentation of "impossible art"; see Chapter V.)

And now BK introduces an issue to which he will return later on:

> The central idea, which has tempted filmmakers from the very beginning, is that with the right equipment it would be possible to document an event as it unfolds in reality. The cameraman, in a sense, becomes an unseen presence within the action; and ideally the film, even as edited, allows the viewer to become a participant in the event rather than an observer of a restructured reality. Whether the film accomplishes that purpose in regard to the Scull auction … it most certainly represents the events of that evening and places them within the context of New York art dealing in which they took place. (50.1–2)

Note BK's slight tinge of skepticism, at this point, about the hope of erasing the art–life distinction.

There is way too much analysis of the film for me to cover. I have therefore chosen to focus on the points in BK's discussion that highlight his formal analysis of techniques of filmmaking.

> Edited from hours of footage, the 72-minute film starts with pre-title shots of the cocktail party opening the exhibition of the sale pieces at the showing room of Sotheby Parke Bernet. As the camera pans the exhibited works, a voice-over network news (CBS) narration is heard reporting the actual auction and the events immediately surrounding it. There is a cut to a TV monitor (black-and-white) showing scenes from the auction.… The emphasis of the report is on protesters blocking the entrance of Sotheby Parke Bernet, and on the record prices brought for individual pieces. With a cut back to the pre-auction party, Robert and Ethel Scull are seen talking with each other in front of and completely surrounded by the white diagonal stripes of Stella's deep blue *Sabine Pass*. (50.2)

BK displays here more than a cursory familiarity with filmmaking, and a keen eye for visual storytelling, allowing him to convey a lot of significance quite concisely.

He then shifts to the import of these scenes, emphasizing the film's manipulation of time:

> The juxtaposition of the pre-sale activities with the network's report of the auction as it took place creates a dramatic tension in the film between an already accomplished event and its unfolding in the film. The present in the film is seen against the background of what we know

from the broadcast actually happened. This knowledge intensifies for the viewer all the behind-the-scenes preparations at Sotheby Parke Bernet: the seating arrangement (the Japanese are next to the Italians), the instructions to the staff (be forceful without being rude), and finally the removal of the works from the exhibition rooms to the storage area of the main auction theater. Women take care of the protocol; black men, mostly, supplied with white cotton gloves, take care of the moving. (50.2)

Here, like the filmmakers themselves, BK shows his eye for the telling details that will cast the event itself as theater.

In fact, as BK now reveals with obvious delight, that is just what it was:

The preparations, which are seen in multiple cuts and fade-outs from place to place and scene to scene, lead to the climax of both the film and the event. On the evening of the auction, as witnessed on the screen, the entrance to Sotheby Parke Bernet is blocked by chanting demonstrators. Rank-and-file cabbies accuse Scull of profiteering at their expense. They carry signs reading "Robbing Cabbies is his Living Buying Artists is his Game" and "Never Trust a Rich Hippie." Art Worker Coalition members stage a street theater event – mock beautiful people exploiting mock artists. Women artists protest that work by only one woman, Lee Bontecou, is included in the sale. The night-time scenes outside Sotheby Parke Bernet are shot with a camera confusion reminiscent of the filmic reporting of the anti-war protests of the late '60s. Demonstrators are contrasted markedly and pointedly with ticket holders pushing by them to get in. Robert and Ethel Scull arrive in a chauffeur-driven Checker limousine.... Ethel wears a long black jersey sheath emblazoned with the emblem of the Scull's Angels taxi fleet. (50.2–51.1)

BK's reference to the Vietnam War protests should not, I think, be dismissed as his own, gratuitous, editorializing. From the beginning of his review, he has made clear how skillfully he thought the makers of the Scull film had deployed their techniques. Although BK did not have to comment on this particular connection, by doing so he was able to make the point indirectly that the events unfolding at SPB were substantive ones, and not just art world spectacle, though they were clearly that also:

The auction itself is remarkable and dramatic in its filming. John Marion, president of Sotheby Parke Bernet and auctioneer for the sale, knocks down each piece emphatically. The camera pans the audience like the auctioneer searching for bids.... Intercut between the shots of bids being made, and as prices rise rapidly in $5,000 increments, the Sculls are shown reacting. He cranes his neck to see from where the bids are coming, while Ethel, less curious, contemplates the event with an almost sad introspection. (51.1)

As his title signals, BK, like the filmmakers, is very interested in the Sculls. And, like the filmmakers, BK draws attention to them in various contexts – arriving at the auction, in the auction theater, at the preauction cocktail party: "Amidst the activity of the party Scull is followed singly [by the camera] as he talks to various people including dealer Leo Castelli…. He [Scull] is clearly pleased with the way the works look together. It was his intention to curate the sale like an exhibition through the selection of particular pieces to be included" (50.2).

BK draws particular attention to an event that transpired involving Scull after the auction itself was over:

At the conclusion of the sale, which comes perhaps a little too rapidly in the film, confrontation breaks out within the house itself. After making a statement in favor of artists' royalties and after kissing Ethel, Robert Rauschenberg engages Scull for the camera and accuses him of profiteering at his and other artists' expense (A combined collage and painting of his, *Double Feature,* bought by Scull for $2500 in 1959, was sold for $90,000.) Drunk, but quite aware of his purpose, he shoves Scull rudely – "I've been working my ass off for you to make that profit." He wants Scull to buy his next piece – "at these prices." Scull concedes that he will look at it anyway. (51.1)

The length of this description marks the beginning a shift in BK's analysis from the film itself to its broader implications: "Both men are obviously conscious of the media presences and therefore the public nature of their pronouncements. Scull maintains that he's done only good for the artists by raising their prices – 'I've been working for you too. We work for each other.' Their points are made and the confrontation ends in a stand-off between them" (51.1–2).

BK is almost done discussing the film as a chronology of the event:

It's over. Just before the Sculls leave they are told [what we already know] that Ben Heller had taken Johns' *Double White Map.* Ethel is saddened by the news – "it's a shame; it should have gone to a museum." Robert comforts her – "it will eventually, it will." A certain tension between them is evident. The Sculls leave, and the camera in a classical movie ending follows the tail lights of their limousine down Madison Avenue. The closing titles are followed … by a brief coda in which workers … are shown packing the pieces. (51.2)

And now, having reported on the event, BK is ready to reconsider *America's Pop Collector: Robert C. Scull,* this time not just as a document. He begins with the issue of the filmmakers' POV:

From the point of view of the film the auction is seen not simply as self-contained historical occurrence but as a media event. The film opens, as already described, with a network report on the auction as seen on a television monitor. In another sequence before the auction Scull is shown on a television talk show which we witness on the bank of monitors in the studio control room…. In other sequences before the auction we witness interviews with the Sculls at their apartment…. In these scenes the camera focuses primarily on the Sculls and their interviewers, but also opens the frame to include the media equipment and personnel. Brief interviews take place at Sotheby Parke Bernet as well, and careful watching of the scenes there reveals the continual presences of reporters, photographers, and film crews. The action is occasionally punctuated by the whiteouts of flash bulbs. (51.2–52.1)

BK lists all these examples, which are actually dispersed throughout the film, to advance his own point of view:

The media presence as externally documented (and one here could discover a kind of infinite regress of filmers filming filmers) creates a disturbing reciprocity between the event as it actually unfolds, and as it will be seen on the 11 o'clock news or reported in the press. The message is clear: news taking continually mediates reality for us. That mediation becomes an active and manipulatory presence in the event itself. To record history requires the recording of that media presence and of the effects of its products on our consciousness. By incorporating the media so insistently the filmmakers seek not to establish their own omniscience, but to offer a compounded view of the event as it took place and as it was otherwise recorded and used. (52.1)

There is an even larger point at which BK is aiming – one that allows him to return to what he sees as central to the event, if not to the film: "Somewhere all wrapped up here is the complex question of the relationship between image and reality. When taken in context of an auction of works of art, that question leads to a different kind of regress: images within images within images" (52.1).

BK is interested in two images in particular. The first is the auction itself: "Through the media and with Scull's cooperation, the auction became a public entertainment. All the elements were present for a good show: irate artists, angry proletariat, incomprehensible art, high profits, prominent persons, international connections, etc. Auctions are like stage events anyway. And this one … was clearly like an opening night spectacular" (52.1).

The second is the "multi-leveled cinematic portrait that emerges from the various views of Robert Scull." BK, devoting almost a page of his four-and-half-page review to deconstructing the filmmakers' complex portrait, finds it to be "that of cultural innocent surprised by what has happened and genuinely upset by the accusations against him" (52.1).

BK seems to find Scull, at least as portrayed in the film, rather sympathetic:

Balding, but still full-bearded, Scull emerges as the well-dressed but aging hippie art freak locked into a particular vocabulary and manner. At home he wears a white flower-decorated shirt open to mid-chest. Acquisition and ownership for him constitute an intimate involvement in the lives of artists. "Art," he tells a *Wall Street Journal* reporter "is a different kind of a high." (52.2)

Not surprisingly, it is the sequence of Scull at work that most appeals to BK, in part because of the quality of the filmmaking:

One of the best sequences in the film takes place at the Scull's Angels garage in the South Bronx. There another but still affable aspect of Scull is revealed. He is the boss, not the executive boss but the kind intimately involved in the operations of his own business. He works daily with the types whose only relation to Madison Avenue is to cruise it for fares. The filmed contrast is intentional and striking — working engine blocks and automobile parts rather than John Chamberlain's auto-part sculpture, which was seen in his studio earlier in the film. Scull is seen at his desk talking on the phone and doing paper work. In voice-over he talks about the upcoming sale and the business of art, while the camera follows the various activities of the garage.

BK clearly admires Scull as a person actively engaged in earning a living. He quotes at length from the voice-over of Scull speaking in this sequence, interpolating a brief visual description:

"Art is supposed to be such a fine, toney, cultured thing, y'know, and suddenly people are bidding wildly like it was a commodity just like any other. And I think at Parke Bernet, that's art without the floss of culture. Over there it is hard, cold money and business and, man, over there you've gotta write a check out" (on the screen woman cashier receiving and counting money turned in by drivers). "There's no fooling around and talking about the aesthetics of art. There they just talk about the money of art." (52.2)

Scull with these words has himself pulled aside the curtain, exposing the reality of the art world, and BK commends him for it:

His [Scull's] comments are not at all cynical, but simply direct in their estimation of the way things are — status and wealth through ownership. His innocence does not lie in lack of knowledge about the world but in his lack of snobbishness. Scull comes off as a man without guile, but also without deep sensitivity or cultivation. Yet he buys art. (52.2)

But if Scull buys art, it is the dealers who sell it, and in the film they comment about Scull as a collector.

> In conversations with and between dealers Ivan Karp and Leo Castelli at Karp's O.K. Harris Gallery in Soho [note how BK locates readers in the city], the film presents the professionals' view of Scull as amateur, parvenu collector. It's the sellers talking about the buyer.... The impression left is that Castelli in particular finds Scull ill-motivated in his collecting and something of a social and cultural climber. (52.2–53.1)

Piece by piece BK is using the film to construct his own portrait, one might say, of the art world in which money circulates and art changes hands. At this point, he reveals a disappointment with the film:

> Between the collector and the dealers, of course, stand the works of art themselves. All the commotion is about these objects, and yet in the film they are sadly diminished. Panning reduces the exhibited pieces to background objects distorted through the motion of the camera. Even in the still shots the works appear pallid and uncompelling, more as objects of curiosity than as important artistic statements. (53.1)

BK does not think this effect is accidental. "The intention of the filmmakers was not to advocate particular styles or particular artists, but to show how art is traded. The attitude toward the pieces, they maintain, emerges not from an editorial position as regards aesthetic quality, but from the nature of the event itself" (53.1).

Anyone with the least familiarity with BK's intellectual and moral convictions can anticipate that he is not going to let this innocence of intent go unchallenged. He is now ready to take up the issue he has let slide throughout his review:

> Despite the professed intention of the filmmakers to document the event as it unfolded in actuality without editorial comment, a particular point of view does emerge, and it emerges largely from the treatment of the works of art. In choosing to emphasize the diminished artistic importance in the works within the context of the sale, the filmmakers invite the audience to take a superior position in regard to the activity played out before them, to question the taste, judgment, and motives of Scull and the potential buyers. The viewer does not achieve the position of participant in the event, is never placed within history itself, but is forced into critical judgment as observer. If the art is questioned, then the whole event can be seen as sham, and those involved either as glamorous opportunists or simply fools. (53.1)

BK points to various sequences within the film, already discussed, that together make it so that "one simply cannot avoid considering the great difference in intrinsic value as opposed to the market value of these objects" (53.2).

And now he makes a point that resonates with his earlier article, "Primitivism and Impossible Art":

In choosing an attitude that raises questions about the whole practice of the commodity exchange of art, the filmmakers align themselves, however gently, with certain radical positions of the late '60s and early '70s. At that time many artists, in reaction to the gallery scene, advocated the making of art which, because it was without direct material manifestation, would have no applicability to the marketplace. (53.2)

Yet having raised this connection, BK decides that is not really to the point:

The film, however, is not a defense of Conceptualism or related movements, or in any way a political propaganda effort against the association of art and wealth. It does not debunk or attempt to rip away the mask of falsehood and hypocrisy by revealing the horrors of capitalist exploitation of art and artists. Its intention, as suggested by Vaughn, is to be descriptive rather than polemical, to be dialectic rather than didactic. (53.2)

Wondering whether the film can actually be considered a documentary, BK's answer is a nuanced one:

But out of that dialectic (at least for this viewer) emerges an image of art-trading which invites challenge. With these considerations in mind, thinking about the film as a historical document immediately raises a major question: is it a primary document, like the sales catalog published by Sotheby Parke Bernet, or is it a secondary description, like an extended news report with editorial overtones? Clearly, it is both. Even as edited, there is no better document of what really happened, say between Rauschenberg and Scull. The film even reveals the way the encounter was staged for, or at least conditioned by the presence of, the news media and film crew. (53.2)

This is the third time BK has evoked the Scull–Rauschenberg encounter, each time to make a different point. The first was to raise the issue of artists' rights to some of the profits when their works are resold; the second was part of his analysis of the filmmakers' portrait of Scull: "Compared to Rauschenberg, who came to the auction with a complaint and staged a confrontation to make it public, Scull remains somehow out of touch with the seriousness of the issues. He is taken aback by the heat of the attack" (52.1). And this last is to endorse the idea that the film does stand as a primary document of the "Scull auction."

However, by allowing that the film is an "encapsulated description," BK has also positioned himself to question the filmmakers' assumption about their dialectic: "[T]here can be no description without judgment. The dialectic is rooted not in the event itself, but in a point of view. Every inclusion, every sequence, every juxtaposition results first from a shooting and then from an editing decision" (53.2). All of BK's descriptions of filmmaking techniques – which make

his descriptions of the film itself, and by extension the event, so compelling –
he has now turned to support a different purpose.

This is still not his conclusion, however:

> Yet despite the ambiguity between primary and secondary source, and
> perhaps because of that very ambiguity, the film offers a composite view
> of history. In viewing it, we witness the way in which any historical
> occurrence is an amalgam of interrelated motives and necessities. In the
> film, the auction is documented not as an isolated phenomenon existing
> in its own restricted time and place, and according to its own limited
> definition of importance, but as a point of confluence of social, cul-
> tural, and economic forces. (53.2)

At this point it may seem that, far from making a point, BK is creating an
immense dialectical tangle that spins round without advancing – and yet that
is not so. The above quotation is in fact to resituate the film into a still larger
discourse:

> In bringing all these elements together, and in directing our awareness
> to their connection, the Scull film, as suggested, offers a synoptic view
> of one particularly significant event in contemporary art. The film thus
> becomes immediately valuable not only as a document of what hap-
> pened at the auction, but also as a source for what has been called con-
> textual art history. (54.1)

BK sees the film as an example of the same phenomenon raised by *An
Anti-Catalog*:

> The contextual approach offers a form of history in which the study
> of the interrelation between historical circumstances, the practice of
> image-making, and the use of images takes precedent over the study
> of individual objects, and even over the development of style as an in-
> dependent phenomenon. Indeed, within the film, works of art are seen
> not in their singularity, but as objects of exchange, inextricably bound
> up with personal motives and with the operation of ownership and sta-
> tus. (54.1)

One might think, given his discussion of this approach in his review of *An
Anti-Catalog* (see Chapter VI), that he would find it to be a problem for the
film. Here, however, his admiration for *America's Pop Collector: Robert C. Scull
– Contemporary Art at Auction* seems to temper not only his reservations about
the film but also his view of this sort of art history:

> To introduce such considerations into the study of art may sully the
> spiritual purity of artistic endeavor, and by extension of art history it-
> self; to ignore them, however, means to accept a view of art historical
> reality and practice which is too narrowly circumscribed and which

supports the myth of its own innocence. In forcing consideration of these issues, whether it does so intentionally or not, the Scull film serves not only as an important art historical document, but as an equally important statement on the nature of art historical studies. (54.1)

However, has not so much shifted his position as broadened it:

And yet there are problems. To view works of art from a too strictly contextual point of view always creates the danger of losing the art for the history or the context. Works of art seen simply as objects like any others, connected with a particular historical or cultural situation, easily degenerate in use into illustrations or simply props of those situations. Distinctions of quality and importance are thereby threatened. Something of that kind happens in the Scull film.... In the use of the film, that potentially damaging effect must be corrected, while at the same time not losing what it tells us so brilliantly about one particular exchange of art in our time. (54.1–2)

This film review, like BK's other articles, may be taken as a manifestation of his outsider position vis-à-vis the institutions of the art world. If art history – no less than galleries, museums, and auction houses – is reducing art merely to a reflection of society, BK will still stand with the artists, who understand art as a force of resistance.

VIII

PHOTO-SYNTHESIS: PHOTOSCULPTURES
AND BLENDS BY DOUG PRINCE (1985)

WERE I TO CATEGORIZE the various types of publication BK wrote, I might divide them into four (overlapping) groups: those that focus on the analysis of works of art; those concerned with the institutions associated with art; those that are revelatory of his work at RISD; and those that review art exhibitions. I have thus far considered all but the last.

According to his CV, BK wrote four such reviews: three were for exhibitions at small colleges, and two were about local exhibitions. Thus they were not likely to have reached a wide audience. Unfortunately, only one of these reviews could be located. Particularly disappointing is the loss of BK's 1976 review "A Boxer's Space" about Mahler Ryder's collages at a gallery in Newport. Ryder, who died at 54, was a Professor of Illustration at RISD.

However, BK's 1985 review of the work of Doug Prince, a visiting faculty member in the Photography Department, has survived. BK's review, "Photo-Synthesis: Photosculptures and Blends by Doug Prince," was published by the RISD Museum for a solo exhibit of Prince's work. Though a scant two columns long, is an exquisite little essay – economical and insightful.[1] It shows, once again, BK's commitment to the images before him, in all their technical, visual, and poetic richness.

Given its brevity and apparent simplicity I could simply replicate this article in full here. However, I am not doing that because I want also to make some points along the way about BK's writing.

BK begins by casting the exhibition's title as an analogy:

The title given to this exhibition "Photo-Synthesis" is particularly appropriate for the work of Doug Prince. In botany, the term refers to that process of chemical reaction by which light is transformed into nourishment, thus sustaining life on earth. The analogy to photography

1 Baruch [D.] Kirschenbaum, "Photo-Synthesis: Photosculptures and Blends by Doug Prince," June 21–September 8, 1985, Museum of Art, Rhode Island School of Design, n.p.

85

is clear, for photographic images are also produced by a chemical reaction to light. In the images of Doug Prince, however, there is an additional implied meaning: through the layering and matching of diverse photographic images, he transforms, through synthesis, literal into metaphoric truth.

BK has just signaled, at the opening of his review, that he will be viewing Prince's work through the lens of rhetorical figures of speech.

He begins by inviting people to put aside their assumptions about photographic images: "Photographs carry a particular weight of authority, for what is shown in a photograph is generally thought to match a reality external to the image. In other words, photographs apparently appropriate reality rather than represent it." And now we see why he is interested in Prince's work: "No such reality and therefore no ordinary 'photographic truth,' however, exists in the work of Doug Prince. The parts are real, but the whole is invented, compiled." BK believes *all* photographs, like other artworks, interpretively represent reality, though he is too canny at this point to say so.

He does continue, however, to elaborate on the technical means by which Prince achieved his images, just as he had explained the filmmaking techniques behind the impact of the Scull auction film:

All the pictures in the exhibition are made from more than a single negative. The smaller pictures are made by the superimposition of parts of two, sometimes three, negatives which are then printed as one. The larger pictures in which leaves and flowers are superimposed on architectural background scenes are made in a series of stages in which two images are combined on a single piece of film which is then printed. For the encased boxes, positives and sometimes negative transparencies are sandwiched between squares of Plexiglas and then spaced with the box to create the desired illusion of intersecting planes in depth.

Even without the photographs reproduced in the review, it is possible, given the simplicity of BK's explanation (he is such a gifted describer) to imagine, if not the photographs themselves, at least the complexity of effects achievable through these techniques.

Then BK changes his rhetorical register. "The power of these created realities to move us rests with the nature of metaphor. Metaphor results from the reciprocal interaction of two terms which may seem at first contradictory. When the poet refers to the 'wine-dark sea' or the 'seeing mouth' [note the use of homophones], each term affects the other and an unexpected, sometimes disturbing meaning emerges."

We are now primed for the first of BK's readings of a Doug Prince image:

When Doug Prince places a giant tortoise amongst the foundation arches of some grand (and one thinks old and European) building (*Tortoise and Arches,* 1985) he creates a visual metaphor. He juxtaposes the prehistorically primitive life form with the vacant remains of human effort. The image unites eonic and human time, the biologically sensate with the insensate stone.[2] The result is to animate the walls, however minimally, and to discover their organic principle. In reverse, the metaphor reveals the architectural principle of this unlikely reptilian creature. No question remains as to which is more enduring. In a more fleeting mode, Prince discovers the metaphoric analogy between three swans and the elegant facade of Palladio's S. Giorgio Maggiore on the Grand Canal in Venice (*Swans in Venice,* 1985).

Having primed us to see and interpret these images, BK moves from the iconographic to the formal:

> The smaller composite pictures like those of the tortoise and the swans glow with a strange black and white irrationality. They are like documented dream images. Because on reflection things in the pictures don't quite match, there occurs a momentary crisis of understanding. In that crisis the visual metaphor works its effect most strongly. Differences in perspective, in lens focal length, and in light of the combined photographic elements become apparent through intersection.

Note how BK's omission from his list of "the" after each "in" gives the word "light" more resonance.

After next giving a straightforward comparison of Prince's three types of image, BK returns to interpreting them as metaphors:

> Both the boxes and the large prints produce what might be called "memory images." They transform the layering of visual elements into the experience of the layering of time. In them, past and present make up the metaphoric terms. The calla lily in the frescoed Italianate bed chamber (*Calla Lily in Bedroom,* 1985) is a ghost of a former presence. It haunts the interior of the room with memory as if something ineffaceable happened there.

I am struck by how Prince's laconic titles seem to unsettle the images. Although BK doesn't make this point, his positioning of the titles suggests he does appreciate them.

> Through layering Prince turns the photographic process, which typically isolates an instant in the flow of time, in on itself. He records not a single moment but a succession of points in times. The elderly couple (*Wedding Chamber,* 1972) seen as vanishing negative presences, kiss in

---

2 The phrase "insensate stone" is BK's misremembering the actual words "insensible rock" in William Cullen Bryant's poem "Thanatopsis." Only when I looked up the poem now did I realize that he had misquoted the lines to me over the years. Giant turtles are central to creation myths in a number of ancient cultures: http://mesosyn.com/myth-1.html.

the dated environment of their past. The nude (*Odalisque,* 1979) looks out at an already accomplished future. Both pictures, as with the calla lily in the bed chamber, result in a presentiment of our own mortality. We are all locked in time, which in a way is the message of all photographs.

For BK images are never not about something larger than themselves.

He follows this with a one-sentence paragraph underscoring what this means: "By joining together separate pieces of photographic reality for metaphoric meaning and effect, Doug Prince simultaneously affirms the essential nature of the photographic image and extends it to an inevitable conclusion."

BK concludes by defining what this "essential nature" is, returning to the point he introduced at the beginning of his review:

> Based upon recorded reality, his images match no discrete actuality outside their own existence. His work both exploits and challenges the whole idea of photographic truth. He twists our expectations. The truth of metaphor is of a different, and perhaps higher, nature than the truth of reality. Metaphoric synthesis lies at the center of the imagination and what we like to call the creative process. "Photo-Synthesis" is not only an appropriate title for this exhibition but one that reveals as well the central artistic concern of Doug Prince and the nature of his inventions.

This review displays in microcosm the purposefulness of BK's writing, his gift for explanation, and the modesty with which he deployed his considerable expertise. It also suggests that he had more than a passing acquaintance with, and interest in, poetry as well as photography.

Fifteen years after he stopped teaching, BK would self-publish *Slippage,* a book of his own poems, written in retirement.[3] On the bookcase to the right of the desk where he wrote the poems is an assortment of stuff, among which is a matted and framed 6.75″ × 8.5″ photograph of the Arch of Titus. This Roman triumphal arch, erected in 81 C.E. on the highest point of the Via Sacra just southeast of the Forum, has on its two *intrados* monumental relief sculptures depicting the processional carrying of the spoils from the Roman sack of the temple in Jerusalem. Because of their subject, some Jews refuse to pass through the arch. In the photograph, the arch, taken on the diagonal, rises from the midpoint of the image. In the far distance through the arch can be seen the Forum, and to the sides its familiar umbrella pines. The foreground is a rising expanse of windblown sand and broken blocks of stone. The relief on the right *intrados* is visible, but cast in shadow, so not legible. The photograph is by Doug Prince.

---

3 This quite different project, like the present one, was also edited by Michael Gnat and with as much insight, expertise, and precision.

IX

REFLECTIONS ON MICHELANGELO'S
DRAWINGS FOR CAVALIERE (1960)

WHEN BK WAS A GRADUATE STUDENT at Harvard, a paper he had written for a seminar with Sydney Freedberg was accepted for the prestigious Frick Symposium on the History of Art for graduate students. The paper was subsequently accepted for publication in *Gazette des Beaux-Arts* and appeared in 1960. In "Reflections on Michelangelo's Drawings for Cavaliere," BK interprets a set of Michelangelo's drawings in light of the sonnets that Michelangelo also wrote to his friend Tomasso dei Cavaliere.[1]

All the qualities of scholarship, close reading, and forthrightness that give his later writing such authority are evident here. Also present are themes of sacred and profane love that anticipate his work on Jan Steen.

BK starts by raising the controversy related to the drawings and sonnets:

From the sixteenth century until the present, speculators have questioned the nature of Michelangelo's love for Cavaliere, and for several other young men also. The opinions which they have offered differ according to the era and the moral outlook of the reviewer. As often happens, original documents have been ignored, or changed to suit the theory. In the sonnets meant for Cavaliere words have been changed; letters full of humble passion have been glaringly misinterpreted; and women have been invented to replace the young nobleman. (99)

Here is BK, a graduate student, charging that the topic he is considering is so deeply implicated in social prejudice as to have compromised scholarly integrity. (It would be nine more years before the Stonewall Riots.)

---

1 Baruch D. Kirschenbaum, "Reflections on Michelangelo's Drawings for Cavaliere," *Gazette des Beaux-Arts* 38 (April–June 1951 [published 1960]): 99–110. surprisingly, there is no mention in the endnotes of him first giving a version of this article at the Frick Symposium; nor is there any note that he was still a graduate student, and wrote it under Sydney Freeberg. It is not clear how much this article is a transcript of the paper. Nowadays, the friend's name is more usually spelled Tommaso dei [*or* de'] Cavalieri.

Having identified the problem, BK then turns to the drawings. "Early in their friendship [notice the neutral term for the relationship] Michelangelo presented Cavaliere with a number of finished drawings in red and black chalk. These are better characterized in Berenson's term, 'pastel paintings,' for they are finished with great care and have not the spontaneity often associated with drawing style" (99). BK writes with assurance, as if on equal footing with the scholars whom he engages through citations and footnotes. He then lists the drawings by subject: "Of the drawings mentioned by Vasari, six have been definitely identified: the *Ganymede*, the *Tityus*, three versions of the *Fall of Phaeton* and the *Children's Bacchanal*" (99).

He states up front what he will spend the rest of the paper demonstrating: "Taken together, the drawings constitute a poetic confession of Michelangelo's love for Cavaliere, and of the elation and guilt, ascent and fall which he associated with love" (99). Those already familiar with the myths no doubt appreciated BK's choice of phrase.

BK continues in this vein:

> For this almost bashful expression of his feelings Michelangelo turned to classical mythology and motif. The association of themes of love and the antique is a natural one, for not only is the antique "classical" but it is also "pagan," and can serve where Christian iconography can not [*sic*] or dare not. That Cavaliere was an amateur of classical art and had a considerable collection, makes it even more natural for Michelangelo to have chosen the classical for these confessional drawings." (99–100)

Of course BK knows he is writing for an audience of experts for whom there was no need to make the antique/classical connection, but stating it allows him to make a point about Christianity's selective appropriation of the antique, which suits his purpose.

After discussing the provenance of the drawings of the *Ganymede* and the *Tityus,* he characterizes Michelangelo's rendering of these myths:

> Michelangelo has chosen two moments representing opposing states of existence: ascension, and fall. It is generally agreed that the drawings constitute a pair symbolizing the dual nature of love. Erwin Panofsky [I think it fair to say no art historian is more famous than he. – EG] finds in them a neo-Platonic program. Thus the *Ganymede* is the ascension of the soul-mind "symbolizing the ecstasy of Platonic love"; and the *Tityus* is the damnation of the lustful body which enslaves the soul. Other critics interpret the drawings as simply the rapture and torture of love. The myths had been so interpreted previously – e.g. by Plato and by Lucretius.[2] (100–101)

2 In Greek mythology Ganymede is the beautiful young boy who was carried off to Olympus by Zeus (in the form of an eagle) and became a cupbearer to the Olympian gods. Tityus was a giant, the offspring of Zeus and the mortal woman Elara, who attempted

Here BK displays his familiarity with the iconology of these subjects and then, having cited various interpretations, positions himself to propose his own. It is also the first instance in his writings of his rejection of easy binaries: "It seems that both Platonism and the confused, ambivalent feeling of love are present, and that to assign a single meaning – or a single impulse – to these works is all too limiting" (101).

To enlist support for his reading of the "admixture of Platonism and physical love," BK quotes in full, without comment, all fourteen lines of one of Michelangelo's love sonnets to Cavaliere (101). Yet to anyone familiar with the myth of Ganymede, these lines in the quoted sonnet – "Wingless upon your pinions forth I fly;/Heavenward your spirit stirreth me to strain;/E'en as you will, I blush and blanch again" – would be identification enough (101).

BK contends in his reading of the drawing that "Ganymede then is not carried off against his will, but rather rises in trance, the powerful strokes of the eagle's wings lifting him into a higher realm. All the energy of flight is concentrated in the gigantic bird. But as if to assist, the body of Ganymede has surrendered all its earthly weight" (102). It is interesting that BK neither points to the drawing (Fig. 1 in the article) nor, as I've noted, isolates or comments on any lines in the sonnet. By making no clear distinction between the drawing and poem, BK seems to imply that his analysis can be applied to both.

His next paragraph starts with an open statement about the source myths:

> Michelangelo departs from myth in one essential. In the story of Ganymede an eagle abducts the boy; but it is a vulture that pecks at Tityus' liver. Yet even a cursory glance at the drawings discovers [note the pointed language] that the bird is the same in both. Closer examination shows that Ganymede and Tityus look remarkably alike, with curly hair and round heads, and full, almost chubby bodies. The bird is the dynamic force in both pictures, Ganymede and Tityus being inert. (102)

BK then broadens his comparison: "As pure energy the bird is amoral and inflicts reward and punishment, with neither benevolence nor malice, upon the same contestant for the same act. Michelangelo seems to be saying that the same amoral forces govern both the positive and negative aspects of a single experience" (102).

To strengthen his argument about Michelangelo's *Tityus* drawing, BK compares it to a Titian painting of the same subject, then swoops in with his conclusion: "This drawing, then, when taken with its companion, the *Ganymede*, depicts a voluntary acceptance of torture, an acceptance of the fall as well as the flight of love and a recognition that one demands the other" (102). Again,

(cont.)
to rape the goddess Leto at the behest of Hera, the wife of Zeus. Tityus was slain by Leto's children, Artemis and Apollo, and then in the underworld staked to the ground, where two vultures perpetually ate his ever-regenerating liver.

In support of his interpretation BK reproduces one of love sonnets that Michelangelo sent Cavaliere. Again, BK does not interpret the poem, beyond pointing out a wordplay reference to Cavaliere.

Having made his case through formal analysis, BK turns again to his conversation with Panofsky:

> In "The Neo-Platonic Movement and Michelangelo," which is both the basis and the inspiration of this essay, Dr. Panofsky sums up his discussion of the two drawings by saying: "In both compositions the traditional allegorical interpretation of a mythological subject was accepted, but it was invested with a deeper meaning of a personal confession, so that both forms of love were conceived as two aspects of one essentially tragic experience." (103)

Due homage paid, BK continues: "This is certainly close to the heart of the matter, but I would qualify the statement: We have here not the representation of sacred and profane love, but rather two inextricable elements to be found in love – to be found indeed, in any intense emotion or experience" (103). This is BK, early in his career, suggesting that to interpret art requires not only close looking but a mind open to accepting the complexity of things – in this case, that the distinctions between the sacred and profane are not so easily parsed, nor the meanings of a work of art so easily constrained in their subject matter.

He then proceeds to a third myth, the *Fall of Phaeton*. Compared to his discussion of the *Ganymede* and the *Tityus*, his analysis of the *Phaeton* is more complicated, as there are three close variants of the same subject.[3] First BK lays out the chronology of the drawings, then he describes the similarities among them:

> In all three versions we find a compositional relationship which expresses the core of the struggle of the individual caught between aspiration and failure. Above, the divine: Zeus mounted on his eagle in position of uncontested power and majesty which Phaeton yearned, against all persuasion, to possess for but a single day. Below, the human: amazement and powerless grief at the moment of disaster. And all this absorbed in the continuity of time – for the river Eridanus [in the form of a river god] flows on. The fall is not only a loss of the divine but also a submersion into anonymity. Between these extremes is the chaotic and agonizing act of falling, in which one is no longer divine, nor yet wholly human. (103–4)

---

3 In Greek myth Phaeton was the son of the water nymph Clymene and (allegedly) Helios, the god of the sun. Phaeton, taunted with illegitimacy, persuaded Helios to let him drive the chariot of the sun across the heaven for a day as a sign of of Helios' paternity. Phaeton, however, was unable to control the chariot's horses, and Zeus, to prevent the sun going off course, threw his thunderbolt at Phaeton, who plunged to his death.

BK's analysis is so emotional that it almost seems he has experienced the same sequence of feelings himself.

He then turns from formal analysis to iconography:

> The changes from version to version of the drawings do, I believe, bear out these feelings. In the first, Michelangelo was much concerned with accuracy of detail. He followed Ovid's narrative strictly. Phaeton falls in an arc; the duality of his state is carried only by his central position. This is even more strongly felt in the second, more despairing version, in which Michelangelo departed radically from Ovid. Phaeton plummets headlong to the ground, losing all contact with the divine.… In the third, and in this interpretation most successful version, Michelangelo abandoned both the asymmetry of the first version and the symmetry of the second, to arrive at a triangular form which connects all the elements into a single experience.[4] (104)

Now he is ready to take up the larger meaning of the myth and its significance for Michelangelo:

> *Hybris* was the sin of Phaeton. He suffered for his presumption to the divine. That Michelangelo declared himself presumptuous in two of his letters to Cavaliere has been pointed out by Panofsky. It would seem that we have in these drawings the fall of the presumptuous lover. Whereas the boy of the myth was caught between attainment and destruction, Michelangelo's tragedy remains potential. He is trapped between immense yearning and the haunting fear of failure. (105)

BK supports this interpretation with quotations from one of the letters Michelangelo wrote to Cavaliere.: "Three versions of this letter survives, which shows how carefully he labored for expression. The making of three versions of the drawing itself, and the anxiety over their acceptability, testify to the same care of execution and humility of approach which are so striking in a man of Michelangelo's external temperament" (106).

Again he returns to Panofsky. If, BK says, the myth of Phaeton was about hubris, then the letters are demonstrations of Michelangelo's humility: "Dr. Panofsky explains this humility neo-Platonically: the youth who is loved becomes the *idea* of beauty, a religious symbol which demands humility. This, then, according to Panofsky, is Michelangelo's approach to Cavaliere, he perishes by fire and fall because of presumption, approach being presumption enough" (106).

As before, BK states his objection to Panofsky's interpretation modestly:

---

4 BK extends his analysis from the divine into the human zone, comparing across the three versions the engagement of Eridanus; the Heliads, Phaeton's sisters by the sun god Helios; and Cycnus (aka Cygnus), king of Liguria, who was Phaeton's friend (or lover) and appears in the third drawing, mourning, as the swan he later became.

Substantially I agree, but would hesitate again on its strictly neo-Platonic approach. If the fatalistic damnation which these drawings depict can be linked with a desire for love, we have yet another reason for use of the words "presumption" and "presumptuous" – a fear of failing by being other than humble. For the unsure lover is always plagued by the fear of losing. (106)

The last sentence is the key that unlocks BK's modest tone. For BK, art, even Michelangelo's, cannot possibly be only about lofty ideas; rather, it is always implicated in actual human experience.

BK offers a final psychological generalization:

The drawings of *Phaeton* express through the single myth the duality within love, as do the *Ganymede* and the *Tityus* taken as a pair. Love, like flight, entails both elation and constant risk. Though Phaeton's presumption brought him death, it brought also a moment in which he partook of the divine. It is as if every action or feeling, for Michelangelo, no matter how fulfilling of the individual, demands its correlated punishment. Positive and negative are inseparable. (106–7)

This declaration does not, however, conclude BK's analysis of the drawings but rather opens them to a bravura comparison to Michelangelo's public works: "Here, I feel, the essence of Michelangelo's Terribilità begins to come into focus. The conflict expands to the act of creation, and becomes the struggle between Michelangelo's demiurgic and destructive urges" (107). After briefly discussing the Sistine Chapel paintings he reinforces this point with Michelangelo's sculpture.

Michelangelo's manner of working in stone, furiously attacking the block so that the image might emerge, is also indicative of the unity of opposite forces. The final act of willful destruction of the last pietàs is the most powerful summation of the opposition of creative and destructive urges, and in a sense the denial of the positive value of art. This speaks of the compulsive yearning for expression and the constant feeling of inadequacy. (108)

BK concludes by suggesting a larger significance for the drawings.

In the Cavaliere drawings, private though they are, and more closely related to Michelangelo's poetry than to his great public works, there appears in microcosm that conflict which achieves Titanic proportions in his massive works. In their smallness, their delicacy of treatment, and perhaps even because of their more personal subject matter, these drawings afford a gentle and gradual approach to the understanding of the struggles in the larger works, which often seem so forbidding. (108)

BK's article about Michelangelo, despite a style that seems at times a bit self-conscious, displays more than a capacity for research, formal analysis, and nuanced and courageous interpretation. It also suggests why BK chose to devote his considerable intellectual capacities to thinking about art. He did so, I believe, because for BK, works of art are always already, first and last, *human* things. As such, they can always be revelatory of the human condition in all its complexities.

I also think that BK could write with such insight about Michelangelo's drawings because he saw them through a deep recognition of human ambition and frailty, including his own. It might be too easy to suggest parallels between Michelangelo's conflict, setting desire against self-doubt, and that of a street kid turned Harvard graduate student. However, I would say that it was BK's belief in the power of art to elevate the human condition, without denying it, that so moved and motivated him – a conclusion fully supported by his writings.

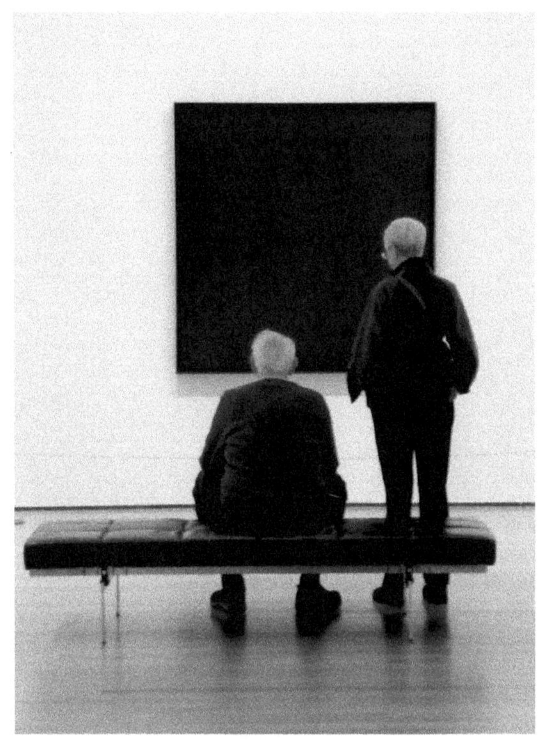

BK and EG at MoMA, NYC. *Photo:* © Ed Brown.

PART TWO

CRITICAL ESSAYS

BARUCH KIRSCHENBAUM

Piss and Light

This paper, which is about Andres Serrano's 1987 photograph called *Piss Christ* (fig. 1), was originally presented at a faculty colloquium on the theme of "Images of Power/Images of Rebellion," held at Rhode Island School of Design in March 1991. As is well known from extensive media coverage (for the most part without reproductions, however), the large (40 x 60 in.) cibachrome photograph of a construction made by Serrano in which he submerged a plastic crucifix in urine (purportedly, his own) caused a major uproar when it was revealed that National Endowment for the Arts (NEA) funding had supported an exhibition in which it had been shown. The Serrano cibachrome, along with the retrospective of the photographs of Robert Mapplethorpe, almost brought down the NEA and the whole apparatus of government support of the arts in this country the previous fall, that is, of 1990.[1]

I had become particularly interested in the Serrano photograph for two reasons. First, because at the height of the NEA funding controversy the issue of art attacked and rejected as blasphemous or inappropriate generated some heated discussion in a course on Italian seventeenth-century art I was then teaching. As is well known to specialists at any rate, a number of Caravaggio's Roman paintings were rejected by the churches for which they had been commissioned because they were thought to lack the decorum believed appropriate for their religious iconography. His *Death of the Virgin* made for the Cherubini Chapel in S. Maria della Scala was removed from the altar because, according to later reports, he was thought to have used the swollen corpse of a common woman—a prostitute according to one source—as a model for the Virgin. The results were apparently considered indecorous by the clergy of the church and, it can be argued, theologically questionable as well. In the case of the *Inspiration of St. Matthew* made for the Contarelli Chapel in S. Luigi dei Francesi, the picture was reportedly removed because the heavy figure of the saint with awkwardly crossed legs and dirty feet seen from below was thought inappropriate for the appearance of St. Matthew, the first among the Evangelists. It can be further surmised that the general characterization of St. Matthew as an illiterate and uncomprehending peasant and the blatant sensuality of the angel—languid and self-caressing—contributed to the rejection of the picture as well. Early sources, however, make no mention of that response.

Both pictures were replaced: the *Death of the Virgin* by that of another artist and the *St. Matthew* by a second, presumably more acceptable, version of the subject by Caravaggio himself, which remains in place in the chapel today. The first version of the *St. Matthew* was destroyed during the Second World War and the *Death of the Virgin* is presently in the Louvre.

The second reason for my interest in Serrano's *Piss Christ* at that time—and also in parallel with Caravaggio—was that for all the fuss made over the photograph little, if any, consideration was given to the meaning that Serrano's self-conscious blasphemy may have been intended to express. Its detractors (among others, The American Family Association and its President the Reverend Donald Wildmon and United States Senator Alfonse D'Amato of New York) simply took its offense as self-evident. On the floor of the Senate, D'Amato in a fit of staged displeasure ripped apart the catalogue of the exhibition in which the photograph had appeared. Its defenders for their part were more concerned with the issues of censorship and constitutional guarantees of freedom of artistic expression than with questions of meaning. This was so although the serious religious content of Serrano's work had received significant critical consideration, most particularly in an article by Lucy Lippard in *Art in America* (April, 1990).[2]

In regard to that meaning and in relation to the theme of the colloquium ("Images of Power/Images of Rebellion"), the power in *Piss Christ* is the power of Catholicism both as a personal faith and as the institution of the church carried by its central icon. The crucifix in Catholic understanding is an object of veneration. Devotion offered to the crucifix (in doctrine anyway, if not always in practice) is offered not to the object itself, but to the actuality of Christ behind the image— the prototype, to use the theological term. The crucifix is not meant as a representation of the historical event of the crucifixion, but as a ritual object that centers attention on the sacrifice of Christ as a sacred event through which, according to Christian belief, the promise of human redemption is fulfilled. As a ritual object it also denotes the power of the church in mediation of that redemption.

That Serrano speaks from the inside of the faith is clear from his background. He is Cuban on his mother's side and Honduran on his father's. He was brought up in Brooklyn largely by his maternal grandmother and, as might be expected, in a strongly Catholic environment. Though he identifies himself as a "lapsed" Catholic, he understands that this only means lapsed from the rituals of the church, not necessarily from personal belief. In an interview in *Contemporanea* with Patrick Finnegan, significantly entitled "Bearing the Cross" (November, 1990),[3] Serrano explained that those unresolved feelings have engendered tensions about his Catholic upbringing that have found, if not resolution, than at least some relief in the creative expression of his art. "I have" he said, "learned that I don't have to embrace the entire philosophy of the Catholic Church, which is often harsh and primitive, to sustain certain feelings of religiosity and spirituality that it cultivated in my life."

If the power of the *Piss Christ* photograph, then, is the power of internalized belief and institutional control, the rebellion is expressed in the emphatic challenge to that power through the obscene defamation of its sacred and central icon. There are several steps involved in that act. First of all, for the image Serrano used a common and cheap plastic crucifix, though one (probably Early Renaissance or Late Gothic in derivation) that presents the body of Christ as delicate and vulnerable. The frailty of the body on the wooden cross intensifies the act of defamation. Next, and what of course has been considered unforgivable, he submerged that bit of plastic and wood in a container of urine again, purportedly his own.

And as if those steps were not in themselves sufficient defamation, he then photographed the construction to be printed in large color format. That transformation from a sculptural construction to photograph changed the essential nature of the image and therefore our response to it. As is well established, photographs are presumed to document an existent actuality whether constructed or natural. That is to say, they are understood as indexical signs. That such a notion is faulty in its assumptions about the nature of the photographic image doesn't make it any the less operative in common valuation. The photograph—more than the construction—implies that we witness the Christ of the crucifix submerged in urine-piss. Further, and in an interesting complication, the nature of the crucifix itself as holy icon reinforces and intensifies the conflation of the plastic figure to begin with and then the photograph with the presumed reality of Christ on the cross. Through the power of the image, what is done to the Christ of the crucifix is done to Christ himself.

As a final and irrevocable act, Serrano affixed a title to the photograph—"Piss Christ"—by which he gives the image a text through which it must be read. If it weren't for the title, the photograph might have been taken as a rather eloquent and moving image of a light-struck crucifix. The defamation is contained, clearly, more in the text of the title than in the image itself.

That Serrano has some difficulty with authority in general can be seen in his other "piss works"—all 40 x 60 in. cibachromes—of the late 1980s to which the *Piss Christ* belongs. In *Female Bust* and *Thinker* both of 1988, just to take two examples out of several (though he did not attach the epithet "piss" to these works, he did in the case of "Piss Discus" and "Piss Elegance" of the same group), he challenges standard cultural and specifically art-historical icons using plastic reproductions that demean them to begin with. One work refers rather distantly to classical sculpture and the other to Rodin's perhaps best known work. That Serrano should respond particularly to sculpture is not surprising. He began making art not as a photographer, but as a sculptor. And the "piss works" (and others as well) rely on his integration of sculptural constructions and photography to achieve their meaning and effect.

But the cultural "piss works" leave the impression that they are actually substitutes for what is really on Serrano's mind. It is not surprising that they are not as successful in their expressive effect as *Piss Christ* or *Piss Pope I* of 1988 or even more *Red Pope* of 1990 (fig. 2). In *Red Pope*, the objects (it's difficult to tell whether they are connected or not, but one assumes it is the mitered Pope Paul who holds the bishop's staff with crucifix for which he is known) are immersed in a mixture of urine and blood which Serrano assures us is animal blood from a local *abattoir*. Defamation by urine is here conflated by Serrano with the bloody history of the Catholic church and simultaneously with the wine of the Eucharist, which in sacramental ritual is miraculously transformed (transubstantiated) into the blood of Christ. In *Red Pope*, and even more strongly in *Two Christs* of 1986, in which he superimposed the bloody skeleton of a butchered animal (a monkey, he reports, which makes the human physical association particularly poignant and disturbing) over a crucifix, Serrano is intent on making the association of blood and Catholicism inescapable and physically repulsive.

Serrano's obsession (if several works can constitute an obsession) with the church and blood can be found also in the 1984 cibachrome called *Heaven and Hell* (fig. 3), in which the painter Leon Golub (known for his harsh paintings of tortures and interrogations) posed for the cardinal and a cousin of Serrano's for the woman. *Heaven and Hell* must be considered a political as well as a religious statement, in which we are confronted with the question of which of the two terms—suffering or official indifference—is heaven and which hell. Being a Latino with family roots in Central America, such a comment by Serrano can be understood as a reference to the support the official church offered (and still offers) to the military right in Nicaragua, Honduras, El Salvador, and elsewhere. It makes reference as well (as Lucy Lippard has pointed out and Serrano affirmed) to the church's indifference to the suffering of women in its positions on divorce, birth control, and abortion. Clearly there is enough blood to go around.

The fluids of the body with which Serrano is so fundamentally concerned function in his images, I believe, as indices of the real bodies that endure the sufferings of the world. In a number of cibachromes from 1986 through 1990, he abstracted those fluids from their bodily sources to give them the quality of color-field paintings. They appear in these works as pure color and flat plane. But once again titles like *Milk, Blood* and *Circle of Blood* serve as texts through which the images in their aestheticized purity must be read. The titles force attention disturbingly back to the human body and its secretions to which Christian symbolic meanings are so often attached. Milk is the purity of the sustaining Virgin; blood the sacrifice of Christ to purge the world of the stain of original sin.

Blood in the contemporary world particularly has two additional charged meanings to which Serrano forces attention. In *Red River* of 1989 (also a large cibachrome; fig. 4), he photographed menstrual blood on a sanitary pad. The suggested ghostly fetal shape in the stain makes the association between menstrual blood and abortion. This is a charged subject particularly for Catholics, whether lapsed or not. There is an inescapable sense of loss in the image. There is also the association of blood with AIDS in the knowledge of which the pure color of *Circle of Blood* loses its aesthetic isolation and innocence to become charged with desperate meanings. And the blood of AIDS is connected also with semen as both intimate and infecting. In a series of cibachromes beginning in 1989, Serrano turned to that bodily, and increasingly social, reality as well. In *Ejaculate in Trajectory*, the blur of color across the dark background becomes (again by virtue of the text of the title) as potentially deadly as it is beautiful. For those aware of the issue, the connection between abstract aestheticized form and harsh reality is clear and intentionally ironic.

In a strange way, all of Serrano's images despite their apparent harshness are saying, "Yes" and "No" and then again "Yes." In *Piss Christ*, that "Yes/No/Yes" can be understood as an expression of Serrano's unresolved conflict with his own Catholicism. The picture is more than a simple power/rebellion opposition, but as suggested at the beginning of this paper, affirms the very belief it appears to attack so meanly. In an interview with Derek Gutherie in the *New Art Examiner* (September 1989), Serrano told the following story:

> You know, a woman said to me recently that when she found out that I had been photographing urine, she laughed and she said, "It strikes me as particularly funny, because I live in the Bowery and I see piss all the time and so I don't understand why." And when she said that, I realized that maybe part of the reason why I'm doing these piss pictures is that I'm trying to come to terms with the difficult or disagreeable aspects of our lives—of my own life.[4]

To put the issue another way, if the crucifix is the power of Catholicism, the piss is the piss of the corruption and suffering of the world through which the image (the icon) of the crucified Christ shines forth as the promise of ultimate redemption. And in the picture, the crucifix is light struck in the golden fluid as if by the presence of divine light.

In the tradition of Christian iconography, the image of the suffering Christ is, of course, very common. And if considered in relationship to that tradition, *Piss Christ* can be understood as a particularly disturbing vision of that basic Christian theme. In historical images, the photograph recalls the light-struck figure of Christ in the pervading darkness of Rembrandt's etching the *Three Crosses* and particularly in its late increasingly dark states. It also recalls in content, though not in image, the intense and painful degradation of Grünewald's tortured body of Christ from the exterior of the Isenheim altarpiece. And there are countless other representations in Christian art of Christ on the cross in his sorrow, of which perhaps none is more physically extreme than the skeletal remains hung on the cross in a late Gothic crucifix at Cologne Cathedral.

Piss Christ, I would argue, far from being an obscene blasphemy, can be located within a long iconographic tradition in Christian art the meaning of which Serrano forces us to

confront with a renewed understanding and passion by the very obscenity of his gesture. He is not alone among contemporary artists in turning to the degraded image of the crucified Christ to comment on the painful realities of the modern world. Barbara Kruger, just to take one example, offers in photo-montage the still struggling female Christ whose face is covered with a gas mask (fig. 5). The point is clear especially given the work's title, *It's our pleasure to disgust you*, and the rest of the text of the image, "forget heroes, forget morality, forget innocence, forget shame."

Barbara Kruger's photo-montage, one may assume, makes reference to a 1928 drawing by George Grosz of the crucified Christ in army boots, whose face is covered with a gas mask (fig. 6). That drawing prompted a sensational group of trials in Berlin between 1928 and 1931, in which Grosz was ultimately found guilty of blasphemy. The text/title of the drawing, *Keep your mouth shut and do your duty*, was taken from a line in the theatrical version of Jaroslav Hasek's novel *The Good Soldier Schweik*, on the design of which Grosz had worked. In the final outcome of the trial, which went all the way to the National Court, Grosz and his publisher (the drawing had been published along with a number of others from the production in a portfolio called *Hintergrund*, that is, "Background") were fined and all the published copies of the drawing along with the printing plates were ordered to be "rendered unusable." In the defense of his work, Grosz maintained that he had conceived of the drawing as being in the German tradition of portraying Christ as a figure denied and rejected. He pleaded that it was a response to the innocence and martyrdom of the men slaughtered during the war. Serrano's *Piss Christ*, I've tried to show, can be understood as a related response to the idea of the figure of the denied and rejected Christ in the world.

It is a sad irony that those who out of Christian respect have attacked Serrano's photograph so violently as blasphemous have so little understanding of the profound Christian meaning that it implies and by which it is energized. Serrano's (like Kruger's and like Grosz's) is an angry and disturbing image, but one that is wrapped in anguished faith.

Finally, there is the nagging suspicion that those who reject images like those of Caravaggio or of Serrano do so not out of a lack of understanding, but out of a clear recognition of their potential for radical political meaning. To accept the image of a plebeian *St. Matthew*, or a common Virgin who seems to die a common death, or an obscenely degraded Christ might reinforce the potential of Christianity to become a voice for social and political discontent. Within the Counter-Reformation church, Caravaggio's religious vision could be understood as reinforcing that potential, and therefore reverberating with Protestant sympathies. And Serrano's religious images come at a time when the Catholic church is again challenged for neglecting the call to a social ministry by those who feel marginalized by their poverty, gender, and by personal choices and orientations.

NOTES

[1] And the controversy continues: in August of 1994, a $20,000 grant to Serrano recommended by the NEA Peer Panel on Photography was overturned by the National Council for the Arts, which was established to oversee NEA grants after the fracas of 1990. Serrano believes that he has been in effect blackballed by the National Council. Litigation is almost certainly to follow, particularly since the National Council used earlier material (presumably *Piss Christ* and other of the "piss works"; see below) in denying a grant for new work. Such use is a violation of NEA guidelines; see Brian Wallis, "Serrano Blackballed by NEA?" *Art in America* 82 (October 1994): 33. His more recent work includes cibachrome portraits of homeless subjects in New York and hooded Klan figures.

[2] Lucy Lippard, "Andres Serrano: The Spirit and the Letter," *Art in America* 78 (April 1990): 230-45.

[3] Patrick Finnegan, "Bearing the Cross," *Contemporanea* 22 (November 1990): 230-45.

[4] Derek Guthrie, "Taboo Artists: Serrano Speaks," *New Art Examiner* 17 (September 1989): 45-46.

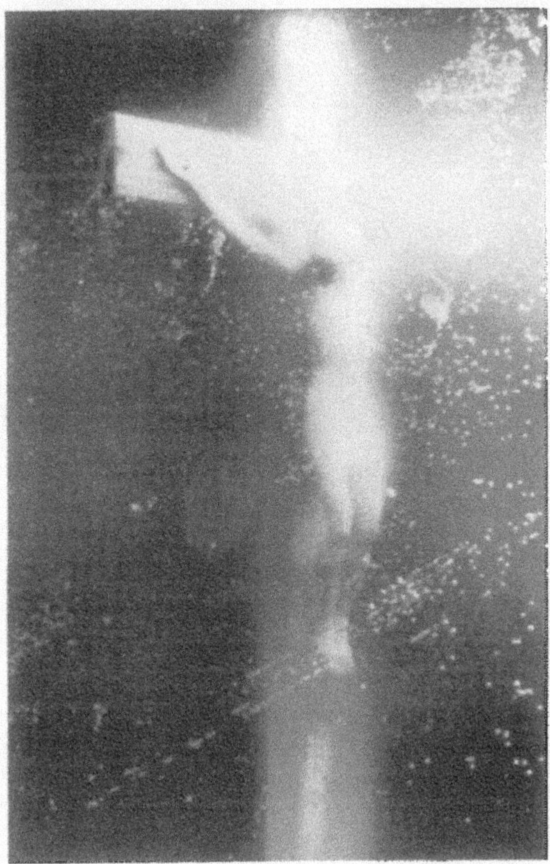

Fig. 1. Andres Serrano, *Piss Christ*, 1987. Paula Cooper Gallery, New York.

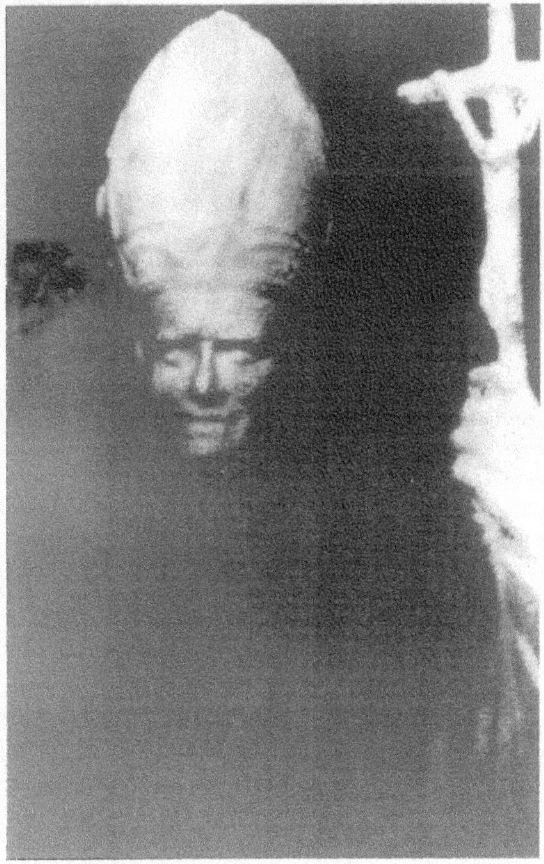

Fig. 2. Andres Serrano, *Red Pope*, 1990. Paula Cooper Gallery, New York.

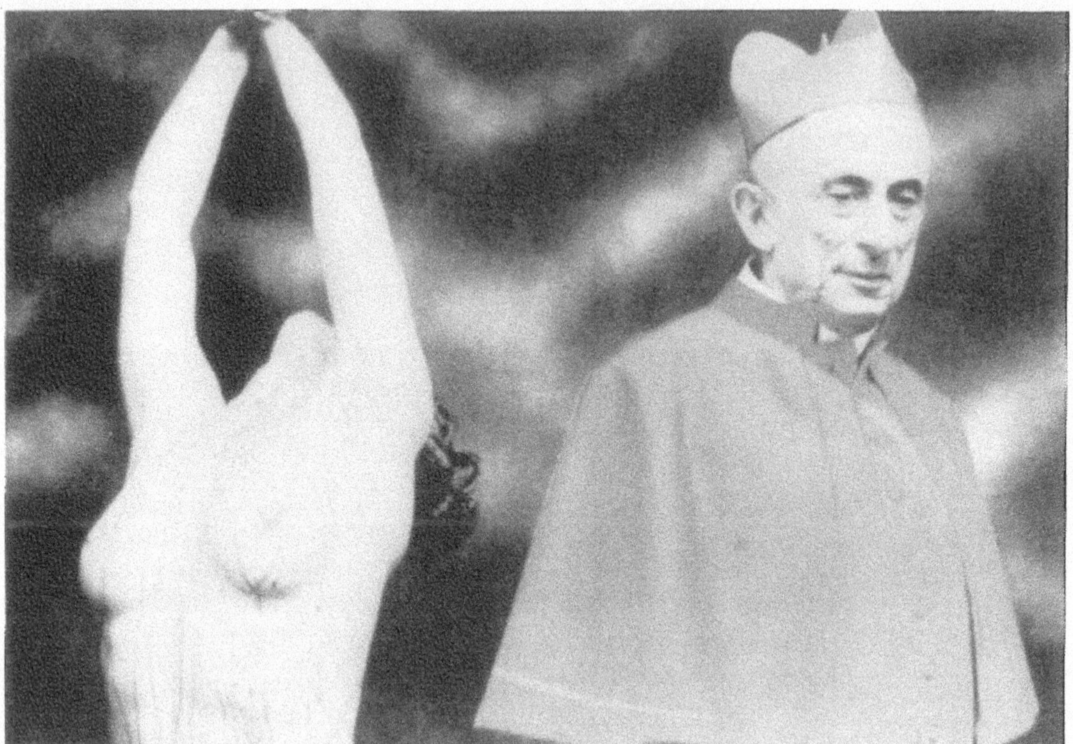

Fig. 3. Andres Serrano, *Heaven and Hell*, 1984. Paula Cooper Gallery, New York.

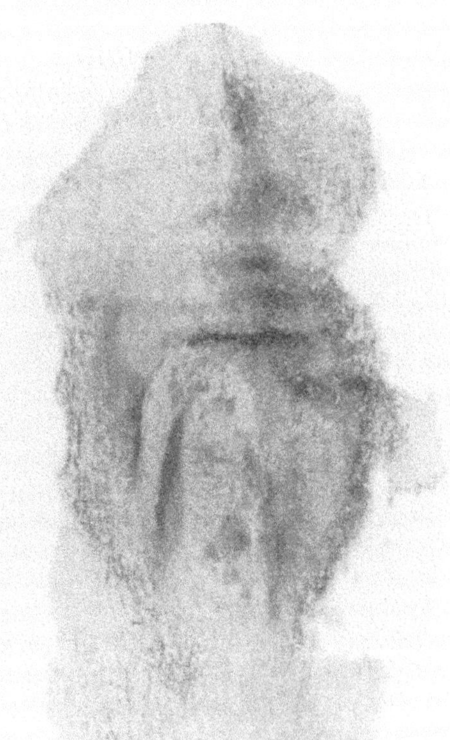

Fig. 4. Andres Serrano, *Red River*, 1989. Paula Cooper
Gallery, New York.

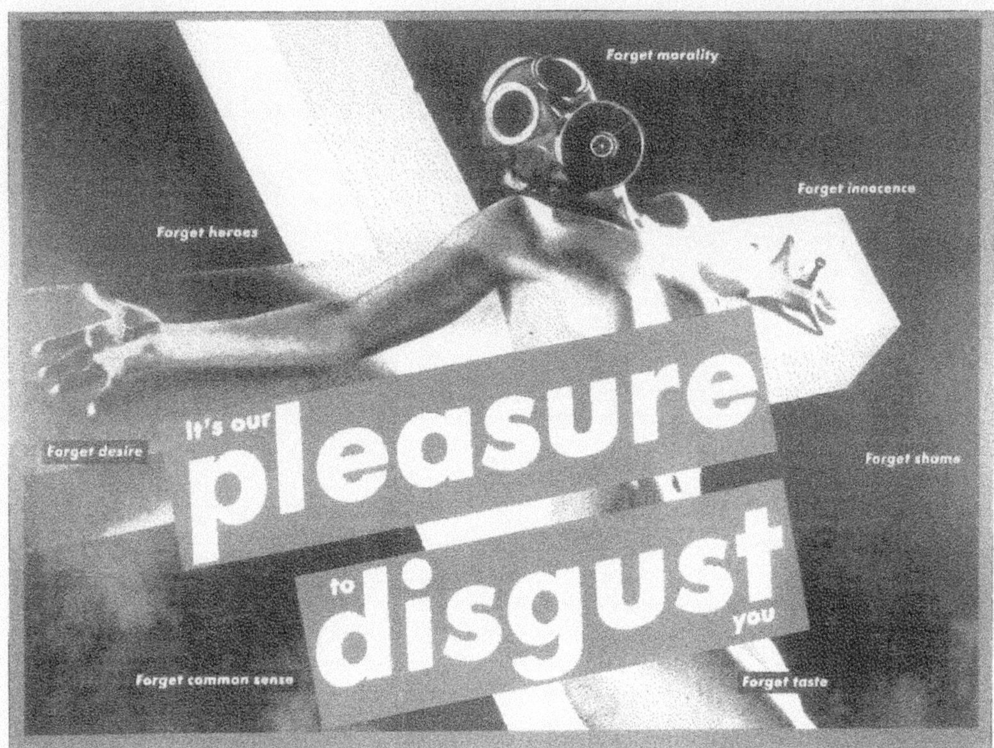

Fig. 5. Barbara Kruger, *It's our pleasure to disgust you*, 1991. Mary Boone Gallery, New York.

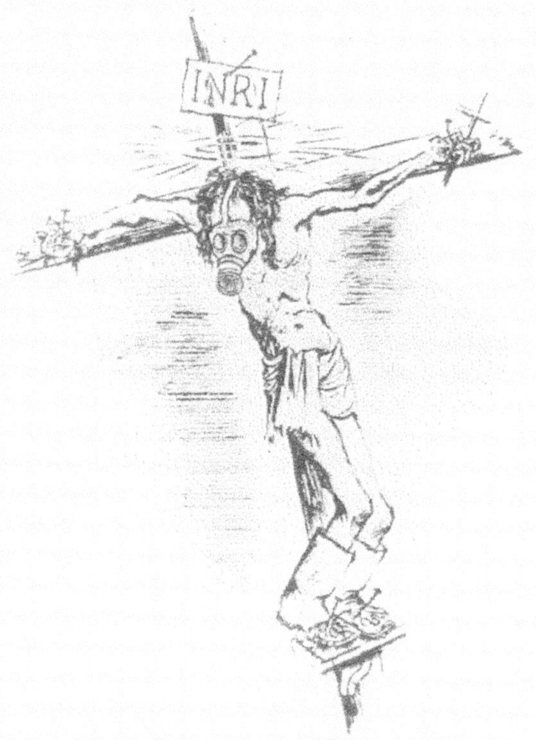

Fig. 6. George Grosz, *Crucified Christ*, 1928. New York, Richard Cohn Collection.

Private Parts and Public Considerations

Baruch D. Kirschenbaum

"RISD show lets you see things you usually don't"

— *Providence Journal-Bulletin*

Saturday, May 13, 1978

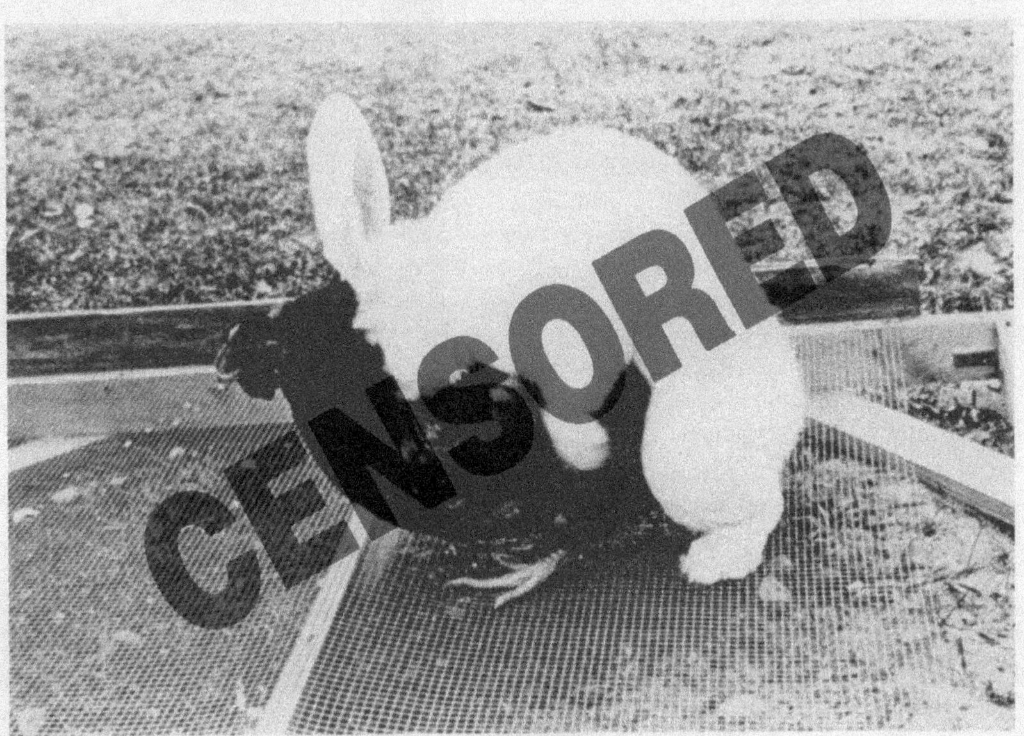

1. Richard Liebowitz, *Rabbit and Chicken*. Seized by police.

In June of 1978, I became involved as an art historian in a court hearing that raised issues about the acceptability of certain kinds of art. The case, which caused considerable local agitation, had to do with an exhibition mounted by students and faculty of the Photography Department at Rhode Island School of Design in Providence. Called "Private Parts," the exhibition contained photographs (mostly) and works in other media which addressed that theme. Most, but not all, were explicitly sexual and/or anatomical. On May 16th, a few days after "Private Parts" opened in a local gallery, it was raided and essentially dismantled by the Providence police acting under a newly adopted state obscenity law. Several exhibitors whose work had been seized brought a class-action suit against the police on behalf of all exhibitors. The first step in the suit was a hearing for preliminary injunction against further action by the police while the case was pending. (The confiscated pieces had been returned under an earlier court order.) My involvement was first as a friend of certain exhibitors and then as an "expert" witness at the hearings, testifying to the artistic nature of the exhibition and therefore to its acceptability under the state law.

  Two factors have moved me to write about the "Private Parts" case and my role in it. First, though a minor and somewhat frivolous event in itself, the show and case that followed raised disturbing questions about relationships among art and prurience and law. Second, while my testimony seemed effective enough in court, it left me feeling ill at ease with the position I had taken and with my arguments in support of that position. The purpose of this paper is to reconsider that position. It is necessary first to describe what happened with the exhibition and to review the legal action including my own testimony.

Part I: The Exhibition and the Raid

  "Erotic art stirs anger over RISD tax status"

   — Providence Journal,
   Monday, May 15

  "Erotic art show raided; 40 photos, objects seized"

   — Providence Journal,
   Wednesday, May 17

The "Private Parts" exhibition was a project of students at Rhode Island School of Design's Photography Department. Intending a show with a thematic basis, two senior students proposed an independent study project to the faculty of the department. They wanted to organize and mount a show that would be a collective effort, involving as many people in the department as cared to be involved. With departmental support the independent study project turned into a departmental effort. The theme exhibition which became "Private Parts" gradually grew more ambitious, however, when its call for submissions extended beyond the department and even beyond the College.

  It is not clear, even to the principals involved, how or exactly when they arrived at the theme of private parts for the exhibition. Once suggested however, it was enthusiastically adopted. It seemed provocative in subject, open to inventive interpretation, both personal and broadly social; and had the capacity to carry a charge which might elicit response outside the boundaries of the art community. Though there was some inkling that in selecting the private-parts theme, the organizers were approaching risky ground, no one anticipated that the show would lead to a police raid and legal action. The exhibition was not

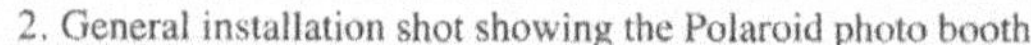

2. General installation shot showing the Polaroid photo booth.

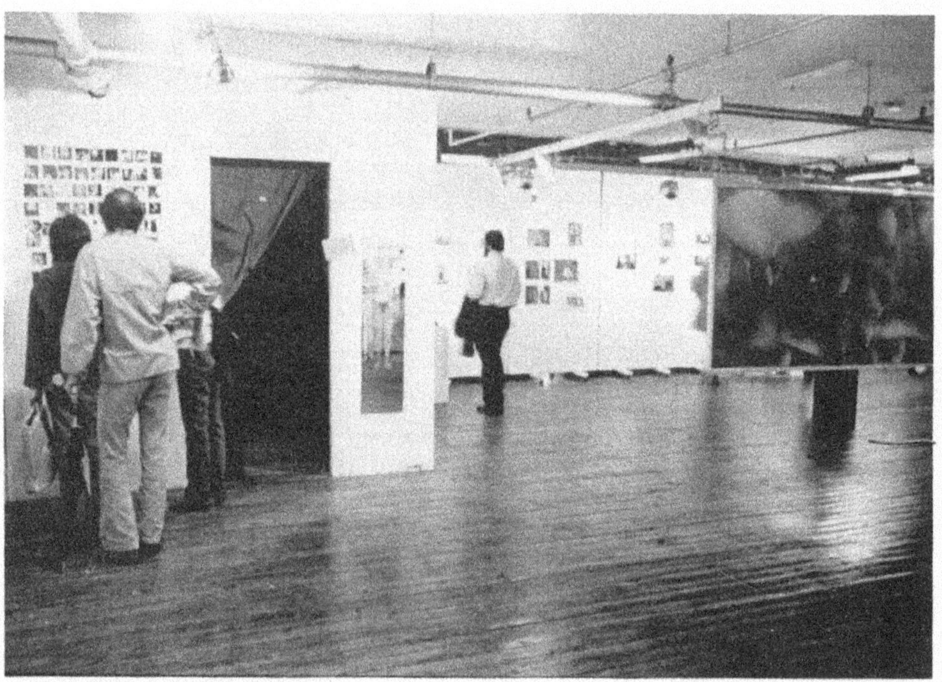

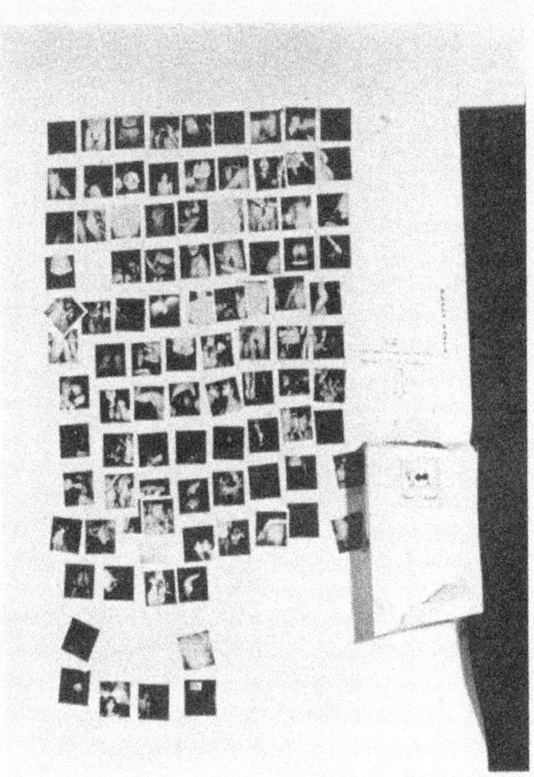

3. The Polaroid photo collage.

mounted to provoke such action nor to challenge the new legislation, which had been signed into law two days before the show opened and which nobody involved knew about beforehand.

As originally conceived, the show offered considerable latitude in the interpretation of the private-parts theme. Flyers soliciting material presented dictionary definitions of the two words of the title, thus:

private (pri' vit) adj. 1. Removed from public view; secluded: a _private_ parlor. 2. Not for public or common use: _private_ property. 3. Having no official rank, character, office, etc.: a _private_ citizen. 4. Not generally known; secret. 5. Not common or usual; special: a _private_ interpretation. 6. Individual; personal: One's _private_ opinion.

_______ n.1. Mil. An enlisted man ranking below a corporal. Abbr. _pvt._ 2. pl. The private parts; genitals. _______ adv. in _private_; in secret; privately. (L. _privatus_, apart from the state, orig. pp. of _privare_, to set apart. _privus_ single, one's own. Doublet of PRIVY) ····pri·vate·ly adv. ···· pri·vate·ness n.

part (part) n. 1. A portion of the whole; piece; segment. 2. Math. One of specific number of equal division; an aliquot division. 3. A distinct piece or portion of a machine that fulfills a specific function in the working order of the whole. 4. Something less than the whole: she has regained _part_ of the weight she lost. 5. An organ, member, or other portion of an animal or plant body. 6. Usually pl. A region; territory: in foreign _parts_. 7. One's proper share, as of obligation, business, or performance: If he'll do his _part_, we'll win. 8. Individual concern or participation in something. 9. The role of lines assigned to an actor in a play; also a role played in actual life. 10. Usually pl. An endorsement of mind or character: a man of _parts_. 11. The dividing line on the scalp made by combing sections of the hair in opposite directions. —etc. —etc. —etc.

At the bottom, this flyer invited submission of works of "ANY SIZE ANY MEDIUM ANY THING ANYONE ANY PRIVATE ANY PART", and gave the assurance "ALL WORK WILL BE SHOWN ANONYMOUSLY·"

Despite the range of possible non-sexual interpretations, most submissions, though by no

private parts

pri·vate (pri'vit) adj. 1.Removed from public view; secluded: a private parlor. 2.Not for public or common use: private property. 3. Having no official rank, character, office, etc: a private citizen. 4.Not generally known; secret. 5.Not common or usual; special: a private interpretation. 6.Individual; personal: one's private opinion. --- n. 1.Mil.An en- listed man ranking below a corporal. Abbr. Pvt. 2.pl. The private parts; genitals. --- in private In secret; privately.(L privatus apart from the state, orig. pp. of privare to set apart --- privus single, one's own. Doublet of PRIVY) --- pri·vate·ly adv. --- pri·vate·ness n.

part (pärt) n. 1.A portion of a whole; piece; segment. 2.Math. One of a specified number of equal divisions: an aliquot division. 3.A distinct piece or portion of a machine that fulfills a specific function in the working order of the whole. 4.Something less than the whole: She has regained part of the weigt she lost. 5.An organ, member, or other portion of an animal or plant body. 6.Usually pl. A region: ter- ritoy: in foreign parts. 7.One's proper share, as ofobligation, business, or performance: If he'll do his part, we'll win. 8.Individual concern or part- icipation in something. 9.The role of lines assign- ed to an actor in a play; also, a role played in actual life. 10.Usually pl. An endowment of mind or character: a man of parts. 11.The dividing line on the the scalp made by combing sections of the hair in opposite directions. --- etc. . . - etc. . . . etc. . . . . etc. . . .etc. . . . .

ANY SIZE ANY MEDIUM ANY THING ANYONE ANY PRIVATE ANY PART

SUBMIT BY APRIL 17th TO TOM YOUNG BENSON HALL 2nd FLOOR

ALL WORK WILL BE SHOWN ANONYMOUSLY AT "ELECTRON MOVERS" MAY 11 - 17

4. *The Private Parts* mailer and poster. It was also blown up and hung at the exhibition.

means all, picked up on the sexual innuendo of the theme and its advertisement. The exhibition's title and the promised freedom of anonymity certainly encouraged that trend and thereby helped to establish the sexual orientation of the show.

Anonymity, of course, implies that there may be something to hide, some reason for public concealment of identity. Indeed the organizers felt that under cover of anonymity, those submitting works would be freer in their attitudes and in possible self-display. Whether it is our own parts or those of others which are shown, the secret or revealing quality of the images is reinforced by the shielding of identity. It is not surprising, therefore, that in the majority of the pictures showing genitals or sexual activity, features were hidden or heads were cropped. The flesh-colored poster for the exhibition, for example, incorporated a tiny photograph of a heavy-set woman seated on a bed cupping her breasts in her hand, her head and face covered by a cloth. Like the black strips placed across the eyes of naked figures in anatomical texts, anonymity served to intensify the privacy of the parts revealed. The anonymity principle (if it can be called that) accorded with the exhibitionist/voyeurist appeal of the theme.

The submissions — there were about 160 of them — were brought to the gallery and the show laid out on the floor in groupings or sub-groupings derived directly from the material: the funky/comic, the conceptual, the high-esthetic, the animal theme, the kinky theme, etc. With on-the-spot haggling, pieces were selected or rejected according to whether they fit into the groupings. The result was an uneven show in terms of quality, but one full of the vigor of collective effort. Some of the pieces included were silly, others a bit pretentious for the occasion, but with an emphasis more in indirectness than directness the show fulfilled both its thematic and collaborative intentions.

Because of sensitive material and late arrangements — it is still not clear which was deter- minant — "Private Parts" was not shown in the College gallery. Instead it was hung a short walk away from the College, in a large loft gallery operated by a local video group. The show opened on Friday night, May 12th, to a large crowd, mostly of students and faculty, who drank wine, munched on erotically shaped bread baked for the occasion, and took polaroids of their various parts (more on that later).

The tone of "Private Parts" was lighthearted and humorous rather than raunchy or obscene. Except for a large photomural of entangled bodily parts (none quite identifiable) and a suspended plastic triangle

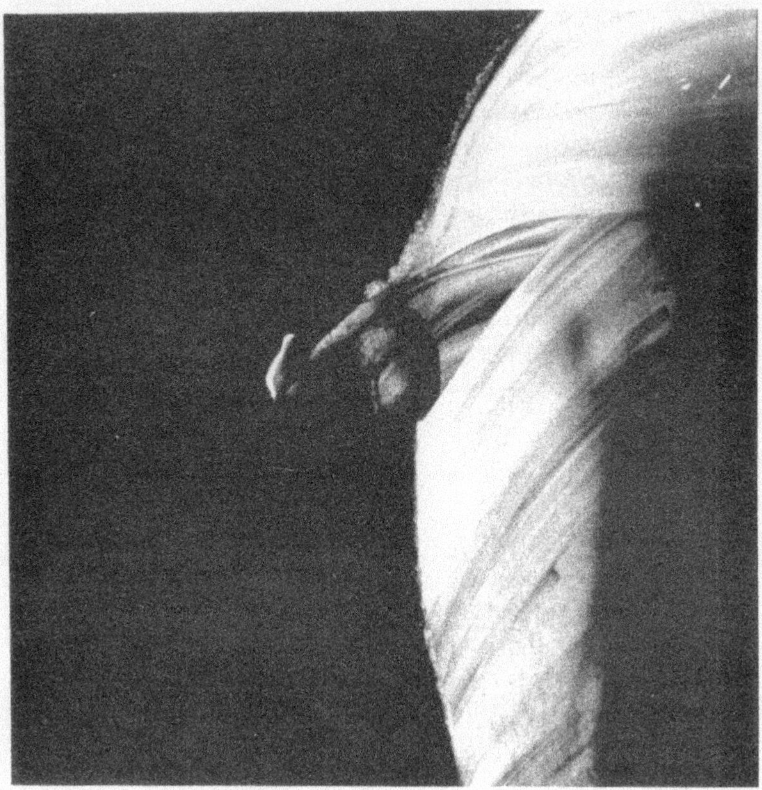

5. William Parker, *Male Nude* (photograph with painting). Seized by police.

covered with black wool (easily identified), most pieces, being photographs, were small and called for close inspection. Some, like William Parker's male nude photograph altered with surface paint, were elegant; others, like a series of "dirty comics" drawings, were crude but entertaining. The delight of the exhibition, which caught everyone's attention, was a photograph of a rabbit trying to mount a chicken, documented from nature (viewers were assured) by Richard Liebowitz. The police later seized it as an infraction of the law. The only item of commercial material was a videotape of a mild 1930's porno movie called *The Magician*. Even that, presented and viewed for its amusement as a period piece, was removed after opening night. As for the rest, it was all home grown — and non-commercial.

One piece became an analogy of the whole show in both tone and content. Near the entrance to the gallery visitors could enter a polaroid photo booth. There, for a quarter, they could individually or in concert photograph whatever they considered to be their private parts. Results were push-pinned on the wall outside the booth as an on-going assemblage, a piece that made itself. The mode of the polaroids was a clowning exhibition of genitals, buttocks, navels, underarms, ear canals, and so forth. Many individual polaroids were seized by the police. The collective piece itself and its identification as a work of art became an issue during the hearings that followed.

Near the entrance also were posted blow-ups of the list of contributors; the dictionary definitions of "private" and "part" already quoted; and three other quotations. Pertinent to the theme of the show, these quotations are worth citing. From Charles Albrecht's *You and Your Wonderful House* (1923):

> **If you see a picture of a nude figure (one without clothes), look at it only for the beauty of it. If the picture is a pure picture, and if you are pure yourself, you will like it more, the more you look at it, and you will have none but nice, pure thoughts about it. If you are pure and the**

picture is not, the very first glance will be enough to make you feel a little uncomfortable, and you won't want to look at it again. Such pictures are never seen in really good books or magazines, or in nice picture stores. They are generally shown in places where pure-minded people never go, except by mistake, and then they get out again, as soon as possible, and never go back.

From William James, *The Varieties of Religious Experience* (1902):

...it always leads to a better understanding of a thing's significance to consider its exaggeration and perversions, its equivalents and substitutes and nearest relatives elsewhere.

From Ludwig Wittgenstein, *Philosophical Investigations* (English, 1953):

...we can easily imagine people amusing themselves in a field by playing with a ball so as to start various existing games, but playing many without finishing them and in between throwing the ball aimlessly into the air, chasing one another with the ball and bombarding one another for a joke and so on. And now someone says: the whole time they are playing a ball-game and following definite rules at every throw.

And is there not also the case where we play and — make up the rules as we go along? And there is even one where we alter them — as we go along.

The *Providence Journal/Bulletin* article which appeared the day following the opening (May

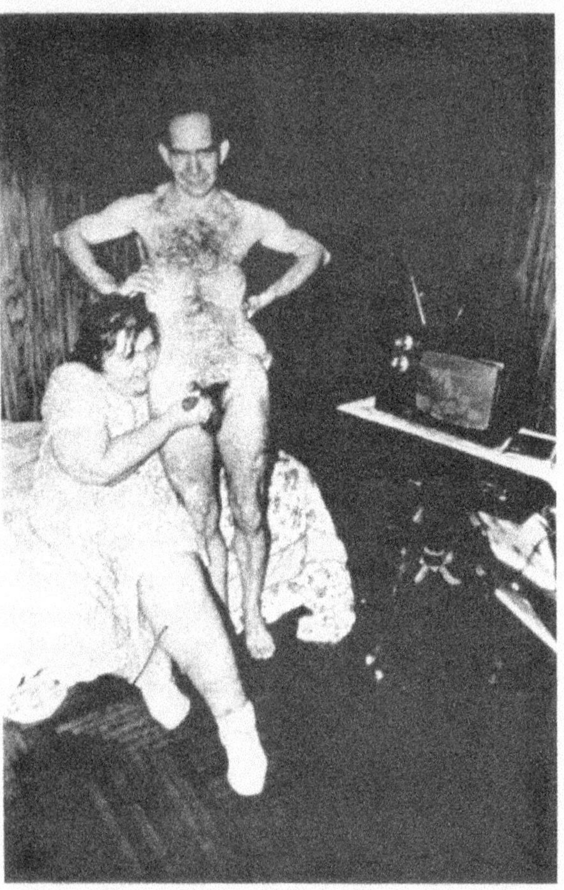

6. Ann Conyngham, *Couple*. Seized by police.

13) was headlines "RISD show lets you see things you usually don't." The reporter closed the review by saying "Unless somebody blows the whistle, the show will continue through Wednesday ...It's open to the public." The headline, to use D.H. Lawrence's description of the prurient, tickled the dirty little secret. The final lines of the article suggested adverse reaction and even the possible closing of the exhibition.

Such reaction was prompt. Thomas Pearlman, a Providence City Councilman, threatened, on the strength of the article alone (for he had not seen the show), to have Rhode Island School of Design's tax-exempt status reviewed and revoked. He called for police action against the show. Pearlman's statements reveal a double focus. He was offended by the public presentation of sexual material and he was outraged that such a a show should have even problematical sponsorship by a school: "Just because a professor does what we arrest operators of well-known bookstores for, does not make it right or permissible." And he added: "At least they're [the bookstore operators are] paying taxes. Not that it [paying taxes] makes it right." In fact, Pearlman and others hold that while the presentation of sexual material is not right, it is righter in some circumstances than in others. Again Pearlman:

> **[The show] is definitely not educational. It's prurient in nature and destructive. [The show] was much more serious [in effect] than are adult bookstores. When you have so-called educators mis-directing our youths in that direction, it's much more serious than a guy in the back alley.**

It should be noted that to be offended by "Private Parts," Pearlman did not need to see the show. The title alone would have been enough, especially given the sponsorship. The question is who gets away with what and under what conditions of privelege.

Providence police chief Angelo Ricci expressed his antagonism as directly and clearly as Pearlman:

> **I think it's wrong. These people [RISD students and faculty] think they can do whatever they want to, and I don't agree...If it's obscene, it's obscene. There is no two ways about it.**

Administrators of the School of Design responded as patly as Pearlman and the police. President Lee Hall, through a spokeswoman, denied all institutional association with the exhibition. She made this disclaimer despite the attack against the students and faculty and despite the unjust impugning of the College's standing in the community and its educational purposes. The denial was a lie. "Private Parts" had emerged from College activities and had received both academic and financial support from the Photography Department, whose head came under threat of arrest once the warrant that led to the raid was issued.

With Pearlman's outrage, Ricci's condemnation, the School of Design's disclaimer, and the media's attention, all the elements were in place for a raid. On the afternoon of May 16th, three days after the show opened to the public (it was to run only a week), the police arrived with a warrant issued on the basis of photographs taken by the police the previous day and a police affidavit describing the material of the exhibition. The warrant described the articles to be seized:

> **Photographs and pictures depicting beasts engaged in sexual intercourse, male genitals in a state of sexual stimulation, masturbation, close up representation of a human genital organ, spread eagle exposure of female genital organ, photographs of devices designed and marketed as useful primarily for stimulation of the human genital organ, oral contact of female breast.**

About forty of the works were removed and carted away in a police van. Selection of offending pieces was made by Lieutenant Paul Yacovone, who was in charge of the operation and would become a defendant in the case. He had written the police affidavit which led to the issuance of the warrant. When someone asked him how he decided what to remove ("Is that what turns you on?") he replied to the effect that having been a cop for thirty years he knew what was obscene and what was not.

Ironically, on May 16th, the day of the raid, the School of Design's Board of Trustees was meeting. While the trustees lunched up the hill, the police were confiscating the work of students and faculty down the hill. After the raid, trustees and officials at the College seemed unconcerned that the police had acted illegally and selectively, and that the law itself might be unconstitutional, and police operations of this kind could subvert the functions of an art school.

Part II: The Legal Action

> "A question of art and pornography — student's exhibition: art or raunch?
> — *Providence Journal,*
> Sunday, May 21

"Federal court orders police to return
Private Parts Art"
— *Providence Journal,*
Tuesday, May 23
*"[Federal Judge] Pettine gets peek at
sex in art"*
Providence Journal,
Wednesday, June 7

Legal action against the police came promptly. During the raid, those responsible for the show had hesitated to identify themselves. They feared harassment and arrest. Once the show closed, however, eight exhibitors joined on behalf of all the exhibitors to bring a class-action suit against the city and the police. They sued in U.S. District Court in Providence to regain the seized work, to recover damages, and to test constitutionality of the new law. The case, brought to the Federal Court even in the initial action, was accepted under that jurisdiction because the plaintiffs claimed infringement of their constitutional rights guaranteed by the First, Fourth, Fifth, and Fourteenth Amendments. The Providence chapter of the American Civil Liberties Union supplied attorney John M. Roney, who was joined in the case for the plaintiffs by private counsel, Lynette Labinger. The defendants were Police Chief Angelo Ricci, Lieutenant Paul Yacavone, and Captain Daniel Barclay.

The first step in the case was to gain a restraining order against the Providence police. In a hearing on May 22nd before Judge Raymond Pettine, plaintiffs questioned whether their rights could be protected under the new statute. On the strength of their arguments, Pettine issued a ten-day order prohibiting further action by the police pending a hearing for preliminary injunction, set for June first. The police were ordered to return all seized work within twenty-four hours and to refrain from interfering with the exhibition of either seized or unseized material. In other words, the show might be re-hung if the plaintiffs desired. The pieces were returned, some in damaged state beyond casual abuse; but the show was not re-hung.

Hearings began before Pettine on June first for a preliminary injunction to restrain police from further action against works or exhibitors, pending trial on the issues involved. Plaintiffs' lawyers presented to the court three main arguments: (1) that the police had violated the terms of the law they were purporting to uphold, and in doing so had denied plaintiffs' constitutional rights

of due process; (2) that the material of the exhibition was legitimate art despite its sexual content and therefore not actionable under the obscenity statute; and (3) that if the statute could be construed to apply to the works exhibited it was over-broad and therefore unconstitutional. Only the first two arguments were pesented, since the injunction was granted on their basis; and no constitutional question was raised.

To follow the first argument, that the police had violated the terms of the very law they were purporting to uphold, it is necessary to refer back to the 1973 U.S. Supreme Court decision in *Miller vs. California.* That case involved the mailing, to people who had not requested them, of advertisements showing men and women engaged in a variety of sexual acts with genitals prominently displayed. In hearing the case, the Supreme Court took on the task of balancing a "commitment to freedom of expression against an acknowledged need to protect society against the effects of obscene materials."[1] In its 5-4 decision, written by Chief Justice Burger, the Court essentially said that it was not the intention of the First Amendment to protect traffic in pornography. The dissenting opinion, written by Justice Douglas, took the firm position that the First Amendment was absolute in its protection of freedom of speech and of the press and allowed for no exceptions. In acknowledging the need and the right to control traffic in pornography, the Court diverged from the findings of the President's Commission on Obscenity and Pornography, which had been established in 1967 by Johnson and continued through the early Nixon years. That 646-page report, published in 1970,[2] recommended with concurrence of 12 out of 17 commission members that "federal, state, and local legislation prohibiting the sale, exhibition, or distribution of sexual materials to consenting adults should be repealed."[3] Through extensive investigation (nine volumes) the commission found no evidence that exposure to pornography contributed to delinquency, criminality, or emotional disturbance — and therefore found reason to exempt it from constitutional guarantees.[4] Hence the *Miller* Decision was itself controversial. In it the Supreme Court, breaking earlier precedent, turned over policy on obscenity to local communities, maintaining that there was no such thing as national standards for what constituted obscenity. At the same time the court offered guidelines on obscenity which might be used in the framing of local statutes: whether the average person, applying contemporary community standards would find that the work, taken as a whole.

appeals to prurient interest; whether the work depicts or describes, in a patently offensive way, sexual conduct specifically defined by state law: whether the work, again taken as a whole, lacks serious artistic, political or scientific value.[5] To assure specificity under the second point two examples were offered by the Court: (1) patently offensive representation of the ultimate sexual acts, normal or perverted, actual or simulated and (2) patently offensive representation or description of masturbation, excretory functions, and lewd exhibition of the genitals.

In the *Miller* Decision the Court reversed itself on its earlier and much more liberal test of obscenity, in *Roth vs. U.S.*, 1956, that a work in order to be found obscene must be "utterly without redeeming social value." That test was so broad as to inhibit almost all prosecution. Almost anything can be shown to have some social importance. In replacing the older test with the need to prove serious artistic, political, or scientific value, the Court opened the possibility for easier and therefore more successful passage of new state laws following the *Miller* Decision guidelines and, concomitantly, more prosecutions against allegedly pornographic activities.

Accordingly to *Miller*, representations and descriptions of sexual activities need not in themselves be considered obscene or patently offensive. They must be judged so by the average person applying contemporary community standards and as so tested in court. Hence it is not the subject itself which is crucial, but its treatment. In offering guidelines on what might be considered patently offensive, the Court did, however, open the way for state legislatures to try to define in law what may be patently offensive. The Rhode Island law under which "Private Parts" had been raided went beyond suggestion by defining certain depictions patently offensive *per se*.[6] Borrowing language directly from *Miller*, it defined an obscene work as follows:

> **A work which taken as a whole appeals to prurient interest in sex, which portrays sexual conduct in a patently offensive way, and which, taken as a whole, does not have serious value. In determining whether or not a work is an obscene work the trier of fact must find (a) the average person, applying contemporary community standards, finds that the work taken as a whole, appeals to the prurient interest and (b) that the work depicts or describes, in a patently offensive way, sexual conduct specifically defined by this chapter or authoritatively construed by the courts of this state as being a portrayal of patently offensive sexual conduct as that phrase is used in the definition of an obscene work and (c) that the work, taken as a whole, lacks serious value.**

As stated in the law, "community standards" means the standards of "the geographical area of the state of Rhode Island and Providence Plantations." "Serious value" is taken to mean "serious literary or artistic or political or scientific value." "Patently offensive sexual conduct" is deemed to include descriptions or representations of any of the following:

> **(a) An act of sexual intercourse, normal or perverted, actual or simulated, including genital-genital, anal-genital, or oral-genital intercourse, whether between human beings or between human beings and an animal.**

> **(b) Sado-masochistic abuse, meaning flagellation or torture by or upon a person who is nude or clad in under-garments or in a revealing costume or the condition of being fettered, bound or otherwise physically restrained on the part of one so clothed, in an act of apparent sexual stimulation or gratification.**

> **(c) Masturbation, excretory functions and lewd exhibitions of the genitals including any**

explicit close-up representation of a human genital organ or spread-eagle exposure of female genital organs.

In defining behavior representations of which are to be taken on their face as patently offensive, the Rhode Island statute contradicted its own requirements and usurped the function of the trier of fact (judge or jury) in deciding whether a representation is indeed "patently offensive." By doing so, as was charged in the complaint entered for the initial restraining order, the law abridged rights to due process and freedom of expression guaranteed by the Constitution.

The same sub-section of the law that defined "patently offensive" representations subjected to prosecution only those who promote or distribute them for the purpose of "commercial gain."

Every person who willfully or knowingly promotes for the purpose of commercial gain within the community any show, motion picture, performance, photograph, book, magazine or other material which is obscene shall upon conviction be punished by a fine of not less than one hundred dollars ($100) nor more than one thousand dollars ($1,000) or by imprisonment for not more than two (2) years or by both such fine and imprisonment.

As was demonstrated in court, the police, and by extension the judge of the District Court who issued the warrant, misapplied the governing commercial-gain stipulation of the law in acting against "Private Parts." In his affidavit in application for the warrant, Yacovone stated that "A charge of twenty-five [sic] (25¢) for polaroid photos were [sic] solicited." The implication was that the charge constituted commercial gain and was therefore grounds for the action. That claim was totally false. Nothing was for sale at the show; no admission was charged; and the quarters collected, which helped limit the use of the booth, covered only in part the cost of the film. Furthermore, the polaroids were not sold but rather became part of an assemblage which itself became part of the exhibition.

There were further and even more serious problems with the warrant. As emerged in court, the police had used an unamended draft of the statute. They had not the bill as passed a few days earlier, but a prior draft. In his affidavit for the warrant Yacovone described what he had seen at the exhibition.

...numerous photographs and pictures depicting beasts engaged in sexual intercourse, male genitals in a state of sexual stimulation, masturbation, close up representation of a human genital organ, spread eagle exposure of female genital organ, photograph of devices designed and marketed as useful primarily for stimulation of the human genital organ, oral contact of female breast...

On the basis of this report and a few photographs, and without viewing the exibition, and certainly without reading the law as passed, the District Court Judge found that "the subject matter was probably in violation" of the obscenity law. He issued a warrant (already quoted) which used language directly from Yacovone's affidavit. In fact, however, several categories of items in both affidavit and warrant had been struck from the definition in the law as passed. Omitted from the law are descriptions of the following:

— Physical contact or simulated physical contact with the clothed or unclothed pubic areas or buttocks of a human male or female, or the breasts of the female...

— A device designed and marketed as useful primarily for stimulation of the human genital organs.

— Male or female genitals in a state of sexual stimulation or arousal.

In neither its amended or unamended version does the law mention intercourse between animals. And yet that was the first item on the warrant as taken from the affidavit.

It may not have been the fault of the police that they received an incorrect copy of the law. It was their fault and the fault of Judge Barretta of the District Court that they so misapplied even what they had. The warrant as issued indicated only categories of actionable materials, leaving the police to decide on the spot which did or did not fit those categories. However, the law specifically required that such decisions be made by a judge and not by police. As shown in court and mentioned earlier, Yacovone seized on his own initiative any image that showed genitals (particularly male genitals) whether close up or distant, and any images that showed or seemed to imply sexual contact. Finally, and this is crucial to this case, the artistic seriousness of the works or of the show as a whole was never considered: not in the complaint, nor the granting of the warrant, nor the subsequent police action.

As the hearings demonstrated, the police blundered on just about every procedure the law requires. Thereby they denied the plaintiffs legal protection. It would seem, then, that they enforced not the law but their own prejudice: to close the show. On the witness stand Yacovone could not explain why the police behaved with such ineptitude — and such zeal. His only position was that the show contained obscenity and should have been closed down. It emerged also from Yacovone's testimony that the police had been advised prior to the May 22nd hearing that they had used an incorrect version of the law in getting the warrant and that it was therefore defective.

For the second argument, to prove artistic merit of "Private Parts," the sides in court divided as follows: The lawyer for the police, an Assistant City Solicitor, argued that the seized material was meant for sexual arousal and was pornographic; it did not therefore have any serious artistic value and should have been confiscated. The plaintiffs' lawyer argued that the works were by art students, faculty, and independent artists; and that the show as a whole had serious artistic and thematic content and should have enjoyed the protection of the law. Supporting the latter position, the plaintiffs individually testified to the artistic intentions of their own works and to the seriousness of the themes in the exhibition as a whole. The quotations mounted with the show were introduced as evidence to indicate philosophical concerns of the organizers and participants.

In the drive to establish the show's artistic intention, the polaroid "do-it-yourself" photo-booth became a stumbling-block. The judge, in a real dilemma, wanted to know how a bunch of Polaroid snapshots of people exposing themselves, pinned as a collection on the wall, could possibly constitute a work of art. To answer that question, William Parker, Professor of Art at University of Connecticut, photographer and photo-historian, one of whose photo-paintings of a male nude had been seized and damaged by the police, and who himself was a plaintiff, was introduced and accepted as an expert witness. In defense of the assemblage and the exhibition as a whole he explained to the court the idea behind process art. He demonstrated how the show was conceived in terms of a process directed towards an iconographic theme. He held that the photo-booth assemblage was only one aspect of the overriding idea. He spoke about Duchampian aesthetics and conceptual art, and how they challenge the idea of set pieces worked over in a traditional artistic manner. In other words, he put the show and its most disturbing inclusion in the context of developments in recent art theory and practice. His comments, though somewhat obscured by a specialist's terminology, constituted an instruction to the court in contemporary artistic concerns and elaborated the idea that classification of something as art does not depend any longer upon the beauty of its subject or the skill of its execution.

Whether Parker's explanation convinced the judge is not clear. But some time after his testimony and that of other plaintiffs, the city indicated that it was willing to let matters rest and to accept a preliminary injunction. The plaintiffs, however, insisted that as part of the injunction they and those in the class they represented be free to exhibit the works seized and others like them and to offer them for sale without threat of harassment or prosecution pending the outcome of the actual trial. The city refused those conditions and the hearing continued on that issue.

The thrust of the argument shifted now to demonstrate that sexual content itself, however explicit, could not be used to discredit representations as works of art. As an art historian I was asked by the plaintiffs' lawyers to prepare a series of slides of historically and critically accepted works of art with sexually explicit content. I put together some forty slides, which I reviewed with the lawyers prior to possible courtroom presentation.

However, before I was to present that material, Yacovone was questioned on the stand as to the criteria for his choices of works to be removed. When it emerged from his testimony that he went mostly on the basis of genital exposure whether or not it was close up or could be considered lewd, I was asked to make a briefer presentation of well known works in which genitals were clearly shown. I chose the usual "masterpieces" — classical sculpture, Donatello, Michelangelo, Ingres, etc. — and presented the material in court, to apparent disappointment of Pettine, who indicated that he and everybody else was aware of all that. He asked whether I didn't have anything else more to the point. On his invitation, then, I elaborated. I showed paleolithic fertility objects; Greek vases with erotic painting; Roman phallic charms; Mochica pottery from Peru; Hindu sculpture; Rembrandt etchings; Boucher paintings; works by Picasso, Bellmer, Klimt, Schiele, and others; and in photography works by Samaras, Arbus, Lazorik. At my conclusion, Pettine called some of it "pretty wild" and more than a little surprising in its extent. He was satisfied also that all pieces were or had been on public display in museums or galleries.

After the slides I took the witness stand. John Roney, lawyer for the plaintiffs, posed some questions the general purpose of which was to elicit from me a distinction between art and pornography. My argument was based on context. That is, I submitted that the context in which a thing appears can alter purpose and therefore effect. What is base, or ordinary, or common, or even patently offensive, changes when its context invites aesthetic or intellectual contemplation. Context, I argued with Duchampian logic, transforms function. Art, even when it features explicit sexual material, transcends its potential prurience by the fact of its identification as art, which implies seriousness of intent if not serious value.

"Private Parts," I further testified, took place in a distinct artistic context. It was held in an art gallery which had been so used before. It was advertised specifically to the Providence art community as an art exhibition. Its contributors were all involved in the practice of art. Hence there could be no doubt that "Private Parts" had been a *bona fide* art exhibition in a *bona fide* art context. Furthermore I maintained, as did William Parker, that the show explored serious thematic concerns, as indicated by a relationship of content to the mounted quotations and especially to the Wittgenstein statement, which raises questions about the rules by which people conduct their lives.

Cross-examined by the defense attorney, I was asked whether in my opinion any of the material in "Private Parts" was in any way prurient or pornographic. I answered that in context of the exhibition the answer had to be, No. He than produced a photograph, or a copy of a photograph, by Ann Conyngham, one of the plaintiffs, which had been seized and admitted into evidence. In black and white, it shows a fat woman in a sloppy chemise seated on an unmade bed; next to her stands a scrawny naked middle-aged man with his hands on his hips; in the corner of the room a television is on. The woman holds the man's penis in her hand as she might if she were masturbating him, though he seems distinctly flaccid. When asked if I did not find this photograph pornographic, I answered that if the intent of pornography is sexual arousal, then this photograph could not be considered pornographic in any context.[7] The scene, though I can't remember whether I said so, was to me poignant and depressing. I was surprised even at the moment of questioning that of all possible images in the show, the lawyer had selected that one to test the consistency of my position.

At the end of my testimony, Pettine also tested the consistency of my argument. Singling out my premise that context, because it can alter purpose and effect, determines prurience, he asked whether, in my opinion, if some materials from "Private Parts" appeared in a "girlie magazine" (his term), they could be taken as prurient. I answered that that might well be the case depending upon the particular pieces. In doing so I affirmed context as the governing factor in establishing acceptability or rejection under the law. Pettine seemed satisfied with that position and its rationale.

The hearing lasted most of five days. Before arriving at his decision Pettine had all the works from "Private Parts" — both seized and unseized — brought to the courtroom and set up for his review. Earlier he had seen slides of the installation; but he wanted direct experience of the pieces so he could judge the whole. He examined them all as they were lined up against the wall and court-room benches. His decision followed. He granted the preliminary injunction as argued for by the plaintiffs, including their continued right to exhibit the works and to offer them for sale even while further legal action was pending. Accepting the argument that context is controlling he added the proviso that pieces could be shown only "in a

art gallery, art show, art festival, art exhibit or art museum."
Accepting too the argument that the assemblage of Polaroid
photos constituted a single piece, he did not extend
protection of the injunction to the individual shots of which
it was composed; nor was such protection sought. In
granting the injunction, he said that the city had presented
no evidence to the effect that "Private Parts" was anything
other than a legitimate art exhibition and no evidence that
the works appealed to prurient interest or portrayed sex in a
patently offensive way. Nor, he added, was evidence
introduced by the defense to determine community
standards on obscenity or to show that "Private Parts" was
held in any way for commercial gain. In short, the city's
case was a total failure.

Part III: Reconsiderations

> "Judge rules 'Private' didn't violate
> anti-porn laws"
>
> *Providence Journal*,
> June 8

For those involved in "Private Parts,"
the hearing was a triumph and an exoneration. Their case
was excellently prepared and well argued. The attorney for
the police, on the other hand, offered little defense, and
police action in retrospect looked foolish. And yet, after the
hearing, I was left with a sense of unease. My dissatisfaction
was not with the outcome, for "Private Parts" should not
have been raided. In closing the show the police violated
the law and did so with bad faith. What nagged at me was
the suspicion that in assessing the show the cops in some
way might have been right. "Private Parts" had in fact
based its appeal upon prurience — whether or not that
prurience was actionable under the law. In defending the
seriousness of the exhibition I had denied that prurience.

The main premise of the argument on
context is that context can change both purpose and effect
of what is presented. The argument implies that the nature
of an object is not fixed, but can sometimes be (or mean)
one thing and under different circumstances something else
entirely. An attendant argument is that art, by force of
seriousness of its intent and its concern with form, redeems
or transcends its own content. That is, when it incorporates
prurient material, it does so for the higher purposes of art.
It would follow, as suggested in the law itself and in the
Supreme Court decisions upon which it is based, that there
are two mutually exclusive categories of things, one of

which we call art, the other pornography. What is art could
not be or even contain pornography, whatever its content
and effect. Conversely, what is identified as pornography
could not be art no matter how serious its intent. Through
such an intellectual and legalistic construct we defend art
from possible profanation and restriction, and pornography
from elevation above its usually accepted station in life.
Art, the argument goes, transcends pornography.

Since my testimony at the hearings,
that distinction has come to seem to me specious. If Picasso
makes a lithograph showing the artist, palette in hand,
involved with the model in such a way that genital
penetration and reception are prominently displayed, that
lithography is iconographically sexual no less than is any
other representation of the same act. That the subject may
express also Picasso's life-long involvement with the
interrelationship between creative and sexual energy — that
both art and sex are acts of possession or appropriation —
does not change the fact of explicit, and in this case
aggressive, sexual activity which reveals physical coupling
in a way that might excite genital response in some viewers
and sexual interest or curiosity in most. Indeed it might be
argued that the formal inventiveness of the piece, the
particular style of figural representation, as is the case also
in Japanese pillow-book woodblocks, is meant to intensify
the possibility of such response. Hans Bellmer's
phantasmagoric drawings of excited and interpenetrating
sexual organs or Lucas Samaras' polaroids or his own
masochistic and exhibitionist compulsions do not negate or
transcend their subject-matter by their artistic intention or
existential themes. They too are what they are with the
capacity, and I think the intention, of sexual focus and
possible arousal. In fact, Samaras picked up some of his
iconography directly from homosexual magazines
obtainable for the most part only in pornographic
bookstores.

Examples of art, both visual and
literary, which contain sexually explicit material can be
itemized indefinitely. Their identification as art — that
they are shown in galleries or museums, sold through art
dealers, reviewed and explained by critics, published by
respected houses, and so forth — does not alter that content
or make it any less prurient. As Morse Peckham has observed
in his brilliant, though infuriatingly convoluted, study of
the subject, the categories of art and pornography are not
mutually exclusive; they are independent categories.
Therefore, as Peckham says, that the attributes of one apply

does not mean that the attributes of the other cannot also apply. Art then can be pornographic, and pornography can be artistic. Even obscenity law recognizes that a work can both be serious art and contain elements of pornography. In practice, however, the usual view is that one identification cancels the other.

Response to sexual description or representation varies from person to person, from mood to mood, and from place to place. Some situations, or contexts, may inspire direct sexual responses; others may inhibit them. Mental set, that is to say pre-established attitudes towards situations and material, may also alter effect because of cultural expectation. We are trained to look at and respond to the category of things called art in a very different way — contemplatively and with deference — from how we regard the much larger category of things lumped together as non-art. Differences in response do not, however, change the nature of the material or its capacity to excite. No more does the context in which the material appears, or the seriousness of its associated themes.

In this I now seem to side with Yacovone, who maintained that after thirty years as a cop he knew perfectly well what was and wasn't obscene, and with the chairman of the Georgia State Literature Commission, who put it this way: "I don't discriminate between nude women whether or not they are art. It's all lustful to me."[9] The obsessed sex avenger and upholder of the morals of the young of the late nineteenth century, Anthony Comstock, was more vehement and more eloquent:

Strychnine is a deadly poison. Its effect when administered sugar-coated is the same as when administered otherwise. When the genius of art reproduces obscene, lewd and lascivious ideas, the deadly effect upon the morals of the young is just as perceptible as when the same ideas are represented by gross expressions in prose or poetry...Art is not above morals. *Morals stand first.* Law ranks next as the defender of public morals. Art only comes in conflict with law when its tendency is obscene, lewd, or indecent.[10]

Unlike Comstock and Yacovone, however, I do not oppose prurient content in art. Nor do I equate pornography with obscenity, as they seem to do and as is often done by those who claim to uphold public morals. I take "pornography" as a descriptive term and "obscenity" as judgmental. Yet the multifarious human sexuality, whether sacred or profane, has always been a subject of artistic expression — as I tried to show in court. What I now oppose is a double standard in judging prurience, one standard for art and a different one for other products. Those who, like Comstock, react intensely and with repugnance to what they see are in a way more honest than those who, in the name of aesthetic purity, dissociate art from its content and from implications of that content.

Often the term "erotic" is used to distinguish prurient content of art from that of pornography.[11] The usual distinction is that the erotic (derived from the Greek, *eros*, love) is the physical manifestation of passionate desire and love, whereas pornography (derived from the Greek roots *porne*, prostitute, and *graphein*, to write — hence, writing about prostitutes) is depersonalized lust divorced from love. The former, the erotic, is upheld as good; the latter, the pornographic, is condemned as bad. Thus the distinction between erotic and pornographic supports the mutually exclusive categories of art and pornography. Prurience in art is erotic, prurience in pornography is obscene. When pornography is thus equated with the obscene, the term "pornography" condemns rather than describes a certain iconography.

Equated with obscenity, pornography is considered unreciprocal, dehumanized. There is no loved other, no object of affection, but only exploitation of genitalia, mouths, anuses, and so forth, variously combined, in rude sexual fantasy the object of which is masturbation. And it is true, as Gloria Steinem and other feminists have written, that pornography often relies for its charge upon situations of dominance and submission, which are expressed in sado-masochistic violence and sexual degradation directed against women.[12] Plenty of horrific stuff is made and distributed to please or attract perverse appetites and compulsions.

Given the tendency to the obscene which seems inherent in pornography, one can understand the desire to draw a distinction between erotica and pornography. That distinction, however, seems to me at best artificial and at worst the result of elitism of class and taste. Are Beardsley's drawings for *Lysistrata* erotic or pornographic? Are passages from Henry Miller's *Tropics* and *Sexus* erotica or practiced pornography? Is *The Story of O.*, with its disciplines and mortifications, simply sado-masochistic pornography, or is there within it, as Susan Sontag suggests, an experience of spiritual elevation gained through physical pain and psychic humiliation?[13] Are Helmut Newton's photographs[14] indulgences in upper-class pornographic fantasies of exhibitionism and sex-murders, or are they exercises in erotic liberation for wealthy connoisseurs? The distinction between erotica and pornography seems ultimately a mechanism for reinforcing the immunities of the intellectual and cultural elite. In such a situation art serves as a mediating device between the acceptably erotic and the distastefully pornographic. The distinction buttresses respectability through euphemism.

The old distinction between soft-core and hard-core, in my way of thinking, is more honest, accurate, and durable than the distinction between the erotic and the pornographic. It is quantitative rather than qualitative. It implies that there is a scale of erotic material and experience that can run from the mild to the extreme, from the suggestive to the blatant, from the bawdy to the obscene. And, disturbing as it may be to certain sensibilities, art when dealing with sexual themes can find its place anywhere along that continuum. In such a construct, location on the continuum is not set by any absolute judgment, but results from subjective predisposition and reaction. Response varies from situation to situation and from person to person. Some, of course, will find any explicit sexual material obscene; others will find everything acceptable and even desirable.

The main reason for problems over the relationship between art and pornography is that art, even modern art with its one-time questionable reputation, has been elevated as an absolute good in society. We cultivate it and support it publicly with millions of dollars. We are urged to venerate it — sometimes idolatrously. Pornography, on the other hand, gets only private support and is considered, in public dictum, if not an absolute evil then certainly a serious social problem. From such a standard, pornography is a dysfunction, a symptom of malady which must be controlled lest it destroy the fabric of social order. Since it is impossible to suppress pornography because it is in continual demand, whether legal or illegal,

it is most often controlled through negation. Pornography becomes taboo. Insistence on what should be often entails denial of what is. Simultaneous knowing and denying may be hypocritical — but, as La Rouchefoucauld observed, hypocrisy is the tribute that vice pays to virtue. To challenge the taboo consequently becomes a political act. The struggle between advocates and opponents of censorship turns out to be a struggle between those who have a vested interest in the status quo and those who, pressing for social change, conceive of freedom of expression as a means to reform. As Andrea Dworkin has put it in a speech on feminist attitudes towards pornography, the male right wants secret access to pornography, the male left public access. The women's movement, on the other hand, and with switch of usual right/left alignments, has attacked pornography because of the degradation that it heaps upon women as it revels in male sexual fantasy.[15] However one looks at it, pornography has ideological potential.[16]

What outraged Councilman Pearlman and the police over "Private Parts" was not that either hard- or soft-core pornography exists, but that they perceived the show as breaking an acceptable frame. It intruded where, in their view, it did not belong. Forbidden or clandestine, pornography does not challenge official values. Rather it upholds them by its very furtiveness. What is declared wrong or immoral can be practiced so long as it is identified as wrong. Occasional police raids against makers, distributors, and retail outlets of pornography confirm that negative moral identification.[17] Restriction of such activities to "combat zones," as in Boston, fulfills the same function. "Night Towns" are where one goes to learn the forbidden: to experience the taboo, but also to confirm it as forbidden. Psychoanalyst William Gaylin, in an article called "Obscenity is more than a four-letter word," recognized that the law operates as an ethical determinant and as a moral force:

Moreover, the attitude of society as reflected in the law has an influence not only on who will read pornography but also on the impact of the literature on those who do...when you make something legal you are doing more than making it allowable or exempt from prosecution. In the unofficial poll I alluded to

earlier, one point was stressed by psychiatrists (and by almost all of them) that was made by no other group. They made a distinction between the reading of pornography, as unlikely to be per se harmful, and the permitting of the reading of pornography, which was conceived as potentially destructive. The child is protected in his reading of pornography by the knowledge that it is pornographic, that is, disapproved. It is outside of parental standards and not a part of his identification processes. To openly permit implies parental approval and even suggests seductive encouragement. If this is so of parental approval, it is equally so of societal approval — another potent influence on the developing ego.[18]

When art adopts prurient iconography usually linked with pornography, it takes that iconography out of its assigned social frame. It presents it as respectable. In doing so art does not sinfully break the taboo; but in jest or in earnest it challenges that taboo with the power, the endorsement, of its own legitimacy as art. That is why prurience in art is so distressing to the forces of social fixity or repression. To make prurience the appeal of art is therefore to bait a particular reaction. Precisely such a challenge provoked Pearlman to declare the show a more serious offense than are adult bookstores or someone selling pornography in a back alley — that is to say, dealing in pornography where it belongs. He did not need to see the show before objecting. Pearlman was correctly representing the common view that recognizes pornography as inevitable and perhaps even needed — but denies its right to public sanction or artistic legitimacy.

Despite protestations after the fact, those who organized "Private Parts" were aware that they risked provoking ideological confrontation. In a way they courted that confrontation. The mounted quotations at the gallery, particularly the message from Wittgenstein, clearly raised ideological questions — as did the very concept of the show. To make public what is usually held to be private is to bait. As I have said, the show based its appeal upon the insinuated prurience of its theme.

The show also tipped the balance of acceptability by being largely photographic. Despite developments of this century, the idea persists that art, particularly visual art, has something to do with skillful manipulation of materials to create objects of surpassing beauty. In popular aesthetic valuation painting, sculpture, drawing, and even printmaking achieve the status of art by virtue of their mediating language, whether or not beauty is accomplished. Photography, however, in ordinary experience and valuation, has not yet achieved that status. As Susan Sontag says, "photographed images do not seem to be statements about the world so much as pieces of it, miniatures of reality that anyone can make and acquire."[19] We do not easily recognize the mediating art in still photographs, which means they have the poignancy of specific reality; and specificity is a powerful ingredient in pornography. In photographs we read not image, but actuality. This is true, I am convinced, even for those who are professionally involved. That is why there were so many cropped heads and obliterated features in "Private Parts." The promised anonymity which protected identity became part of the prurient appeal for both contributors and spectators. Photography is a voyeuristic and exhibitionistic medium.[20] "Private Parts" exploited both those tendencies and did so, I think, with good humor, and clear effect.

The main residual meaning of "Private Parts" inheres precisely in its prurience. To neutralize that prurience, as I did in court by an argument on context (based on aesthetic theories of transformation) is to destroy that potential meaning. It is, so to speak, when things get tough, one can hide behind the protective skirts of art as an inviolate, autonomous, and self-justifying activity. The strategy, though prudent, expedient, and offered with conviction, is ultimately evasive. The principle of anonymity as part of the show contributed as well to such evasion. The thrust of "Private Parts" was to challenge artistic loftiness through engagement with a charged theme based upon common experience. The show flaunted exposure, teased conventional distinctions between image and actuality, and invited redefinition of what should be called decent and respectable. But its good humor was not appreciated by those who are already quite sure of and committed to their own standards of decency and respectability — and who do not wish the question reopened.

Art in the modern world, whatever else it may have accomplished, has been a way of dealing with our pathologies. It deals with them through the acts of revelation and objectification. Like pornography even at its most obscene, it is symptomatic, descriptive, articulating, and inviting of collaboration. We may not always like what we see, but we need not close our eyes or shake our heads; we should see what is there to be seen and call it by its right name without pretense. In a world where corruption and collective horror so outweigh the effect of private compulsion, sex and sexuality have become a preoccupation of our psychic and physical behavior and intuition. We live in a pornographic environment. Art often, as in this case, serves to close the gap between our professed values and our actual behavior. It is an antidote or palliative to schizophrenia. Therefore a show like "Private Parts" can be regarded at once as symptomatic — and curative.

Reconsideration of my role in the "Private Parts" case leaves this quandary. I now consider my testimony fallacious, mistaken; but the outcome of the case I consider right. "Private Parts" should never have been raided and indeed was protected under the law used to attack it. That should have been enough. There was no reason to argue that its status as art altered its content or possible effects of that content. Were I asked again to testify in such a case, I would have to take the position that to deny prurience on the basis of context would be to deny the nature of the particular material. Such testimony might not help the plaintiff, but it would help focus concern where it belongs. And where it belongs, in my estimation, is on the actual life-content of works of art whatever that might be, unprotected by special status or the circumlocutions of criticism and defense. Without such awareness art loses its effective power.

Endnotes

1   Lane V. Sunderland, *Obscenity, The Court, The Congress and the President's Commission*, Washington, 1975, p. 1.

2   *The Report of the Commission on Obscenity and Pornography*, William B. Lockhart, Chairman, Government Printing Office, Washington, D.C., 1970. There was also a nine-volume Technical Report published in 1971-72.

3   Sunderland, *Obscenity*, p. 74.

4   *Ibid.*, pp. 74-75.

5   *Ibid.*, p.10.

6   Subsequently that law was challenged in the state supreme court under cases involving commercial distribution of pornography and found unconstitutional precisely because of its attempt to define the patently offensive. The law was rapidly rewritten eliminating such definitions. It was passed by the General Assembly and signed into law once again by the Governor.

7   In her testimony Ann Conyngham explained that the photograph was only one of a series which she had made documenting the life of these two people and that they had asked particularly for such a picture.

8   Morse Peckham, *Art and Pornography*, New York, 1969, p. 4.

9   *Ibid.*, p. 12.

10   Heyward Broun and Margaret Leech, *Anthony Comstock, Roundsman of the Lord*, New York, 1927, p. 223.

11   Eberhard and Phyllis Kronhausen, *Pornography and the Law*, New York, 1959, p. 18.

12   Gloria Steinem, "Erotica and Pornography, A Clear and Present Difference," *Ms.*, November 1978, p. 75 ff.

13   Susan Sontag, "The Pornographic Imagination," *Styles of Radical Will*, New York, 1966, p. 48 ff.

14   Helmut Newton, *White Women*, New York, 1978.

15   See *Off Our Backs*, February 1972, p.1 and also the Gloria Steinem article already cited.

16   In this observation and what follows I am once again indebted to Morse Peckham's *Art and Pornography*, particularly to his first chapter, "What is Pornography." See also Felix Pollak, "Pornography: A Trip Around the Half-World," *Perspectives on Pornography* (ed. Douglas A. Hughes), New York, 1970, p. 183.

17   At times, following periods of permissiveness, police and court actions become serious in reestablishing social stability and moral authority. I believe this to be such a time.

18   Quoted in Sunderland, *Obscenity*, p. 79.

19   Susan Sontag, *On Photography*, New York, 1972, p. 4.

20   Sontag, *On Photography*, p. 10.

Baruch D. Kirschenbaum is Professor of Art History at Rhode Island School of Design, Providence, R.I.

Baruch D. Kirschenbaum

A Divergent View
on Art School Humanities

For five years I have taught in and helped shape the humanities program at Rhode Island School of Design. On the basis of that experience I should like to respond to Kenneth Lash's "A New Approach to Teaching Humanities in an Art School" (Spring '67 XXVI, 3, pp. 252-6). Like the San Francisco Art Institute where Mr. Lash teaches, the Rhode Island School of Design is a degree-granting professional school in the arts; and we have in common certain problems in structuring a program in the humanities. While questions of order, relevance, and purpose plague liberal education in general, they are more acute at the professional school because the amount of time devoted to the humanities there is fractional. Yet the need of the student is quite as urgent, and art school students, as Mr. Lash recognizes, often demand a personal significance in what is required of them. Though our problems arising out of parallel situations are similar, there are differences in our solutions which I think are worth commenting on now.

Mr. Lash advocates a four-year humanities package. His program of interrelated materials ranges from the prehistoric to the contemporary in time, space from the Far East to the Asian Steppes and Western Europe. In short "little less than a cultural history of the world" is to be given in a four-year sequence of courses taught in concert by several instructors and visiting lecturers. He presents this program as experimental. The goal might be called total education.

One section is described in his article thus:

> . . . instead of studying Homer in a course called Western Literature, the student will come upon him in the midst of a series of interrelated lectures on early Greek history, society, religion and mythology, art, ancient science. Further, he will have worked his way to this point through a study of prehistory and of whatever major civilization predate the Greek. Thus the linear effect of cumulated learning is given full scope, yet this learning is at each moment being achieved by study in depth, by organic examination of cultural objects and events in context.

And from here in the same semester they go on to study, or so I gather from the outline of courses, the

The author (Ph.D. Harvard, 1966) teaches history of art elective courses at the Rhode Island School of Design where he helped to fashion the present humanities program. ∎

classical Greeks and the Romans and their history, society, religion, art, science, etc., all interrelated and structured in depth.

In sum, what we have here, though Mr. Lash understandably avoids the term, is a cross-disciplinary survey course. Such a course, I protest, has to be only a collection of necessary generalizations with glimpses of a rapid scattering of items and data: a cultural patchwork stitched together into the pattern of classical civilization. Claims for study in depth cannot be convincingly defended. The "linear effect of cumulated learning" is just another way of noting the traditional chronological development in such courses. The whole program, it seems to me, is a sequence of surveys strung together chronologically. Surveys are surveys by any name. When cross-disciplinary they are likely to suffer even more from the shortcomings of condensation.

I have no argument here with such courses, though I do find Mr. Lash's section on Homeric Greece overwhelmingly ambitious and would caution against the pitfalls of *hubris*. What troubles me is his advocacy of a series of such courses as a complete liberal arts program. It is true that most college curricula in this area are a chaotic hodge-podge of courses thrown together on professorial whim without regard for general instructional purpose. For all that, there is still something to be said for specialized courses in which limited material is studied in detail, with a closeness, intensity, and reflection that the broad sweep simply forbids. I do believe that Mr. Lash's well worked over, well condensed, sixty minutes on Dostoyevsky and the Russian Novel would be fascinating and informative, but his ninety minutes on *Crime and Punishment,* even though delivered on the spur of the moment, might just hold something of more particular worth even for the novice.

Specialized courses are my concern here. Whether taught to art students or anyone else, they are not *ipso facto* irrelevant, dull, or useless. They serve notice that things can be studied critically in depth for themselves, and that most areas have internal histories which can be separated from broader considerations, and that men of spirit and intelligence have sometimes spent their lives in pursuit of what might appear to be minor considerations, especially when viewed from the panoramic perspective of human culture. Cumulative knowledge originates in meticulous endeavor. The seven-league-boots approach ignores all that; and I feel that it is important and even exciting to learn some new things in detail, to acquire some more specialized knowledge, and to grapple with the intricacies of a subject.

It is disheartening after a while to see things always in the context of broader themes, always in terms of other things, always nicely syllabized for their place in the overall picture and in total education. In emphasizing connectives between a variety of things and events, such courses as Mr. Lash describes tend to give students a false sense of security about the nature of historical reality. Some things just don't connect. For the most part we simply leave them out, but sometimes in our eagerness for order we give them Procrustean treatment and come out with mutilated truth. History is an immense tangle, and it is presumptuous and misleading to give the impression that we can untangle it by the coherence of our survey syllabi. Though perhaps students are negligent in making certain kinds of connections between things, probably they make too many connections with too little thought and too little information. They need to be saved from hasty or glib concludings also even if they pick up the tendency from us.

In regard to content Mr. Lash feels it necessary to include nonwestern material in the syllabus. He accepts the idea from a report ("The College and World Affairs," Education and World Affairs, Inc., New York, 1964) that the responsibility of liberal studies should be to break the present provincialism of our learning and to "divest it of its preoccupation with the western heritage." (The quotation is a paraphrase by Mr. Lash of the report.) While I salute his far-eastern inclusions and agree that our shrinking world demands a new internationalism in learning, I don't know why he thinks we should divest ourselves of the just preoccupation with our own past. That past truly belongs to us and we rightly give it our deepest consideration. How else shall we know what we look like? How else shall we recognize our unique contributions to the whole culture of the world? I accept the idea of cultural comparison for increased richness, as well as for other values. I wish only to correct what might be called a misplaced globalism.

My objection, then, to the program as described by Mr. Lash, is that it pretends to accomplish more than it can, and to be more than it is, and that in its broadness it necessarily ignores much of the depth required for advanced learning. The use of the word "experimental" will just not alter survey education into thorough education—if such can be said to exist. On that score also much of what Mr. Lash describes as experimental is really quite common. Cross-disciplinary humanities is an old idea; the chronological organization by semester is as traditional as you can get, and the arrangement of two-lectures-one-discussion-section-per-week is standard procedure for such courses. The only thing that is new perhaps is the extension of a usually shorter introductory program into a four-year sequence and the attempt to make it an all-in-one educational package.

Having declared my objections and reservations, let me briefly describe as an alternative the program now in force at Rhode Island School of Design. It has been in effect with some revision since 1962, and I have been involved with it since that time. I make no great claims of originality for it, but do feel that it supplies some of the diversity which I find lacking in Mr. Lash's program. In recognition of the need for a general cultural background, freshmen and sophomores are required to take a cultural survey similar to that described by Mr. Lash. Given in two years rather than in four, the program has a coverage less ambitious. Deliberately the emphasis is placed on art history, literature, and philosophical ideas. Each year's program is staffed by two lecturers and discussion-section assistants. Readings consist mostly of primary materials with some critical commentary on specific items. There is no text.

Along with the two-year sequence students are required to take twenty-four additional credits (eight semester-courses) elected from three possible areas: art history, literature, and history of ideas. (We are presently working towards offerings in science.) These courses may be quite specialized, such as a seminar in the paintings of Rubens and Rembrandt, or a study of the Victorian novel; or they may be more inclusive, such as *Modern French Painting* or *Aesthetics Theory.* Some are strictly historical in organization; others, like *The Image of the Child in Fiction* or *Myths of Creation and Fall,* are thematic. Offerings in these elective areas do not pretend to anything like a complete coverage of the fields involved, but each gives some idea of the discipline and what it means to work within it.

The requiring of such courses may mar a student's educational complexion, as Mr. Lash suggests, but from my point of view the diversity of learning and experience derived from them is worth any resultant blemishes. While I admire efforts to achieve smoothness and integration in education, I personally prefer a gentle anarchy. It is more like life. I know that in this age of totalism (total thought, total nourishment, total entertainment) and the big experience (the car ride that's more than a car ride, the insight that's more than an insight)—in this age of totalism, diversity and complexity are frowned upon. That may be reason enough to pursue and conserve them.

In his article Mr. Lash is also at some pains to describe the art students at San Francisco. His description fits those in Providence as well. He sees them as a new breed of disaffected, alienated young, mistrustful of their culture and their elders, but eager to grab what "gets" to them. Often, as he says, they are antagonistic to required liberal studies, feeling that they interfere with their deep studio involvement, and that these studies furthermore tend to be overly analytical. The description is a good one, and it is refreshing to hear some praise for these students' directness, their energy, and their willingness to engage in what is relevant to

(Continued on page 175)

ART SCHOOL HUMANITIES

(Continued from page 167)

them. I like to think that it is our advocacy of student freedom, and their own dedication to artistic ideas, that create that verve; but who knows where it comes from.

For all that I agree here with Mr. Lash and share his enthusiasms, there is another side of the matter which also needs mentioning. Often in their freedom these students are pitifully lost without discipline in a sargasso of dripping subjectivity. They mistake their own instantaneous reactions for "vital" (a student word) responses, as though the less thought one gave, the better and more genuine the result. Intense, immediate, and sometimes humorously outrageous, they are too often narrow-minded and ungenerous in their judgments. The classroom revelation, which Mr. Lash admiringly calls "epiphany-on-the-spot" learning, may be very inspiring and exciting. However I find it frequently accompanied by a nihilism towards all except what scores, what grabs. It is part of the current instantness cult—instant coffee, instant communication, instant intimacy. I mistrust its substantiality and its staying power.

In his method as well as in his style of writing Mr. Lash seems to be aligning himself with the new breed of student in a kind of bread-and-circuses desire to please—make it relevant man, or humanities turned on. It may be, as a friend of mine suggests, that he has been touched by the "over-30 paranoia syndrome" with the attendant fear of being thought square. Much of the criticism leveled against the liberal arts is justifiable, and I admire Mr. Lash's energetic response to it. I do suggest only that his program for total education needs some tempering in depth and diversity, even if that means it will not be so immediately attractive.

Primitivism and Impossible Art

Baruch D. Kirschenbaum

> If the guilt accumulated in the civilized domination of man by man can ever be redeemed by freedom, then the 'original sin' must be committed again . . . .
>
> Herbert Marcuse, *Eros and Civilization*

Primitivism refers to an attitude of mind working from a cultural state to an imagined pre-cultural state uncontaminated by the ills of civilization. It arises out of the suspicion (even conviction, depending on how bad things appear) that civilization has brought with it a progressive deterioration of the true state of being. It then becomes necessary to return to an exemplary pre-civilized (primitive) state in order to rediscover the fundamental realities of life, which will obviate the ills and restore modern fragmentation to wholeness. Within such thought, the essential human condition always precedes the actual; this idea shapes our location within the infinity of time, for we move continually forward to an ultimate return (Mircea Eliade). More abstractly, the Millennium always achieves the past—a perfected, mythologized past.

The kind of primitivism that sees the beginnings as idyllic has been characterized as "soft primitivism" and can be opposed to the "hard" view that sees the beginnings as bestial and therefore unenviable in any way. Thomas Hobbes, with his Nature red in tooth and claw, is perhaps the progenitor of "hard primitivism" for modern thought. More recently Robert Ardrey, in trying to explain and even to justify current political bestiality, has sought to prove (never successfully) the brutality of our beginnings as weapons-makers and killers. In this hard-headedly practical view civilization, for all that may be wrong with it, is the only salvation from continual self-mutilation; civilization saves us from barbarism. The "soft" view however, with its millennial tendencies, has dominated imagination. Perhaps this is because it supplies some relief from the responsibilities of civilization and a comforting sense that things will fulfill themselves. It is in the "soft" sense that the word primitivism is used here.

All periods of what might be called high or advanced civilization have had such primitivistic longings, though some more vigorously than others. For the ancients of our tradition, Theocritus and, later, Virgil invented the mythical sweetly-sad world of Arcady where the honey and wine of eternal evening would relieve them of the burden of their own crass culture. The Renaissance pre-empted that pastoral world for its own pagan and boisterous longings. It was for that time an antidote to the sado-masochistic compulsions of medieval Christianity. Christianity itself had made this life of the earthly city a vale of tears between Edenic beginnings and eventual return to them after the retributive holocaust of judgment. Never has the longing for the future/past been so destructively conceived. Cities crumble, rain turns to fire, bellicosity rages, and for every soul saved for the state of innocence thousands are sucked into the burning ass-hole of hell. All the delicate fantasies of paradise and the saved enjoying eternal bliss cannot make up for the horror of that image.

For the eighteenth and nineteenth centuries, intent on enlightened education, Rousseau constructed the concept of the Noble Savage, and would educate Émile in the precepts of primitive necessities. Even as they were slaughtered as heathen, the Indians of America were idealized as dwellers in innocence close to paradise. Ironically, even some of those people whom Europeans regarded as living in a perfected state of nature felt themselves removed from the essential perfections of their own beginnings, and mythologized for themselves an eventual return to a purer state (Mircea Eliade). In face of aggressively advancing industrial and technological civilization, our own century has been absorbed with counter-notions of the primitive as a means to some sort of salvation.

At one time it might have been possible to look at modern primitivism as an extension of a wayward romanticism. But as the problems of modern society deepen, the desperation of reaching out for the "primal sanities" becomes more and more intense. Always the desire has been for a freedom that seems denied the individual in the structure of things as they exist. In this most free of times, it seems always that freedom evades us.

Artistically these preoccupations with the primitive have gone in two different directions: one (the earlier) leading to expressive freedom through primitivized form, a kind of millennium of artistic language; and the other leading to rediscovery of creative capacity through primitivized behavior, perhaps a millennium of self. In the loss of religious consciousness, art and its practice have become the means to spiritual awareness and accomplishment. If art could be free then we could be free and the millennium would be achieved.

The earlier primitivism, which Robert Goldwater has written about, involved the use and incorporation of primitive motifs and primitivising ideas of form in painting and sculpture. Though there has been considerable

Baruch Kirschenbaum *is director of the European Honors Program of the Rhode Island School of Design. He taught history of art courses at RISD for several years before moving to Rome two years ago. He received his Ph.D. degree at Harvard in 1966.* ■

quibbling on the subject, it makes little difference whether it was Vlaminck in a Paris bistro, Kirchner in the Ethnological Museum in Dresden, Matisse or Picasso at Derain's or at the Trocadéro who first discovered primitive sculpture, or whether it was in 1904, 1905, 1906. . . . Probably if one wished to argue it out the credit should go to Gauguin, who already at the end of the nineteenth century incorporated primitive and archaic pieces in his own work. He insisted that art could find its "nourishing milk" only in the mysterious anti-naturalism of its own primitive (for him barbaric) beginnings, which he struggled to re-invent. What makes a difference is the creation, simultaneously, of a new primitivized imagery and a new sense of the inventive possibilities of form. It would not be too much to claim that the whole transformation of artistic language of the early century had its beginning in primitivizing attitudes, and developed specifically from the increasing awareness of primitive art and particularly of West African sculpture. Everywhere expressive freedom came to be associated with primitivized invention.

These transformations in form were part of a general primitivizing trend that was to grow throughout the first part of the century. The new biology (up from Darwin), the new anthropology (up from Frazer), the new psychology (up from Freud), even the new politics (Engels was a great primitivizer) directed attention to the origin of things as the source of their true explanation. Revelation of origins would strip away the layers of civilization and restraint which have kept us from our truer, more fundamental selves and open up whole new areas of recognition and meaning. Neurosis was the price of civilization; and though Freud might conclude that it was worth the price, there remained a strong tendency to reject the bargain.

With African sculpture as inspiration, the struggle in art became one for directness, immediacy, and economy of means. It seemed necessary to break through whatever stood between the artist and his work, whether pre-conception of rendering and color, or self-consciousness of intent, or the responsibilities to tradition. All that intervened in that sacred communication could be overcome by what Robert Goldwater speaking of the Fauves called a "reduction of means" and by what later became a kind of aesthetic rallying-cry: "truth to materials." Paint should look like paint, wood like wood, stone like stone, whatever else might be involved. The real error (already identified by Gauguin, and as Henry Moore among others would later agree) seemed to be the classical, with its insistence on imitation. Starting with the primitive, the means to expression could be equated with expression itself. Those means might be primitivized, even crude, but they had the intensity of discovery and in some cases really did escape most pre-conceptions with regard to the craft and purpose of art.

To read a painting like *Les Demoiselles d'Avignon*

simply as an essay in the application of African sculpture to the new painting, or as an experiment in primitivized means, is, however, accurate only up to a point. Picasso's women accomplish far more. They establish their own mythical/primitive existence through a ritual display of themselves. The almost animalistic figures in Matisse's *Le Luxe*—particularly the painting in Copenhagen—though so different in their primitivism from Picasso's, share something of the same feeling. They are ritual participants in a certain coming of age, or coming to form. We are given to witness a hieratic experience of birth. Still, these paintings are at least as much about painting itself, and their concern on one important level remains that of formal means. The lines are clear. For Picasso and those around him the primitive leads to cubism and its formal rigors; for Matisse, to arabesque for pure color and a celebration of surface.

The development was similar for others too. Inspired by masks and children's drawings, Klee created an art of incredibly frail purity. Beginning with stiff, block-like Peruvian carving, Moore ends with autonomous sculptural statements abstracted from that initial idea. Even where the concern lay with dream images or fantasy (surrealism is a kind of primitivism which seeks meaning through non-rational pre-analytic experience, which according to the practitioners of psycho-ontology around Freud establishes mythic and primitive connections), the problems of formal invention were most immediate, and hence Miró's canvasses can be regarded as form structured to pre-analytical fantasy.

Whatever the source and whatever the particular need, primitive images and primitivizing ideas were used to instruct art to new possibilities. This was a primitivism of form or formal primitivism that would (as already suggested) bring about the millennium of artistic language. In the drive for formalistic autonomy or pure form primitive affinities were left behind or, perhaps better, outrun; and there emerges a highly sophisticated art and criticism bereft of earlier primitive sensitivities and purpose. Minimalism is a direct line from economy of means. Even what could be thought of as the latter-day primitivism of abstract expressionism—a primitivism of kinetic response which obliterates the distinction between subject and object—ends in provocative patterning. Only Dubuffet manages an insistent primitive vision, through an equally insistent denial of culture.

Within the context of primitivism, the predominance of formalistic or stylistic thinking makes for a certain conflict. In argument the desire may have been for release from self-conscious intent, but style is the result of analytical and critical processes. These processes assure pre-consideration of intent. That is, art cannot be accidental; accident must be transformed into discovery; and someplace along the line the artist becomes the critical respondent to his own work. No one makes this clearer than Albers, with his system of color squares so deliberately calculated as to be reproducible by formula. From here follows (within the concept of style) the self-evident distinction between art and life. Art is purposeful (criticism will make it so), life is fortuitous. The whole critical and commercial apparatus of artists and appreciators, creators and consumers (collectors) which supports the art world as we know it, stems from that distinction.

A possible way to break the distinction between art and life, assuming that one should purpose to do so, is to turn from style to behavior as the essential means to expression. This, I surmise, is one of the developments presently going on. It results from, or leads to (a difficult judgment here), a second kind of primitivism, which in counter-distinction to formal primitivism might be called behavioral primitivism. If earlier the means to expression were equated with expression itself, now the tendency is to equate behavior with expression. The important thing is *to do art*. Any resultant thing or object becomes a by-product of that activity to be more or less valued as a document of something that happened, rather than as anything of intrinsic worth or as an end in itself: e.g., the ice-man's bill which Rafael Ferrer suggested might do for a collector's drawing for his ice-blocks melting on leaves at the Whitney. It is enough, as Jill Johnson put it, back in 1965, to stake out a claim (through behavior) to be an artist. In this case, lying on one's back and criticizing the constellations.

Almost always the results of art behavior (activity, action, event—any of these terms apply) are, like the melting ice-blocks, ephemeral. The best one can do is subject the behavior to recall. Thus if a number of people gather together in a large room (called studio) with bales of rags and the express purpose of doing something with them (individually, together or how it happens) for a period of time, the outcome (a certain redistribution of the rags) does not constitute a statement. All that exists is an encapsulated period of time during which something took place, and other things did not take place, and in which energy was expended in the way of gratuitous activity. It would be nice to let it go simply at that, but either because the truly ephemeral is difficult to accept, or because of outrageous narcissism, the whole enterprise is filmed and photographed (slides no doubt for some pocket-portfolio). There follows the inexplicable but happy assumption that the cameras have recorded things as they are. The celluloid (viewed in darkness, lights flashing, faces weird with shadow) becomes the non-object object, the non-image image, a spur to total recall (document) of a primary and now mythologized event. The experience of seeing the films and slides becomes a kind of post-ritual reliving. With video-tape the event and its external consideration can exist simultaneously, creating the *ne plus ultra* of self-consciousness hiding under the cover of extreme spontaneity.

Either in recall or in event itself, the new art exists for those involved in it. The experience (like the expension of energy) is theirs and not that of some imagined audience responding to what passes before them. The piling up of earth and the remains of excavation (Robert Morris), the burial of a steel cube (Sol Lewitt), the dissolving of detergent-soaked sugar cubes in the sea (Dan Graham), the distribution of hot-dogs on a Manhattan street (Hanna Wiener), are the rites of initiates engaged in ritual activity. Several thousand people may have gone to Little Bay, near Sydney, to see Christo Javacheff's wrapped cliffs, but clearly they were outside the action and witnessed only a curious reminder of expended energy. The wrapping of the cliffs, and before them of buildings, may bring us momentarily into a new awareness of their existence, or create a new sense of their bulk, but those reactions must be minor compared to the reaction of having organized and completed the work of wrapping with all the statistics of plastic yardage, rope, and man-hours. Richard Long walked in a straight line in southwest England for ten miles shooting every half-hour—or so the photograph asserts.

The more "impossible" art becomes, the more its meaning is resident only in its own activity. The exhibition of such activities or their results in galleries or museums either in process or, as more often, in photograph would, when pushed to the extreme, have to be seen as an absurd left-over of another orientation and involves everybody in cross-purposes. The very antiseptic quality of most modern galleries seems to deny the earth orientation of much of the new art. (The Italian term "arte povera" would seem to deny in its origin the whole commercialism of galleries.) Jannis Kounellis's horses at Attico in Rome struck that note of incongruity. The point of course may have been just that, a disturbing articulation of the mod (almost all galleries presently) and the primitive. Still out of community, the whole thing rests upon documentation and publication. It is still, like it or not, for sale in one way or another; and Robert Scull shall become patron for that which he cannot purchase—i.e., Michael Heizer's thirty tons of granite with rain-water fill.

Outside of the gallery or the publication, art as participatory ritual is at once more public in that it takes place in the context of life (Dennis Oppenheim convinced a farmer to let him plot a harvester's course) and more private in that it truly absorbs only those actively engaged in its doing. Ultimately, in a world crammed full of things almost to saturation, *to do art* may be far more satisfactory than *to make objects*. We may have a parallel here with the increased economic demand for services rather than goods. At least one adds less to the accumulation, while at the same time making for purposeful labor. But that brings us to the question of art and garbage, which is another consideration altogether.

Whichever way one looks at these new tendencies, the result is the blurring of the line between art and life. To accept the life situations as art itself rather than the subject of art (Douglas Davis),—to think of life as a qualitative event at the expense of art (Gregory Battcock),—derives from a desire to find a new integration of meaning and activity in our lives. Art becomes more mundane, less intellectually and commercially sacred, and life hopefully becomes more filled with significance. The new integration of creative activity with life will bring about the rediscovery of center and a return to an imagined primitive wholeness in which all things are part of all other things, and one need not worry too much about definitions. It is then possible to image art as out of the studios, their isolation, and their fretful individualism. Given how long in our tradition artists have been on the outs with society, separated both by social hypocrisies and by the artists' own smugness, the desire for a new place, however ludicrous for the moment the results may appear to some, is not only understandable, but sorely welcome. The vision of course may be impossibly idealistic.

Released from image, art can reach out to encompass the elemental forces of the earth: the action of the sea (Jan Dibbets), the contours of the land (Dennis Oppenheim), the sky (Forrest Myers), and by extension our own place within it all. Nature becomes a norm—a space-age nature in which for the first time we can experience the earth as a shared whole. We can, perhaps we must, see ourselves living within its state not as isolated personalities struggling for self-identification, but jointly in service to the whole. The sophistication of our technology has brought us back to a primitive recognition of the center of the universe which we occupy.

While technology thrusts us willingly or unwillingly into a terracentric primitivism, its white-sleeve impersonality and brave-new-world potentials are challenged by a growing band of primitivized street people who antithesize technological values. Indians of the city, frontier types, astrological romantics, Myshkin-like holy idiots, narcotized and progressively anarchistic, they seek in the most urban of places release from the pressures and imperatives of urban civilization. In many ways they are the displaced people of technology. Some would even drop back (or out—Leary is one of the high priests of the new primitivism) into a state of insouciant stupidity or further into an animalism of grunts and howls and aberrant sexuality in order to come in touch with a truer sense of their own being. Sometimes it seems that we have all become type-cast movie-extras in continual search for parts.

Street people like street works are made simply by identifying them as such (John Perreault). Anything, anyone can be a street work. Without manifestos, without theory, but only through declaration it is possible to turn oneself and whatever else one wishes into art. Behavior becomes expression not only through doing but simply through being; and all the rest seems beside the point. Style is transferred from object to person, and thus the burdens of ordinariness, boredom, and displacement are lifted. The tribalism of the streets carries its art with it in a ritual of instant meaning and purpose. Just to be able to live on the streets (a word fast coming to mean the whole alternative place to the home/classroom/office/ home structure) becomes a creative act.

There is something desperate about it all. Image-making for the moment seems almost impossible. The instantaneous communication of every effort defeats itself in anxiety over meaning and originality while assuring us that no one is indispensible. Ability seems more and more a horned devil to be exorcised, especially as the forces of technology and corporate politics absorb everything in massive homogeneity. The art/life, life/art equation could conceivably be a way out from these dilemmas except for one glaring mis-conception. Art, modern no less than primitive, has always served to delineate areas of sacredness and significance from the rest of life. This had been its force and its importance. Its elevating and even revolutionary power derives from intensification. We need that separating-out of the sacred to relieve the leveling power of the ordinary, and to bring us beyond ourselves in thought and sensitivity. Primitive artists operated outside the bounds of ordinary life, and their objects became efficacious in part through the sacred position of the artists themselves. The distinction between art and life is what sustains us, and what sustains art. If all things are art, and art is all things, we may end up with the same bloodless homogeneity with which technology threatens us.

Still the new primitivism is deeply impressive, perhaps because, even in its chaos, it focuses on life itself (the art I think is sometimes an excuse), and not simply on poetic or intellectual yearnings, or formal problems. If earlier, primitive examples were used to instruct art, primitivizing ideas are now used to instruct life, and have run over into a politics of confrontation and political confrontation with the civilization which has spawned them. The millennium will be one of rediscovered creative capacity of being—a millennium of self located in wholeness. If impressive, these visions are also deeply saddening as all reachings-out for the Edenic dream must inevitably be.

Perhaps there remains no more to say. The comparison between earlier formal primitivism and present behavioral primitivism has been drawn with at least some of its implications. Still some leftover thoughts fit in here somewhere. First, a little more on the contradictions of technology and primitivism. Primitivism stands as an insistent counter-force to the homogeneity of technological style. It is the wild man dancing defiantly in the face of the juggernaut of progress. (The music may be electronically filtered and expanded, but the current is conceived as some magical force, a new mana, or spiritual fluid to be shaped into sound.) Nevertheless technology, as suggested, may be the only means of bringing us to a sense of our oneness as inhabitants of this planet. The barrenness of the moon alone, I should think, would drive us into that embrace. On a somewhat more earthbound level, McLuhan, another of the high priests of the new primitivism, may be correct in believing that a new global tribalism will result from our electronic media.

Still technology and more specifically electronic technology is fast relieving us of the measure of our lives, and a whole generation (only the first) is faced with the nagging sense of its own superfluousness. In terms of work, the world's work—not simply labor or employment, though that too—the prognosis for the future is grim. Thus we have tribes of young wanderers, the nomads of advanced technological society, seeking grazing grounds for their own spirits—another Woodstock, a gathering of tribes (Abbie Hoffman), a new or at any rate relived archetypal event that will connect up the future with the past, and avoid revolution. These are not the unemployed, like the Blacks, who having been for so long denied the goods and services of society continue to seek them as a means to personal and social salvation; they are the non-employed. We have no need for their labor, or their ability, and we offer them no future. School, long a means of relieving pressure on the labor market, is recognized as socially required busy-work that keeps people uselessly penned up and destroys sensitivity. Intensity of vocation leads to grace; vocation being denied, there results a hatred of work in the traditional sense. Not to work even at what might be offered becomes a political act of a new disenfranchised mass, for to accept employment is to participate within the system which has created that disenfranchisement.

This aspect of the new primitivism, if I am not being overly dramatic, is part of an impassioned and confused search for some possible place within the total structure, and for continuity where all signs suggest that no continuity exists. It is not that life is too organized, but that it is too arbitrary, too haphazard; the random sample dominates. The alternative image is that of a primitivized life in which all labor is needed and in which each individual finds place within the continuous round of activity upon which life depends. The inaccuracy of this image of primitive life matters little. We have already once before experienced the Noble Savage as exemplary image. Another alternative is that of the emancipated peasant, emancipated by his labor-earth-folk realities long sacrificed for the goods and services of urban civilization. Almost in Wordsworthian terms he too is reinvented, and endowed with intellectual and even spiritual (especially Eastern-religious) virtue. But the children

of the adults are leaving the communes; and where to for them?

What started out as a reaction against the mass-produced mass-merchandised look has already been commercially taken over and advertised as the anti-Establishment style. Popular, abundant, for sale everywhere, the primitive comes to seem faddish and insignificant (Indian maidens posture in *Vogue*). Still, underneath, the problem of loss of place and ultimate boredom remains. One possible escape from that hell is to transform activity and being into art. If ordinary acts can be elevated to the level of expression just by their doing, if people can in themselves become art, then a life of meaningful existence can be conceived and stretched into the future. Art as labor—the producing of objects—is measured in terms of critical and hopefully financial recognition. Art as behavior is invested with meaning for the participants through the quality and shape of time created. It is primitive-ritualistic.

If I were to be most harsh in my estimation, such art constitutes the playtime/work-fun activities of the superfluous child/adults of our age. If I were to be most open and accepting in my judgment, it is the primitivized beginning of a liberation from old forms and concepts—the first step in breaking the work/labor/success syndrome which has enslaved our spirits and lives and has set us as individuals in counter-stance to society. The latter sounds too grand, the former too dismal. Meanwhile, we remain desperately in need of new structures for our creative energies.

Karl E. Meyer. *The Art Museum: Power, Money, Ethics.* A Twentieth Century Fund Report. New York: William Morrow, 1979. 352 pp.; illustrations, appendices, bibliography, index. $15.00.

The Catalog Committee. *An* Anti-*Catalog.* New York: The Catalog Committee of Artists Meeting for Cultural Change, 1977. 79 pp.; illustrations. $3.50.

Sponsored by and published for the Twentieth Century Fund, Karl Meyer's study of the American art museum and its current problems carries the subtitle *Power, Money, Ethics.* My reaction is that while the book makes abundantly clear the role of money and power in museums (their order is better reversed), it reveals little of the ethics. The story of burgeoning art museums since World War II, which Meyer documents with an array of impressive and convincing statistics, turns out to be one of self-serving cupidity, conflict of interest, influence mongering, competitive status seeking, overkill commercialism, and simple greed. By way of illustration, Meyer recounts Thomas Hoving's attempted sinecure at the Metropolitan Museum of Art with Walter Annenberg's support; the takeover of the Pasadena Museum by the Norton Simon organization; Nelson Rockefeller's role in reversing the New York State legislature's decision not to allow the building of an apartment tower over the Museum of Modern Art, a project that reeked with trustees' conflicts of interest; the self-congratulatory smuggling of a Raphael painting out of Italy and into the Museum of Fine Arts, Boston, by its director and chief curator; and the splashy no-holds-barred commercialism of "blockbuster" shows like the "Treasures of Tutankhamun."

Given the ethical abuses and attitudes of those in power (particularly trustees), one might expect an angry book or at least one derived in part from a deep anger carefully controlled. Meyer's is no such book. In place of what would be justifiable moral outrage, he offers sweet reasonableness based upon historical explanation. He admonishes and cautions; but on issue after issue he refuses to take a stand. The result is a book more apologetic than demanding, one which smacks of the complicity of understanding. But to understand is not necessarily to forgive. The point here is not that Meyer's book is weak because he does not get angry but that in it he avoids the moral, intellectual, and aesthetic issues that shriek from his own pages. While proposing governmental control to soften abuses, he upholds the status quo of a system shot through with corruption.

Meyer deals at some length with the question of acquisition policies. He cautions against the continuing competitive chase after prestigious works, which has led to enormously inflated prices, to collusion between dealers and museum officials, and, I believe, to the idea that artistic value is established by price. He accedes, however, to the argument that a museum's lifeblood depends upon the continued building of collections through purchases as well as through gifts. Only a moratorium on market acquisitions could clean out that mess, but Meyer does not recommend it or even suggest it as a possibility, perhaps because such a recommendation would go unheeded. Yet the great museums of Europe do not purchase and have hardly become moribund. Furthermore, as Meyer indicates, major American museums cannot properly care for all the objects that tax incentives (a form of indirect federal subsidy) have brought into their galleries and storerooms. It is tax policy and not purchases, no matter how dramatic and self-congratulatory, that has built the great collections of this country. Meyer is very good at making this clear.

Cataloguing ethical abuses is neither the purpose nor the central theme of Meyer's book. He cites them in various sections of his study only as examples of the practices of museum directors, curators, and trustees that have contributed to the present difficulties. It is those difficulties themselves on which Meyer focuses. American art museums are in serious financial trouble. While there is a lot of money for sensational acquisitions, at least in the major institutions, there is not enough to maintain buildings, keep the lights on, and in some cases even keep the doors open. As might be expected, the cry for help has been directed to the federal government. Museum dissatisfaction with the restricted and often capricious funding by the National Endowment for the Arts, which, following the pattern of private patronage, prefers to support special projects rather than operating expenses, led to the establishment of the Institute of Museum Services (IMS) in 1977.

A federal agency with a first-year budget in excess of $4 million, the IMS at last allows for direct federal support of museums. With this direct involvement Meyer sees the need, as many have before him, for the creation of a federal policy on the arts. He recommends the establishment of a private commission to formulate such a policy along the lines of the Carnegie Commission's study of public television. He recommends an expanded mandate for the IMS to oversee museum operations and practices. Despite their eagerness for federal support, this is just the kind of accountability and control museum people have always wished to avoid. As S. Dillon Ripley, secretary of the Smithsonian Institution, warned in 1976, he who pays the piper calls the tune. Such fears are not to be taken lightly. A recent report to the House Appropriations Committee on the operations of the National Endowment for the Arts took that organization to task for the looseness of its operations, particularly with regard to accountability, and for its lack of initiative in establishing policy. And Dick Netzer, in *The Subsidized Muse*—his study of public support for the arts which was likewise funded by the Twentieth Century Fund—recognized that increased support will inevitably demand increased accountability, while at the same time raising serious questions, particularly economic, about the effectiveness of governmental support.[1]

There is great irony in concluding that direct governmental support for art museums is necessary to save them from financial ruin. Art museums, as Meyer shows so well, have always been the cultural precinct of the superrich from J. P. Morgan and Andrew Mellon to Joseph Hirshhorn and Norton Simon. Art, in the form of European masterpieces in particular, assured the cultural respectability of the few enormous industrial fortunes created in this country. There are those who feel strongly that the association of art with

[1] Dick Netzer, *The Subsidized Muse: Public Support for the Arts in the United States* (New York: Cambridge University Press, 1978).

capitalistic wealth has resulted in the loss of art's political and cultural meaning; thus museums have become repositories of the art of those in power: art officially defined and interpreted. For those who share this view the museum becomes an arena for ideological confrontation.

New York's Whitney Museum of American Art became such an arena in 1976 when it decided (along with the de Young Museum in San Francisco) to show as part of its bicentennial fare the collection of American art formed by Mr. and Mrs. John D. Rockefeller III. Not only were there letters of protest and street demonstrations boycotting the show by those who felt affronted and disenfranchised, but the catalogue of the exhibition, authored by E. P. Richardson, was countered by the publication in 1977 of *An* Anti-*Catalog*. Written by a committee of artists associated in a group called Artists Meeting for Cultural Change, *An* Anti-*Catalog*, like Meyer's book, addresses power, money, and ethics in museum practices. Unlike Meyer, however, the writers of *An* Anti-*Catalog* take an emphatic stand against the ethical and intellectual abuses arising from the association of art and wealth.

At first glance *An* Anti-*Catalog* may seem merely a diatribe against the entire concept of the fine arts and its supporting class structure. It is, however, much more than that. The issues it raises are important. The main contention is that by showing the Rockefeller collection as American art, the Whitney Museum legitimized it as an adequate sampling of the art of this country and thereby supported the interpretation of American history explicit in that selection. The committee also charges that the exhibition and catalogue pretend political and cultural neutrality although just the opposite is true. The Rockefeller collection, the authors of *An* Anti-*Catalog* maintain, ignores minority artists, including women, and offers a vision of America in which the poor are sentimentalized, the land is romanticized, and the rich and powerful are celebrated for their beauty and gentility.

With heavy reliance on English critic John Berger's *Ways of Seeing* (a book taken from his BBC television series), the writers of *An* Anti-*Catalog* maintain that the emphasis on formal appreciation in Richardson's catalogue leads to mystification of art (Berger's term) and deprives it of other meaning.[2] The object becomes more important than its

both past and present meaning. In looking at a Copley or a Sargent portrait, for instance, we are asked to appreciate the artist's ability to render stuff or flesh rather than to react to the people represented and their stance in the world as conveyed by the artist. With such an approach (and *An* Anti-*Catalog* is very insistent on this point), value inheres in the thing itself rather than in what the object may reveal, and art becomes simply the precious object. There is nothing terribly disturbing about that—art has always been made as a commodity—but if that is all there is, appreciation assumes a merely monetary value. In art, "priceless" has come to mean enormously expensive rather than without regard to price. It is no wonder that our new museums, as the committee points out, look more like vaults and fortresses than temples of art.

There is much quasi-Marxist rhetoric in *An* Anti-*Catalog* and, to my way of thinking, an overemphasis on social and cultural meaning as opposed to artistic accomplishment and purpose. It is possible to react to Copley's and Sargent's brilliance as painters without losing sight of broader historical implications of their paintings. The purpose of the patron need not be the purpose of the artist. The converse is true as well. The use to which art is put often separates the intention of the artist from that of both owner and interpreter. In exegesis there is always the danger of sacrificing the art to an insisted-upon meaning. Besides such cautions, it should be said that current art history is much more aware and concerned with the latent values inherent in all images and their use than the writers of *An* Anti-*Catalog* admit.

Still, what is said is important. *An* Anti-*Catalog* raises questions about the effect of museums on their growing audiences. What do people learn in museums? And is it as good and worth the bargain as Meyer implies when he recommends that we pick up the tab? The issue is not the populist-elitist split, but who holds the power, to what end, and with what idea about art and for whose benefit. Meyer raises such questions in his last few pages and worries about the possible adverse effect of museum hoopla. He ends, however, by offering the standard lighthouse analogy: the light is available to all alike and for the common benefit, abuses of the system notwithstanding.

Last year was the fiftieth anniversary of the founding of the Museum of Modern Art. It was established with Rockefeller money and support at a time when "modern art" was not exactly popular in this country. No one, not even the writers of *An*

---

[2] John Berger, *Ways of Seeing* (New York: Viking Press, 1973).

Anti-*Catalog,* despite their disagreement with museum policy, could hold that the effect of that institution has been detrimental to American artistic consciousness. There have been disputes and accusations enough, but often in ignorance of the politically radical nature of much of the art, both American and European, that has been brought to our awareness on 53d Street. For the most part, American art museums have served well, if not brilliantly, in bringing art and knowledge of it to a broad audience. That is not at issue.

What is at issue, and what is brought into focus by these two books, is that success has often been accompanied by intellectual and moral failure. And it looks as if the situation is getting worse rather than better as museums compete for greater attendance and increased revenues. Neither government control nor the new museum code of ethics (1978, included as an appendix by Meyer), nor the polemics of *An* Anti-*Catalog* will solve the problem. What is needed is leadership willing to forego the attractions of power and the hierarchy of taste for the sake of transcendent ideals of what is right and what is wrong in the world.

Art has often been considered, along with religion, as a means to spiritual revelation. For many who could not stand the corruption of the earthly church, it was the only means to such knowledge. If that collapses, we are left only vast collections of overvalued stuff, mass idolatry, and the reactive threat of violent iconoclasm.

BARUCH D. KIRSCHENBAUM
Rhode Island School of Design

The Scull Auction and the Scull Film

BARUCH D. KIRSCHENBAUM

On the evening of October 18, 1973, at Sotheby Parke Bernet, taxi-fleet owner Robert C. Scull sold 50 works from his well-known collection of contemporary American painting and sculpture. The sale brought record prices for works by living artists and earned a total of $2,242,900. Jasper Johns' *Double White Map*, which Scull bought around 1965 for $10,200, brought the highest price of the evening, $240,000 from dealer Ben Heller, who that summer had sold Jackson Pollock's *Blue Poles* to the Australian National Gallery for $2,000,000. The auction raised issues of substance about the practice and exchange of art, and brought demonstrators and street theater to the entrance of Sotheby Parke Bernet. Outraged by the implications of the sale, Barbara Rose titled her stinging report of the auction in *New York Magazine* "Profit Without Honor."[1]

The auction itself, the pre-sale activities and preparations, and the protests and confrontations are all documented in a remarkable film originated and produced by E.J. Vaughn in collaboration with John Schott. The identification of this film, *America's Pop Collector: Robert C. Scull —Contemporary Art at Auction*, as an important, indeed irreplaceable art historical document is the direct subject of this paper.

The film does more than simply document the sale. It offers an idea of the broader social, cultural, and economic context in which the events of that evening took place. In doing so it suggests the complex interconnections of the "art world," which reach far beyond the making and even the exchange of art itself. It also integrates within the action a series of cinematic portraits of the principals involved, particularly Robert and Ethel Scull. The study of the individuals raises the question of personal motivation and introduces a psychological dimension to the description of what took place.

In short, the film offers a synoptic view of a significant event of our time involving the exchange of art. In studying past art the retrieval of such information is an arduous task. Connections between apparently disparate elements of social/cultural/political/economic and artistic activities must often be made speculatively rather than as certainly documented. With a view to future history, then, and certainly for our own understanding, it is worthwhile to identify contemporary documents which in themselves establish such cultural interconnections. The Scull film is such a document.

The film was conceived and directed by E.J. Vaughn and John Schott and filmed by Susan and Alan Raymond along with Ron Dorfman.[2] It was edited by John Schott and Leah Siegal. The cinematic philosophy followed by the group has been called "direct cinema" and sometimes referred to as "reality filmmaking." It is based on the ideas of Richard Leacock, who with others in the late '50s and early '60s pioneered the use of portable, hand-held and synchronous sound equipment in the making of documentaries. The central idea, which has tempted

filmmakers from the very beginning, is that with the right equipment it would be possible to document an event as it unfolds in reality. The cameraman, in a sense, becomes an unseen presence within the action; and ideally the film, even as edited, allows the viewer to become a participant in the event rather than an observer of a restructured reality. Whether the film accomplishes that purpose in regard to the Scull auction will be discussed below. Whether it does or not, it most certainly represents the events of that evening and places them within the context of New York art dealing in which they took place.

Edited from hours of footage, the 72-minute film starts with pre-title shots of the cocktail party opening the exhibition of the sale pieces at the showing rooms at Sotheby Parke Bernet. As the camera pans the exhibited works, a voice-over network news (CBS) narration is heard reporting the actual auction and the events immediately surrounding it. There is a cut to a TV monitor (black-and-white) showing scenes from the auction along with continued narration. The emphasis of the report is on protesters blocking the entrance of Sotheby Parke Bernet, and on the record prices brought for individual pieces. With a cut back to the pre-auction party, Robert and Ethel Scull are seen talking with each other in front of and completely surrounded by the white diagonal stripes of Stella's deep blue *Sabine Pass*. Amidst the activity of the party Scull is followed singly as he talks to various people including dealer Leo Castelli, and explains to a woman acquaintance that he thinks the sale is the right thing at the right moment and will benefit the artists. He is clearly pleased with the way the works look together. It was his intention to curate the sale like an exhibition through the selection of particular pieces to be included.

The juxtaposition of the pre-sale activities with the network's report of the auction as it took place creates a dramatic tension in the film between an already accomplished event and its unfolding in the film. The present in the film is seen against the background of what we know from the broadcast actually happened. This knowledge intensifies for the viewer all the behind-the-scenes preparations at Sotheby Parke Bernet: the seating arrangement (the Japanese are next to the Italians), instructions to the staff (be forceful without being rude), and finally the removal of the works from the exhibition rooms to the storage area of the main auction theater. Women take care of the protocol; black men, mostly, supplied with white cotton gloves, take care of the moving. The viewing rooms are panned again empty of people and emptied of the works.

The preparations, which are seen in multiple cuts and fade-outs from place to place and scene to scene, lead to the climax of both the film and the event. On the evening of the auction, as witnessed on the screen, the entrance to Sotheby Parke Bernet is blocked by chanting demonstrators. Rank-and-file cabbies accuse Scull of profiteering at their expense. They carry signs reading "Robbing Cabbies is his Living Buying Artists is his Game" and "Never Trust a Rich Hippie." Art Worker Coalition members stage a street theater event—mock beautiful people exploiting mock artists. Women artists protest that work by only one woman, Lee Bontecou, is included in the sale. The night-time scenes outside Sotheby Parke Bernet are shot with a camera confusion reminiscent of the filmic reporting of the anti-war protests of the late '60s. Demonstrators are contrasted markedly and pointedly with ticket holders pushing by them to get in. Robert and Ethel Scull arrive in a chauffeur-driven Checker limousine. They are ushered in the back way, and up in the freight elevator. Ethel wears a long black jersey sheath emblazoned with the emblem of the Scull's Angels taxi fleet.

The auction itself is remarkable and dramatic in its filming. John Marion, president of Sotheby Parke Bernet and auctioneer for the sale, knocks down each piece emphatically. The camera pans the audience like the auctioneer searching for bids. It follows the intense round of bidding on de Kooning's *Police Gazette* ($180,000) and on Johns' *Double White Map* ($240,000). Intercut between the shots of bids being made, and as prices rise rapidly in $5,000 increments, the Sculls are shown reacting. He cranes his neck to see from where the bids are coming, while Ethel, less curious, contemplates the event with an almost sad introspection.

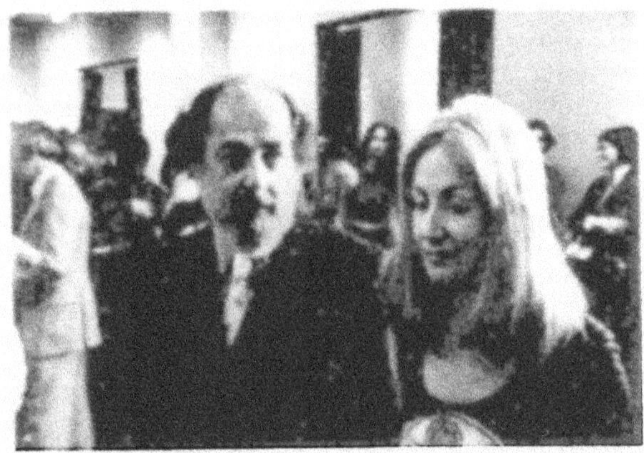

Robert and Ethel Scull at the auction.

At the conclusion of the sale, which comes perhaps a little too rapidly in the film, confrontation breaks out within the house itself. After making a statement in favor of artists' royalties and after kissing Ethel, Robert Rauschenberg engages Scull for the camera and accuses him of profiteering at his and other artists' expense. (A combined collage and painting of his, *Double Feature*, bought by Scull for $2500 in 1959, was sold for $90,000.) Drunk, but quite aware of his purpose, he shoves Scull rudely—"I've been working my ass off for you to make that profit." He wants Scull to buy his next piece—"at these prices." Scull concedes that he will look at it anyway. Both men are obviously conscious of the media presences and therefore the public nature of their pronouncements. Scull maintains that he's done only good for the artists by raising their prices—"I've been working for you too. We work for each other." Their

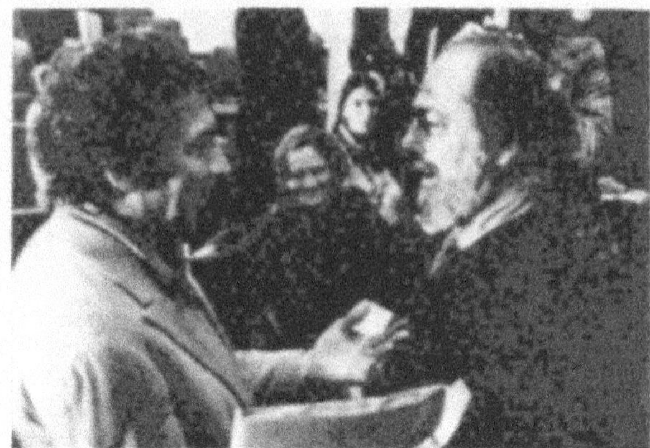

Robert Rauschenberg and Scull.

points are made and the confrontation ends in a stand-off between them. Scull, however, is clearly angered when a young, unknown man (perhaps a reporter) challenges him on the same issue of exploitation and profiteering. A yelling match takes place—"who the hell do you think you're talking to?"

It's over. Just before the Sculls leave they are told that Ben Heller had taken Johns' *Double White Map*. Ethel is saddened by the news—"it's a shame; it should have gone to a museum." Robert comforts her—"it will eventually. It will." A certain tension between them is evident. The Sculls leave, and the camera in a classical movie ending follows the tail lights of their limousine down Madison Avenue. The closing titles are followed (somewhat awkwardly for the edgy viewer) by a brief coda in which workers (again mostly black) are shown packing the pieces—most obviously Johns' bronze *Ale Cans* ($90,000)— for shipment. A worker avoids removing an awkwardly placed sticker from the bronze base of the cans—"if the patina comes off, I don't want to know about it." The finished crates, stacked against one another, are stenciled:

"Keep Dry"
"Work of Art"
"FRAGILE"

From the point of view of the film the auction is seen not simply as self-contained historical occurrence, but as a media event. The film opens, as already described, with a network report on the auction as seen on a television monitor. In another sequence before the auction Scull is shown on a television talk show which we witness on the bank of monitors in the studio control room. There, in answer to a question about his cabs, he says that his cabs will pick you up anywhere and take you to your door—"you don't have to walk anywhere." That remark ironically and unwittingly sets Scull's own privileged situation against the larger reality of the city and its common fears.

In other sequences before the auction we witness interviews with the Sculls at their apartment, where Alfred Leslie's giant portrait of Scull and Warhol's multiple photo-booth portrait of a younger and more spirited Ethel are incorporated as part of their domestic environment. In these scenes the camera focuses primarily on the Sculls and their interviewers, but also opens the frame to include the media equipment and personnel. Brief interviews take place at Sotheby Parke Bernet as well, and careful watching of the scenes there reveals the continual presences of reporters, photographers, and film crews. The action is occasionally punctuated by the whiteouts of flash bulbs.

The media presence as externally documented (and one here could discover a kind of infinite regress of filmers filming filmers) creates a disturbing reciprocity between the event as it actually unfolds, and as it will be seen on the 11 o'clock news or reported in the press. The message is clear: news taking continually mediates reality for us. That mediation becomes an active and manipulatory presence in the event itself. To record history requires the recording of that media presence and of the potential effects of its products on our consciousness. By incorporating the media so insistently the filmmakers seek not to establish their own omniscience, but to offer a compounded view of the event as it took place and as it was otherwise recorded and used. Somewhere all wrapped up here is the complex question of the relationship between image and reality. When taken in context of an auction of works of art, that question leads to a different kind of regress: images within images within images.

Through the media and with Scull's cooperation, the auction became a public entertainment. All the elements were present for a good show: irate artists, angry proletariat, incomprehensible art, high profits, prominent persons, international connections, etc. Auctions are like stage events anyway. And this one with its crowded (SRO) main theater, auxiliary television rooms, and ushered audience was clearly like an opening-night spectacular.[3] In the film Scull himself seems caught up, or at least seems to feel that he should be caught up, in the entertainment. As he and Ethel leave their apartment for the auction, he counters the rather somber mood by saying, "If you can't enjoy it, why bother?" The answer seems somehow obvious.

The multi-leveled cinematic portrait that emerges from the various views of Robert Scull—in interviews with the press, in personal exchange, at Sotheby Parke Bernet, at his office at the taxi garage—is that of cultural innocent surprised by what has happened and genuinely upset by the accusations against him. Compared to Rauschenberg, who came to the auction with a complaint and staged a confrontation to make it public, Scull remains somehow out of touch with the seriousness of the issues. He is taken aback by the heat of the attack. He leaves the impression of a rather gentle, unaffected man who wishes to hurt nobody, and who simply wants people to like him. Above all, as he says in a dark interview filmed in the interior of his car as it negotiates New York traffic and the light streets flash by outside, he doesn't want to make an idiot of himself.

Nowhere in the film is to be found even a recollection of Tom Wolfe's aggressive pleasure-and-status seekers, "Bob and Spike," as he described the Sculls of the '60s in *The Pump House Gang*.[4] The titles of two of de Kooning's paintings sold at the auction, *Spike's Folly I* (1959) and *Spike's Folly II* (1960), are the only reminders of that old identity. Despite the excitement of the sale, there is the sense of something having passed. "The Sculls," Rauschenberg says in a moment of reflection, "were miracles, and there will be others." They were miracles not only because they bought courageously, but because they advocated the type of art they bought and the artists who made it.

When it comes to art and what might be called art behavior, Scull is surprisingly without sophistication and without pre-

tense. Self-made with his wife's help, and off the streets, he seems to repeat stock opinions about art almost as if rehearsed. His answer to the continual questions about his motive in selling is that he is liberating these works for the world at large now that they have reached maturity through his attention. Europeans, he is sure, will buy; and they did. The sale, he is convinced, will establish contemporary American art at the proper level of its power, vitality, and value. The artists will benefit through recognition and higher prices. Scull, one is convinced, believes in the truth of these assertions and in the honesty of his own motivation, which is not to say that he is unaware of the benefits to himself either in profits or in reputation.

Superimposed on Scull's rather simple directness is the style of the '60s. Balding, but still full-bearded, Scull emerges as the well-dressed but aging hippie art freak locked into a particular vocabulary and manner. At home he wears a white flower-decorated shirt open to mid-chest. Acquisition and ownership for him constitute an intimate involvement in the lives of artists. "Art," he tells a *Wall Street Journal* reporter, "is a different kind of a high." He describes how Larry Poons' *Wildcat Arrival* knocks him out, and to demonstrators he calls "hi'ya boys, right on" even though he is visibly annoyed by their presence.

One of the best sequences in the film takes place at the Scull's Angels garage in the South Bronx. There another but still affable aspect of Scull is revealed. He is the boss, not the executive boss but the kind intimately involved in the operations of his own business. He works daily with types whose only relation to Madison Avenue is to cruise it for fares. The filmed contrast is intentional and striking—working engine blocks and automobile parts rather than John Chamberlain's auto-part sculpture, which was seen in his studio earlier in the film. Scull is seen at his desk talking on the phone and doing paper work. In voice-over he talks about the upcoming sale and the business of art, while the camera follows the various activities of the garage.

> Art is supposed to be such a fine, toney, cultured thing, y'know, and suddenly people are bidding wildly like it was a commodity just like any other. And I think at Parke Bernet, that's art without the floss of culture. Over there it is hard, cold money and business and, man, over there you've gotta write a check out (on the screen woman cashier receiving and counting money turned in by drivers). There's no fooling around and talking about the aesthetics of art. There they just talk about the money of art.

In this perhaps more natural habitat, Scull appears at ease as the urban realist in a tough business. His comments are not at all cynical, but simply direct in their estimation of the way things are—status and wealth through ownership. His innocence does not lie in lack of knowledge about the world, but in his lack of snobbishness. Scull comes off as a man without guile, but also without deep sensitivity or cultivation. Yet he buys art. He is an anomaly, and though audience reaction to Scull is sometimes very negative, the film in no way vilifies him.

In conversations with and between dealers Ivan Karp and Leo Castelli at Karp's O.K. Harris Gallery in SoHo, the film presents the professionals' view of Scull as amateur, parvenu collector. It's the sellers talking about the buyer. Castelli characterizes Scull as a voracious and compulsive buyer (anality is implied) who wanted to collect everything—works, artists, galleries, even dealers—at very low prices. "You know that Scull never had much money, really, he didn't have much money." Karp opposes the sale (pictures will go abroad) and finds Scull's intended presence at the auction a breach of both sensitivity and decorum. Castelli, who doesn't mind pictures going abroad, finds Scull's motive in collecting not the cultivation of art, but the gaining of notoriety and attention. He sees the sale as Scull's "final grand gesture to get an incredible amount of attention." The impression left is that Castelli in particular finds Scull ill-motivated in his collecting and something of a social and cultural climber.

Between the collector and the dealers, of course, stand the works of art themselves. All the commotion is about these objects, and yet in the film they are sadly diminished. Panning reduces the exhibited pieces to background objects distorted through the motion of the camera. Even in the still shots the works appear pallid and uncompelling, more as objects of curiosity than as important artistic statements. In short, as seen in the film, within the context of the auction house the works become merchandise displayed for sale. The intention of the filmmakers was not to advocate particular styles or particular artists, but to show how art is traded. The attitude toward the pieces, they maintain, emerges not from an editorial position as regards aesthetic quality, but from the nature of the event itself.

Despite the professed intention of the filmmakers to document the event as it unfolded in actuality without editorial comment, a particular point of view does emerge, and it emerges largely from the treatment of the works of art. In choosing to emphasize the diminished artistic importance of the works within the context of the sale, the filmmakers invite the audience to take a superior position in regard to the activity played out before them, to question the taste, judgment, and motives of Scull and the potential buyers. The viewer does not achieve the position of participant in the event, is never placed within history itself, but is forced into critical judgment as observer. If the art is questioned, then the whole event can be seen as sham, and those involved either as glamorous opportunists or simply fools.[5] In either case, the film stresses the denial of the images in favor of the play of personalities and the drama of events. That may well be the essential truth of the whole affair and therefore the most important realization one can gain from it as regards the exchange of art in the contemporary world, but the film determinedly reinforces that position. In a particularly unfortunate inclusion, from the point of view of objectivity, the camera cuts to a close-up of a dollar sign in one of Scull's pictures at his home. Its meaning is clear and explicit: in the upper reaches of our society art functions as a medium of exchange, and as a successful form of high investment.

In showing the works being moved from place to place by employees and in closing with the packing of the objects for shipment, the film enforces a consideration of the distinction between the objects for sale as material things—say, six yards of canvas covered with pigment and stretched on a wooden frame—and as works of art. In light of the social swirl, the intense bidding, and the prices brought, that distinction must be seen as intentionally ironic. During preparation for the auction, employees hanging Poons' large (116 × 190") *Wildcat Arrival* drop the canvas and one corner hits the floor with a thud. The sequence is accompanied by a voice-over explanation by John Marion of bidding procedures and price estimates. When the Poons slips, or when Jasper Johns' bronze *Ale Cans*

slide off their pedestal with a clank into the lap of one of the movers, one simply cannot avoid considering the great difference in intrinsic value as opposed to the market value of these objects.

In raising the issue of value so directly and consciously through documentation, the film reveals the way in which contemporary object-art functions as inflated commodity stuff to be traded by the wealthy for their own potential profit and status. By extension, the question of the artist's contribution to the monetary value of an object and what should be his or her share of the profits is also suggested. These were volatile issues in New York in 1973, and were brought to a head by the auction, because of the 26 artists represented, all but two (Barnett Newman and Franz Kline) were alive to see their pictures sold to Scull's considerable benefit. His argument that the sale is to the benefit of the artists because it will raise prices on their future work, while true, is simply not satisfying. The confrontation between Scull and Rauschenberg at the conclusion of the sale and the latter's call for federal legislation to establish artists' royalties on subsequent sales of their work made these issues part of the auction as an historical event.[6]

In choosing an attitude that raises questions about the whole practice of the commodity exchange of art, the filmmakers align themselves, however gently, with certain radical positions of the late '60s and early '70s. At that time many artists, in reaction to the gallery scene, advocated the making of art which, because it was without direct material manifestation, would have no applicability to the marketplace. It would thereby be free of the taint of profit taking and capitalism. The film, however, is not a defense of Conceptualism or related movements, or in any way a political propaganda effort against the association of art and wealth. It does not debunk or attempt to rip away the mask of falsehood and hypocrisy by revealing the horrors of capitalist exploitation of art and artists. Its intention, as suggested by Vaughn, is to be descriptive rather than polemical, to be dialectic rather than didactic. But out of that dialectic (at least for this viewer) emerges an image of art-trading which invites challenge.

With these considerations in mind, thinking about the film as a historical document immediately raises a major question: is it a primary document, like the sales catalog published by Sotheby Parke Bernet, or is it a secondary description, like an extended news report with editorial overtones? Clearly it is both. Even as edited, there is no better document of what really happened, say, between Rauschenberg and Scull. The film even reveals the way the encounter was staged for, or at least conditioned by the presence of, the news media and film crew. That simply is unavailable elsewhere, except perhaps in individual memory. But the film is just as clearly an encapsulated description, and there can be no description without judgment. The dialectic is rooted not in the event itself, but in a point of view. Every inclusion, every sequence, every juxtaposition results first from a shooting and then from an editing decision.

Yet despite the ambiguity between primary and secondary source, and perhaps because of that very ambiguity, the film offers a composite view of history. In viewing it, we witness the way in which any historical occurrence is an amalgam of interrelated motives and necessities. In the film, the auction is documented not as an isolated phenomenon existing in its own restricted time and place, and according to its own limited definition of importance, but as a point of confluence of social, cultural, and economic forces. If, for instance, the film forces a comparison between John Chamberlain's auto-part sculpture and the operation of Scull's taxi garage, that comparison, or more accurately that connection, is established in actuality by the insignia of Scull's Angels on Ethel Scull's dress. New York taxicabs and New York art somewhere occupy a common ground. The ordinary life of the city, the hassle, the paranoia ("you don't have to walk anywhere"), the caste system (it's blacks who move the pieces), the disenfranchised of the art world, interact with international exchange and cultivated taste.

In bringing all these elements together, and in directing our awareness to their connection, the Scull film, as suggested, offers a synoptic view of one particularly significant event in contemporary art. The film thus becomes immediately valuable not only as a document of what happened at the auction, but also as a source for what has been called contextual art history. The contextual approach offers a form of history in which the study of the interrelation between historical circumstances, the practice of image-making, and the use of images takes precedent over the study of individual objects, and even over the development of style as an independent phenomenon.[7] Indeed, within the film, works of art are seen not in their singularity, but as objects of exchange, inextricably bound up with personal motives and with the operation of ownership and status. To introduce such considerations into the study of art may sully the spiritual purity of artistic endeavor, and by extension of art history itself; to ignore them, however, means to accept a view of art historical reality and practice which is too narrowly circumscribed and which supports the myth of its own innocence.[8] In forcing consideration of these issues, whether it does so intentionally or not, the Scull film serves not only as an important art historical document, but as an equally important statement on the nature of art historical studies.

And yet there are problems. To view works of art from a too strictly contextual point of view always creates the danger of losing the art for the history or the context. Works of art seen simply as objects like any others, connected with a particular historical or cultural situation, easily degenerate in use into illustrations or simply props of those situations. Distinctions of quality and importance are thereby threatened. Something of

that kind happens in the Scull film, with an effect that has already been discussed. In the use of the film, that potentially damaging effect must be corrected, while at the same time not losing what it tells us so brilliantly about one particular exchange of art in our time.[9] ■

1. *New York Magazine*, November 5, 1973, p. 80 ff. See also J.E. Patterson, "Facts, Figures, Questions about the Scull Sale," *Art News*, December, 1973, pp. 78–80; S. Spector, "Sotheby-Parke-Bernet: The Scull Collection," *Art in America*, September, 1973, pp. 25–26; Katherine Kuh, "New Art and Its Collectors," *Saturday Review/World*, December 4, 1973, pp. 38–40; John Tancock, "The Robert C. Scull Auction," *Art at Auction: The Year at Sotheby Parke Bernet*, 1973, p. 138 ff.
2. The Raymonds were responsible earlier for the series "An American Family," which introduced the Louds to television audiences via NET.
3. That even scholarly exhibitions have recently taken on the quality of theatrical entertainments can be seen in the ad run by The Museum of Modern Art for its exhibition of the late works of Cézanne. Critics are quoted in the ad as if reviewing a movie or play. The implicit promise in the ad is of cultural fulfillment, but the form connects it, however discreetly, with the hoopla of the entertainment industry: don't miss this one.
4. Tom Wolfe, *The Pump House Gang*, New York, 1968, pp. 139–60.
5. I am indebted to my friend and colleague Robert Horvitz for this observation.
6. In 1976 California passed the Resale Royalties Act, to be effective January 1, 1977. The first such state law, it calls for 5 percent royalty to be paid artists by owners who sell their work for a profit and above a base price of $1,000. The law, which requires artists to sue owners if they do not receive royalty payment, has proved impossible to enforce and is unpopular with dealers and collectors as well as with some younger artists, who fear it can injure their careers by inhibiting both primary and secondary sales. Despite the problems with the California law and intended challenges to it in the courts, a number of other states are considering pending legislation, and there are plans for the introduction of federal legislation as well. In the battle over the passage of the California Resale Royalties Act the Scull film was used by those advocating its passage.
7. For a discussion of contextual art history see Svetlana Alpers, "Is Art History?," *Daedalus*, Summer, 1977, pp. 1–13.
8. Art history, as Albert Elsen has recently pointed out and as many have privately known, is not so academically pure. It has always had a connection with the market in art and antiquities both legitimate and illegitimate. See "Bomb the Church? What We Don't Tell Our Students in Art I," *Art Journal*, Fall, 1977, p. 28 ff.
9. The film is available through Cinema Five in New York.

Baruch D. Kirschenbaum is Chairman of the Division of Liberal Arts, Rhode Island School of Design.

Photo-Synthesis: Photosculptures and Blends by Doug Prince

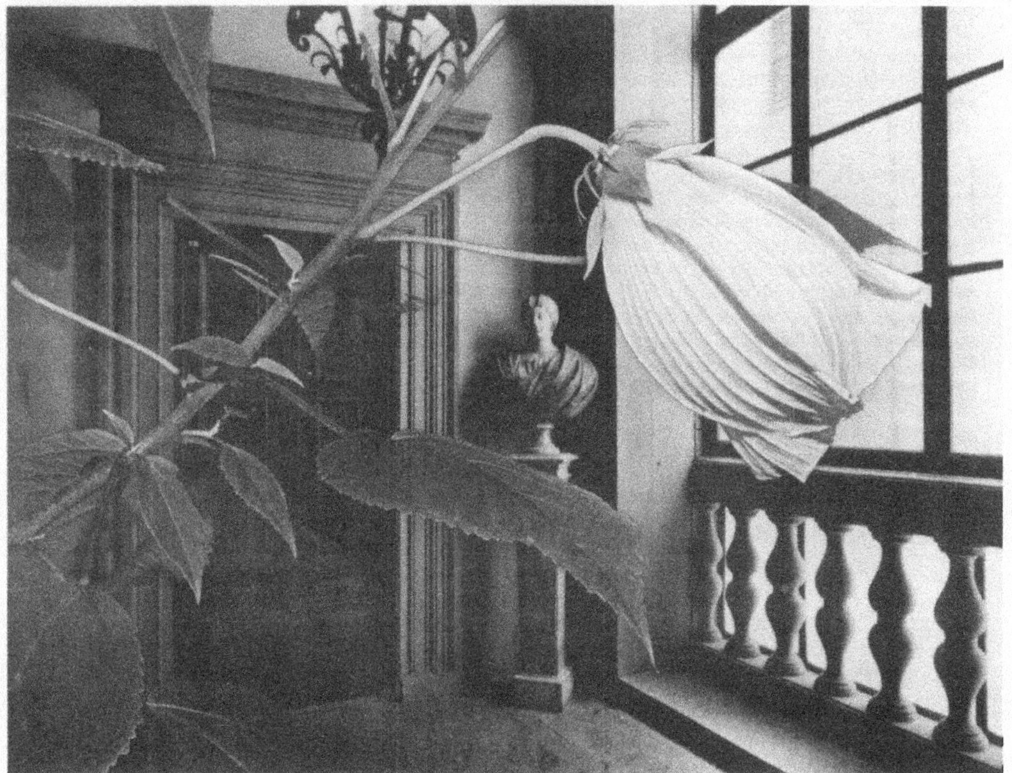

White Flower and Sculpture, 1984

June 21 - September 8, 1985

Museum of Art
Rhode Island School of Design
Providence, Rhode Island

Doug Prince

The title given to this exhibition, ''Photo-Synthesis,'' is particularly appropriate for the work of Doug Prince. In botany, the term refers to that process of chemical reaction by which light is transformed into nourishment, thus sustaining life on earth. The analogy to photography is clear, for photographic images are also produced by a chemical reaction to light. In the images of Doug Prince, however, there is an additional implied meaning: through the layering and matching of diverse photographic images, he transforms, through synthesis, literal into metaphoric truth.

Photographs carry a particular weight of authority, for what is shown in a photograph is generally thought to match a reality external to the image. In other words, photographs apparently appropriate reality rather than represent it. No such reality and therefore no ordinary ''photographic truth,'' however, exists in the work of Doug Prince. The parts are real, but the whole is invented, compiled.

All the pictures in the exhibition are made from more than a single negative. The smaller pictures are made by the superimposition of parts of two, sometimes three, negatives which are then printed as one. The large pictures in which leaves and flowers are superimposed on architectural background scenes are made in a series of stages in which two images are combined on a single piece of film which is then printed. For the encased boxes, positives and sometimes negative transparencies are sandwiched between squares of Plexiglas and then spaced within the box to create the desired illusion of intersecting planes in depth.

The power of these created realities to move us rests with the nature of metaphor. Metaphor results from the reciprocal interaction of two terms which may seem at first contradictory. When the poet refers to the ''wine-dark sea'' or the ''seeing mouth,'' each term affects the other and an unexpected, sometimes disturbing meaning emerges. When Doug Prince places a giant tortoise amongst the foundation arches of some grand (and one thinks old and European) building *(Tortoise and Arches,* 1985), he creates a visual metaphor. He juxtaposes the prehistorically primitive life form with the vacant remains of human effort. The image unites eonic and human time, the biologically sensate with the insensate stone. The result is to animate the walls, however minimally, and to discover their organic principle. In reverse, the metaphor reveals the architectural principle of this unlikely reptilian creature. No question remains as to which is more enduring. In a more fleeting mode, Prince discovers the metaphoric analogy between three swans and the elegant facade of Palladio's S. Giorgio Maggiore on the Grand Canal in Venice *(Swans in Venice,* 1985).

The smaller composite pictures like those of the tortoise and the swans glow with a strange black and white irrationality. They are like documented dream images. Because on reflection things in the pictures don't quite match, there occurs a momentary crisis of understanding. In that crisis the visual metaphor works its effect most strongly. Differences in perspec-

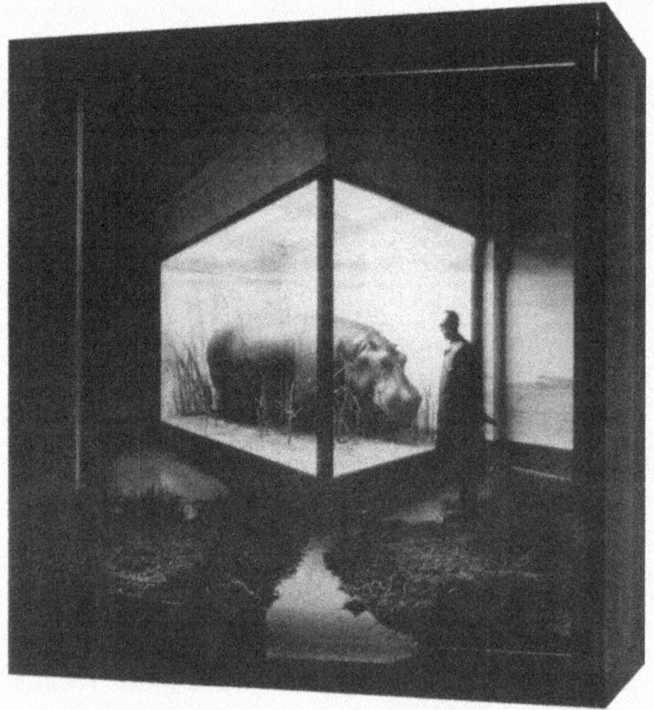

Hippopotamus and Man, 1983

tive, in lens focal length, and in light of the combined photographic elements become apparent through intersection.

If the composite nature of the small pictures is not immediately apparent, that of the large pictures and the boxes is discernible at once. The boxes which Prince conceives of as miniaturized environments are constructed, as already noted, of layered transparencies seen one through the other. In the large prints, the plants and flowers are independent images which float on the surface of the pictures. Details of architecture under-images are seen through the leaves and petals that seem to be in the process of disappearance. In their layering, the large photographs are like two-dimensional versions of the boxes. Though they don't have quite the same effect of environmental depth, they achieve a similar integration of elements.

Both the boxes and the large prints produce what might be called "memory images." They transform the layering of visual elements into the experience of the layering of time. In them, past and present make up the metaphoric terms. The calla lily in the frescoed Italianate bed chamber *(Calla Lily in Bedroom,* 1984) is a ghost of a former presence. It haunts the interior of the room with memory as if something ineffaceable happened there.

Through layering Prince turns the photographic process, which typically isolates an instant in the flow of time, in on itself. He records not a single moment but a succession of points in time. The elderly couple *(Wedding Chamber,* 1972,) seen as vanishing negative presences, kiss in the dated environment of their past. The nude *(Odalisque,* 1979) looks out at an already accomplished future. Both pictures, as with the calla lily in the bed chamber, result in a presentiment of our own mortality. We are all locked in time, which in a way is the message of all photographs.

By joining together separate pieces of photographic reality for metaphoric meaning and effect, Doug Prince simultaneously affirms the essential nature of the photographic image and extends it to an inevitable conclusion.

Based upon recorded reality, his images match no discrete actuality outside their own existence. His work both exploits and challenges the whole idea of photographic truth. He twists our expectations. The truth of metaphor is of a different, and perhaps higher, nature than the truth of reality. Metaphoric synthesis lies at the center of the imagination and what we like to call the creative process. "Photo-Synthesis" is not only an appropriate title for this exhibition but one that reveals as well the central artistic concern of Doug Prince and the nature of his inventions.

Baruch Kirschenbaum
Professor of Art History
Rhode Island School of Design

Doug Prince

A note about dates: The date following the title of each work refers to the year the image was compiled; the numbers in parentheses refer to the years in which the negatives were made.

Black & white silver prints, 8" x 10"
1. White Calf in Pen, 1979 (71-66-71)
2. Swans in Venice, 1985 (81-79)
3. Footprints with Houses, 1985 (83-80)
4. Case in Pebbles with Statues, 1985 (81-81)
5. Sky-writing over Forum, 1985, (78-80)
6. Collie on Cape Cod, 1985 (78-78)
7. Brice on Frozen Beach, 1985 (78-79)
8. Deer in Ruins, 1985 (79-78)
9. Case with Cow, 1985 (79-80)
10. Tortoise and Arches, 1985 (80-81)
11. Case on Blanket with Ocean, 1985 (79-80)
12. Train Set and Balloon, 1985 (78-78)
13. Swan in Winter, 1978 (74-66)
14. Young Woman with Lightning, 1979 (79-79)
15. White Horse in Fog, 1979 (78-78)
16. Brice and Brian under Vines, 1978 (72-73)
17. Brice and Brian with Ship, 1978 (73-73)
18. Brian, Snake and Mountains, 1979 (79-74)

Black & white silver prints, 11" x 14"
19. Morning Glory with Sculpture, 1985
20. Calla Lily in Bedroom, 1984
21. Rose with Arch, 1984
22. Trumpet Flower and Angel, 1984
23. Morning Glories and Landscape, 1984
24. Hibiscus Interior, 1985
25. White Flower and Sculpture, 1984

Photo-sculptures, 5" x 5" x 2 1/2"
1. Wedding Chamber, 1972
2. Magnolia Chamber, 1973
3. Summer Interior, 1980
4. Floating Fan, 1972
5. Palace Window, 1982
6. Hippopotamus and Man, 1983
7. Floating Doll, 1979
8. Man with Tulips, 1982
9. Rattle and Carriage in Hallway, 1982

Photo-sculptures, 8" x 8" x 3 1/2"
10. Floating Rose, 1978
11. Florida Room, 1983
12. Odalisque, 1979
13. Nautilus Chamber, 1984
14. Roman Forum, 1985
15. Key Chamber, 1983
16. Case in the Heavens, 1985
17. Observation Room, 1983
18. Projection Screen, 1983
19. Delivery Room, 1982

Doug Prince

EDUCATION

1968 M.A. University of Iowa
1965 B.A. University of Iowa

TEACHING EXPERIENCE

1984 - 1985
University of Rhode Island, Department of Art, Kingston, RI; Visiting Artist.

1982 - 1983
Northern Kentucky University, Department of Fine Art, Highland Heights, Kentucky; Visiting Associate Professor.

1976 - 1979
Rhode Island School of Design, Photography Department, Providence, Rhode Island; Assistant Professor.

1968 - 1976
University of Florida, Department of Fine Arts, Gainesville, Florida; Assistant Professor.

SELECT ONE-PERSON EXHIBITIONS

1983   "Doug Prince: Selected Works 1971 - 1983," Witkin Gallery, New York.
Carl Solway Gallery, Cincinnati, Ohio.
1981   Rondanini Galleria d'Arte Contemporanea, Rome, Italy.
1980   Witkin Gallery, New York.
Addison Gallery of American Art, Phillips Academy, Andover, MA.
1975   Light Gallery, New York.
1973   Light Gallery, New York.
1968   Gallery for the Advancement of Photography, Iowa City, Iowa.
1967   Des Moines Art Center, Des Moines, Iowa.
1966   Art Gallery, University of Iowa, Iowa City.

HONORS AND AWARDS

1979   National Endowment for the Arts Photography Fellowship
1977   National Endowment for the Arts Photography Fellowship
1972   Le Prix de la Ville D'Avignon

PERMANENT COLLECTIONS

Museum of Modern Art, New York
National Exchange Bank of Chicago
International Museum of Photography, George Eastman House, Rochester
Philadelphia Museum of Art
Photographic Archives, University of Louisville, Kentucky
International Center of Photography
Museum of Art, Rhode Island School of Design
Universita' di Parma, Parma, Italy
University of New Mexico, Albuquerque
Addison Gallery of American Art, Andover
Princeton Art Museum
Worcester Art Museum, Worcester, MA
Virginia Museum of Fine Art, Richmond
Australian National Gallery, Australia
The Israel Museum, Jerusalem
Museum of Fine Arts, Boston

Museum of Art
2 College Street
Providence, RI 02903

Non-Profit Org.
U.S. Postage
PAID
Providence, R.I.
Permit No. 408

REFLECTIONS ON MICHELANGELO'S DRAWINGS FOR CAVALIERE

BY BARUCH D. KIRSCHENBAUM

URING MICHELANGELO's stay in Rome from late summer of 1532 to June 1533, Cavaliere as "... a young Rome Cavaliere. Benedetto Varchi describes he was introduced to Tomasso dan of noble birth in whom I recognized while in Rome not only incomparable beauty, but so much elegance of manner, such excellence and such grace of behavior, that he well deserved and still deserves to win more love the better he is known[1]." Giorgio Vasari, in mentioning a portrait from life of Cavaliere, also testifies to the young man's beauty: "for he [Michelangelo] abhorred drawing anything from life unless it was of the utmost beauty[2]." Michelangelo, then fifty-seven, became enamored.

From the sixteenth century until the present, speculators have questioned the nature of Michelangelo's love for Cavaliere, and for several other young men also. The opinions which they have offered differ according to the era and the moral outlook of the reviewer. As often happens, original documents have been ignored, or changed to suit the theory. In the sonnets meant for Cavaliere words have been changed; letters full of humble passion have been glaringly misinterpreted; and women have been invented to replace the young nobleman[3].

Early in their friendship, Michelangelo presented Cavaliere with a number of finished drawings in red and black chalk. These are better characterized in Berenson's term, "pastel paintings," for they are finished with great care and have not the spontaneity often associated with drawing style. Of the drawings mentioned by Vasari, six have been definitely identified: the *Ganymede*, the *Tityus*, three versions of the *Fall of Phaeton*, and the *Children's Bacchanal*[4].

Taken together, the drawings constitute a poetic confession of Michelangelo's love for Cavaliere, and of the elation and guilt, ascent and fall which he associated with love. For this almost bashful expression of his feelings Michelangelo turned to classical mythology and motif. The association of themes of love and the antique

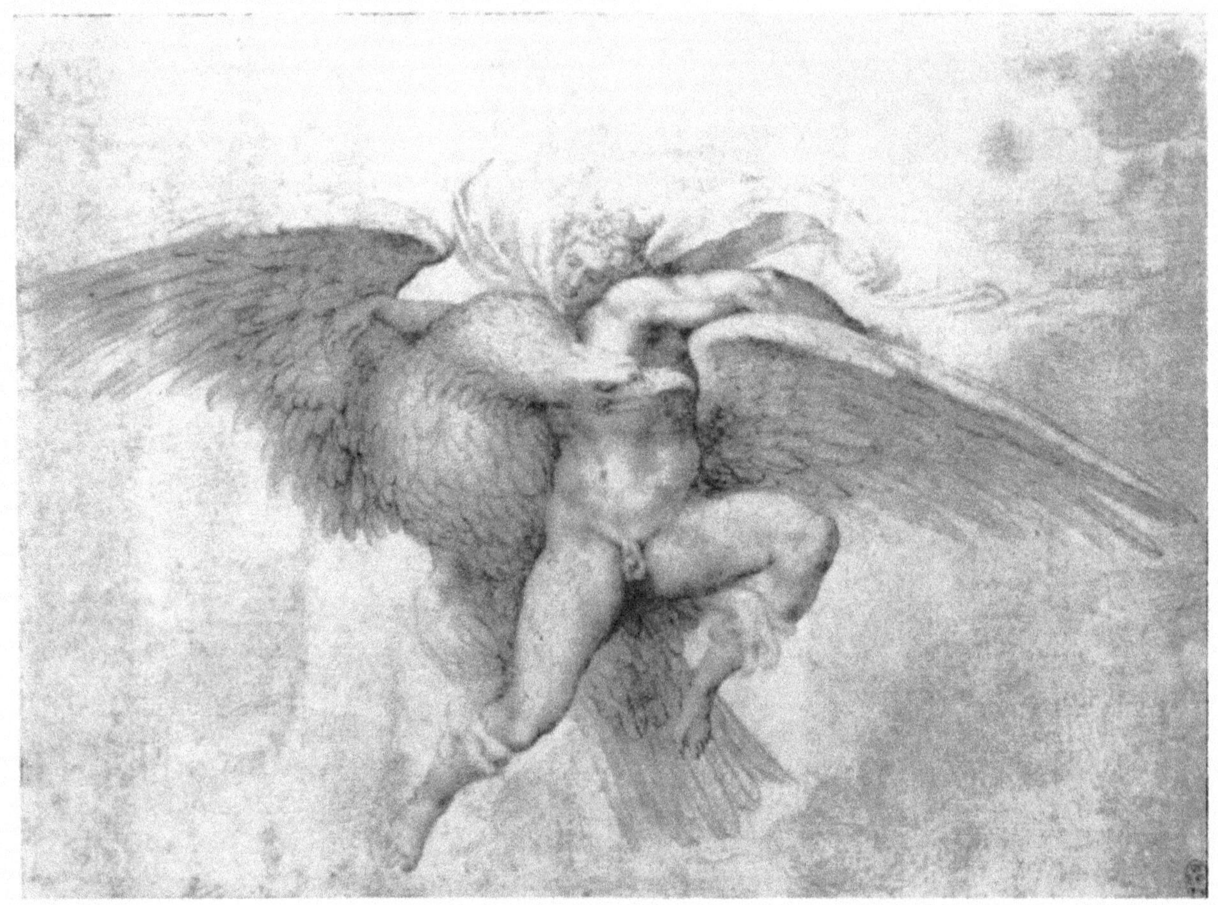

FIG. 1.—Copy after Michelangelo, *Ganymede*, Windsor.
Royal Collection, Windsor Castle. Copyright reserved.

is a natural one, for not only is the antique "classical" but it is also "pagan," and can serve where Christian iconography can not or dare not. That Cavaliere was an amateur of classical art and had a considerable collection, makes it even more natural for Michelangelo to have chosen the classical for these confessional drawings [5].

At the end of 1532 he sent to Cavaliere the *Ganymede* (fig. 1) and the *Tityus* (fig. 2). It is generally agreed that the *Ganymede* at Windsor Castle is a copy, but the best of several; however, it has been cut and does not show the landscape, the barking dog, the sheep and the equipment of the young shepherd, which were part of the original drawing [6]. The *Tityus*, also at Windsor Castle, is considered original.

Michelangelo has chosen two moments representing opposing states of existence: ascension, and fall. It is generally agreed that the drawings constitute a pair symbolizing the dual nature of love. Erwin Panofsky finds in them a neo-Platonic program. Thus the *Ganymede* is the ascension of the soul-mind "symbolizing the ecstasy of Platonic love"; and the *Tityus* is the damnation of the lustful body which enslaves the soul [7]. Other critics interpret the drawings as simply the rapture and torture of love [8].

REFLECTIONS ON MICHELANGELO'S DRAWINGS FOR CAVALIERE   IOI

The myths had been so interpreted previously—e.g. by Plato and by Lucretius".

It seems that both Platonism and the confused, ambivalent feeling of love are present, and that to assign a single meaning—or a single impulse—to these works is all too limiting. The same admixture of Platonism and physical love is found in one of the first love sonnets addressed to Cavaliere:

> *With your fair eyes a charming light I see,*
> *For which my own blind eyes would peer in vain;*
> *Stayed by your feet, the burden I sustain*
> *Which my lame feet find all too strong for me;*
> *Wingless upon your pinions forth I fly;*
> *Heavenward your spirit stirreth me to strain;*
> *E'en as you will, I blush and blanch again,*
> *Freeze in the sun, burn'neath a frosty sky.*
> *Your will includes and is the lord of mine;*
> *Life to my thoughts within your heart is given;*
> *My words begin to breathe upon your breath:*
> *Like to the moon am I, that cannot shine*
> *Alone; for, lo! our eyes see naught in heaven*
> *Save what the living sun illumineth* [10].

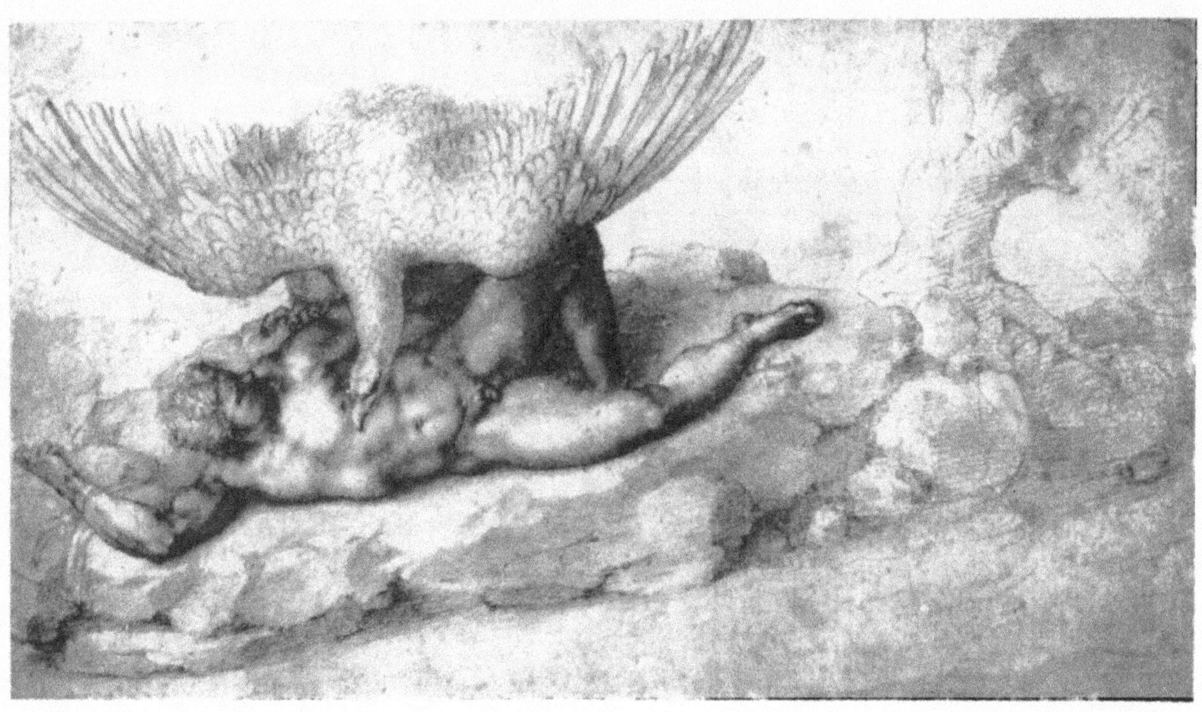

FIG. 2.—Michelangelo, *Tityus*. Royal Collection,
Windsor Castle. Copyright reserved.

Ganymede then is not carried off against his will, but rather rises in trance, the powerful strokes of the eagle's wings lifting him into a higher realm. All the energy of flight is concentrated in the gigantic bird. But as if to assist, the body of Ganymede has surrendered all its earthly weight.

Michelangelo departs from myth in one essential. In the story of Ganymede an eagle abducts the boy; but it is a vulture that pecks at Tityus' liver [11]. Yet even a cursory glance at the drawings discovers that the bird is the same in both. Closer examination shows that Ganymede and Tityus look remarkably alike, with curly hair and round heads, and full, almost chubby bodies. The bird is the dynamic force in both pictures, Ganymede and Tityus being inert. As pure energy the bird is amoral and inflicts reward and punishment, with neither benevolence nor malice, upon the same contestant for the same act. Michelangelo seems to be saying that the same amoral forces govern both positive and negative aspects of a single experience.

By contrast, in Titian's painting at the Prado (fig. 3) which Panofsky shows to be Tityus rather than the commonly accepted Prometheus [12], the contour of the vulture is quite easily distinguished. Clearly and purposefully Michelangelo changed the bird for his own meaning: to equate the forces in the two drawings. But more important, the comparison emphasizes the lack of struggle on the part of Michelangelo's Tityus. The damned in Titian writhes to escape the sharp beak of the vulture, his muscles taut with strain. In the drawing there is an element of struggle: Tityus raises his head, he clenches his fist; but at the same time his position is almost relaxed, especially the legs, and the muscles are loose. This is all the more surprising since, compared with the prominence which Titian gives his chains, we have to seek out the bonds in Michelangelo. Faint lines alone bind Tityus to his rock; indeed, one of the fetters lies unused on the ground (by the left leg). Despite this, Michelangelo's Tityus chooses only token resistance. This drawing, then, when taken with its companion, the *Ganymede*, depicts a voluntary acceptance of torture, an acceptance of the fall as well as the flight of love and a recognition that one demands the other. A second love sonnet sent to Cavaliere supports this contention:

> *Why should I seek to ease intense desire*
> *With still more tears and windy words of grief,*
> *When heaven, or late or soon, sends no relief*
> *To souls whom love hath robed around with fire?*
> *Why need my aching heart to death aspire,*
> *When all must die? Nay, death beyond belief*
> *Unto these eyes would be both sweet and brief,*
> *Since in my sum of woes all joys expire!*
> *Therefore, because I cannot shun the blow*
> *I rather seek, say who must rule my breast,*

REFLECTIONS ON MICHELANGELO'S DRAWINGS FOR CAVALIERE   103

Gliding between her gladness and her woe?
If only chains and bands can make me blest,
No marvel if alone and bare I go,
An armèd KNIGHT'S captive and slave confessed [13].

The last line of the sonnet is a play on the name of Cavaliere.

In "The Neo-Platonic Movement and Michelangelo," which is both the basis and the inspiration of this essay, Dr. Panofsky sums up his discussion of the two drawings by saying: "In both compositions the traditional allegorical interpretation of a mythological subject was accepted, but it was invested with a deeper meaning of a personal confession, so that both forms of love were conceived as two aspects of one essentially tragic experience [14]." This is certainly close to the heart of the matter, but I would qualify the statement: We have here not the representation of sacred and profane love, but rather two inextricable elements to be found in love—to be found, indeed, in any intense emotion or experience. The next group of drawings given to Cavaliere bears out this feeling by uniting the antithetical elements in a single theme.

Michelangelo sent to Cavaliere three versions of the *Fall of Phaeton*. They are in the British Museum (fig. 4); in the Accademia at Venice (fig. 5) —badly preserved; and at Windsor Castle (fig. 6). All three are considered original. The sequence of the drawings has been generally accepted as given here [15]—the first dating somewhere in the autumn of 1532 and the latter two between June and September of 1533. From a formal point of view this would seem accurate, since the last version appears to solve the problems of the preceding two. Furthermore, the first two bear inscriptions in Michelangelo's own hand promising variants if they did not please.

In all three versions we find a compositional relationship which expresses the core of the struggle of the individual caught between aspiration and failure. Above, the

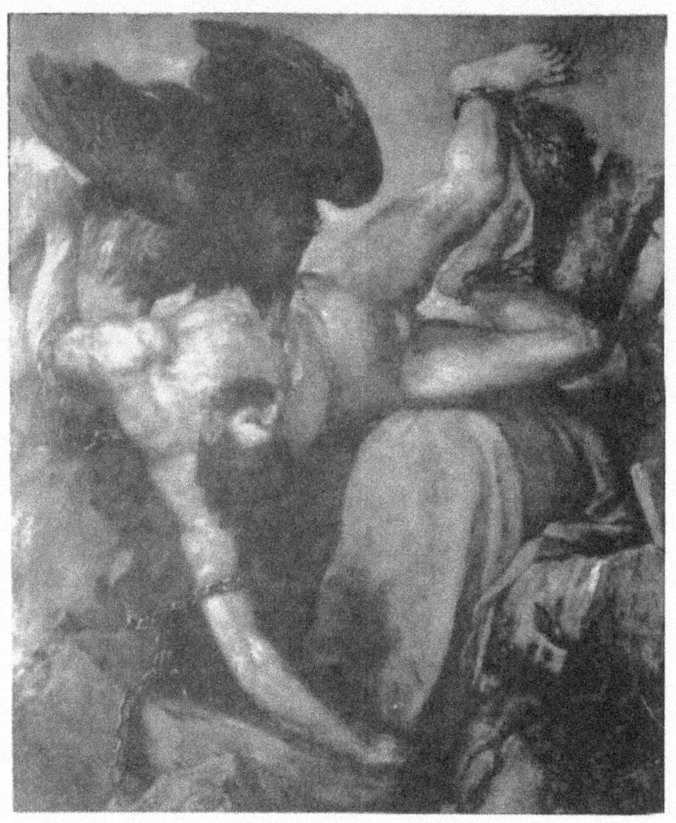

FIG. 3.—Titian, *Tityus*. Madrid, Prado.

divine: Zeus mounted on his eagle in position of uncontested power and majesty which Phaeton yearned, against all persuasion, to possess for but a single day. Below, the human: amazement and powerless grief at the moment of disaster. And all this absorbed in the continuity of time—for the river Eridanus flows on. The fall is not only a loss of the divine but also a submersion into anonymity. Between these extremes is the chaotic and agonizing act of falling, in which one is no longer divine, nor yet wholly human.

The changes from version to version of the drawing do, I believe, bear out these feelings. In the first, Michelangelo was much concerned with accuracy of detail. He followed Ovid's narrative strictly [16]. Phaeton falls in an arc; the duality of his state is carried only by his central position. This is even more strongly felt in the second, more despairing version, in which Michelangelo departed radically from Ovid. Phaeton plummets headlong to the ground, losing all contact with the divine. He is symmetrically flanked by animal flesh; this juxtaposition intensifies the animal aspect of his own nature. In the third, and in this interpretation most successful version, Michelangelo abandoned both the asymmetry of the first version and the symmetry of the second, to arrive at a triangular form which connects all the elements into a single experience. Phaeton falls not headlong, but to the side, his position reminiscent of his once-free flight. His separation from the falling horses allows dissociation of flesh, though certainly not so much as in the first version. These changes emphasize the dual nature of the moment of fall.

The changes in the lower part of the drawings also show an increasing awareness of this meaning. In the first version, Eridanus looks up interested if not concerned with the happenings. In the second version, placed on the same axis as Phaeton, he reaches out as if to break the fall. Here he is the real third party in the drama. In

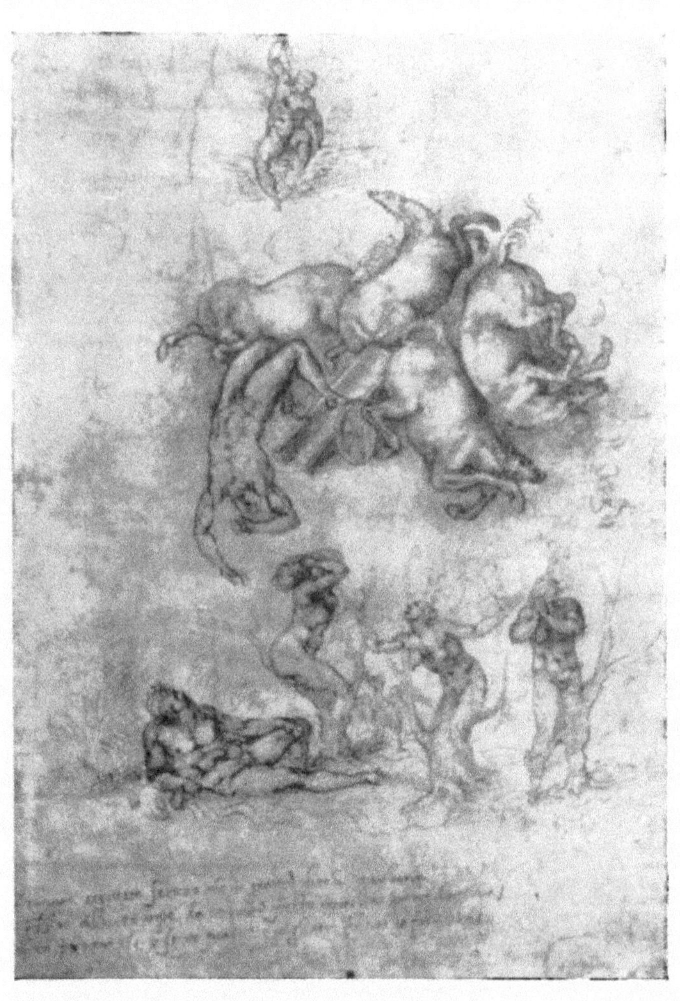

FIG. 4.—Michelangelo, *Fall of Phaeton* (first version).
London, British Museum.

the last version, Eridanus symbolizes instead the flow of time and the practical world which proceeds indifferent to personal tragedy, however profound, like the ploughman in Breughel's *Fall of Icarus.*

The metamorphosis of the Heliads in the first version denies, to a degree, the human element in the lower part. These sisters of Phaeton suffer by association. Therefore they cannot symbolize the human as opposed to the divine. The vague lower half in the second version seems to be a transition. In the third, no metamorphosis has taken place. Only transformed Cycnus reminds us of the completion of the myth. The lower part of the third version thus symbolizes the whole of the human state —its grief and its evanescence.

Hybris was the sin of Phaeton. He suffered for his presumption to the divine. That Michelangelo declared himself presumptuous in two of his letters to Cavaliere has been pointed out by Panofsky[17]. It would seem that we have in these drawings the fall of the presumptuous lover. Whereas the boy of the myth was caught between attainment and destruction, Michelangelo's tragedy remains potential. He is trapped between immense yearning and the haunting fear of failure. In his first letter to Cavaliere, dated January 1, 1533, Michelangelo wrote:

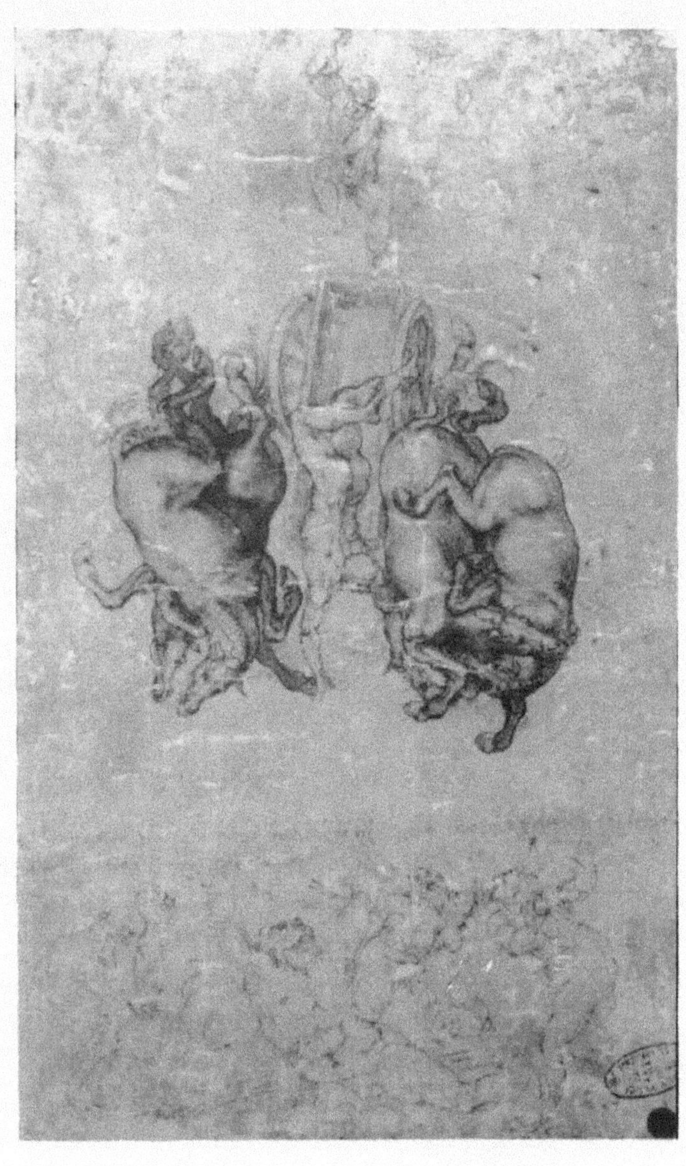

FIG. 5 — Michelangelo, *Fall of Phaeton* (second version) Venice, Accademia delle Belle Arti.

Without due consideration, Messer Tomao, my very dear lord, I was moved to write to your lordship, not by way of answer to any letter received from you, but being myself the first to make advances, as though I felt bound to cross a little stream with dry feet, or a ford made manifest by paucity of water. But now that I have left the

> *shore, instead of the trifling river I expected, the ocean with its tower-*
> *ing waves appears before me, so that, if it were possible, in order to*
> *avoid drowning, I would gladly retrace my steps to the dry land*
> *whence I started. Still, as I am here, I will e'en make of my heart a*
> *rock, and proceed farther; and if I shall not display the art of sailing*
> *on the sea of your powerful genius, that genius itself will excuse me,*
> *nor will be disdainful of my inferiority in parts, nor desire from me*
> *that which I do not possess, inasmuch as he who is unique in all things*
> *can have peers in none* . . . [18].

Three versions of this letter survive [19], which shows how carefully he labored for
expression. The making of three versions of the drawing itself, and the anxiety
over their acceptability, testify to the same care of execution and humility of
approach which are so striking in a man of Michelangelo's external temperament.
The inscription on the first version reads:

> *Messer Tomasso, if this sketch does not please you, tell Urbino*
> *[Francesco Urbino, Michelangelo's servant], so that I may have time*
> *to make another by tomorrow evening—as I have promised; and if it*
> *pleases you and you want me to finish it tell him so* [20].

The inscription on the second version is barely discernible, but seems to indicate a
third version [21]. The final version bears no inscription.

Dr. Panofsky explains this humility neo-Platonically: the youth who is loved
becomes the *idea* of beauty, a religious symbol which demands humility [22]. This, then,
according to Panofsky, is Michelangelo's approach to Cavaliere; he perishes by fire
and fall because of presumption, approach being presumption enough. Substantially
I agree, but would hesitate again on its strictly neo-Platonic approach. If the fatalistic damnation which these drawings depict can be linked with a desire for love,
we have yet another reason for use of the words "presumption" and "presumptuous"
—a fear of failing by being other than humble. For the unsure lover is always
plagued by the fear of losing.

Indeed it would seem that in the only other drawing which we definitely know
Michelangelo made for Cavaliere, the *Children's Bacchanal* [23] (fig. 7), at Windsor
Castle, his humility sinks to possible self-abasement. Several of the groups are
taken directly from the Sistine frescoes, in particular from the *Sacrifice of Noah*
and the *Drunkenness of Noah*. Consciously or not, Michelangelo has taken these
exalted motifs and used them to depict a base semi-human orgy.

The drawings of *Phaeton* express through the single myth the duality within
love, as do the *Ganymede* and the *Tityus* taken as a pair. Love, like flight, entails
both elation and constant risk. Though Phaeton's presumption brought him death,
it brought also a moment in which he partook of the divine. It is as if every action

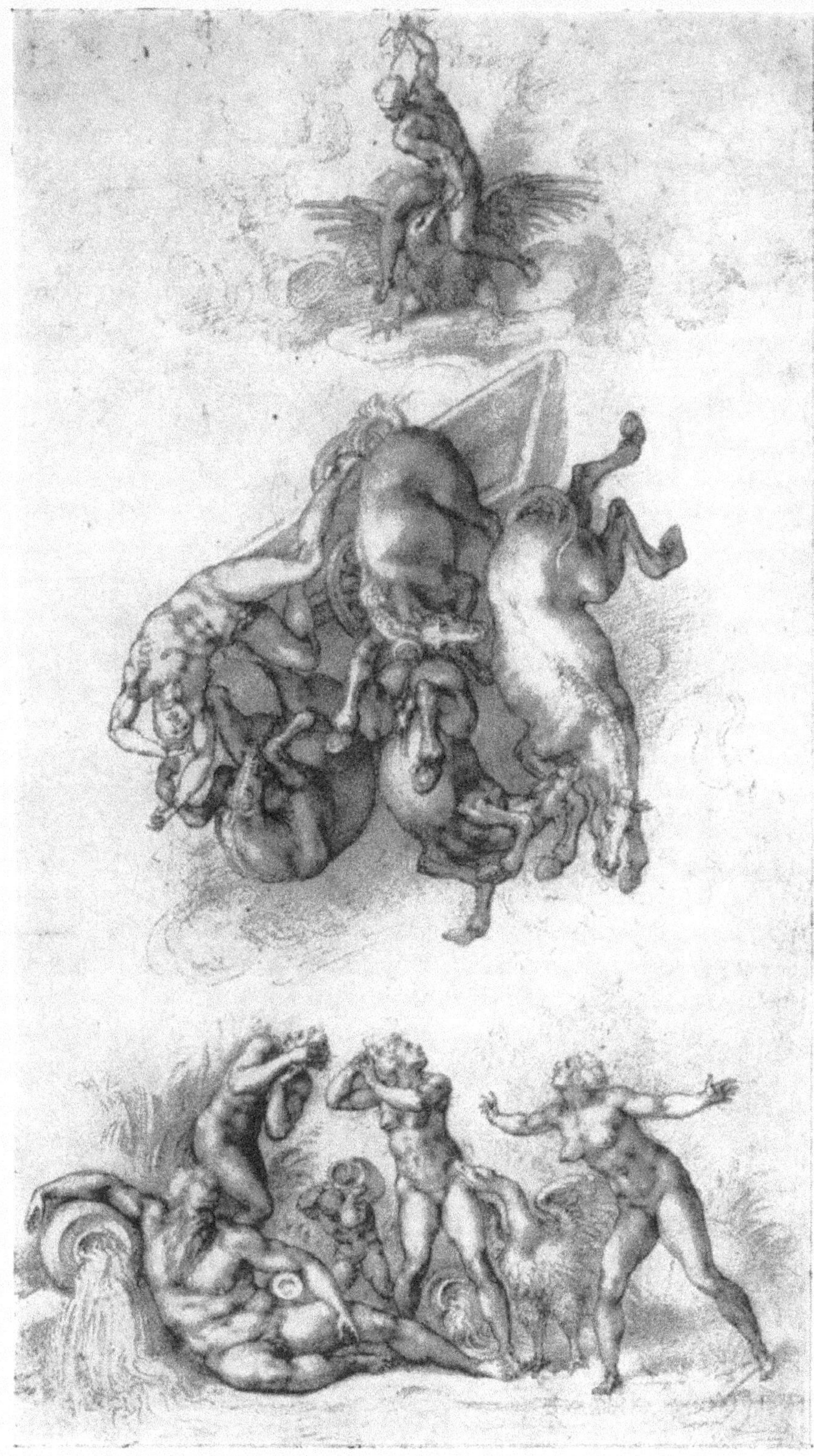

FIG. 6.—Michelangelo, *Fall of Phaeton* (third version).
Royal Collection, Windsor Castle, Copyright reserved.

or feeling, for Michelangelo, no matter how fulfilling of the individual, demands its correlated punishment. Positive and negative are inseparable.

Here, I feel, the essence of Michelangelo's Terribilità begins to come into focus. The conflict expands to the act of creation, and becomes the struggle between Michelangelo's demiurgic and destructive impulses. Thus in the Sistine Ceiling, all the powers summoned for creation lead first to the fall of man and finally to the drunkenness and degradation of Noah. In the *Last Judgment*, salvation and damnation form a convective circuit. Michelangelo's manner of working in stone, furiously attacking the block so that the image might emerge, is also indicative of the unity of opposite forces. The final act of willful destruction of the last pietàs is the most powerful summation of the opposition of creative and destructive urges, and in a sense the denial of the positive value of art. This speaks of the compulsive yearning for expression, and the constant feeling of inadequacy.

In the Cavaliere drawings, private though they are, and more closely related to Michelangelo's poetry than to his great public works, there appears in microcosm that conflict which achieves Titanic proportions in his massive works. In their smallness, their delicacy of treatment, and perhaps even because of their more personal subject matter, these drawings afford a gentle and gradual approach to the understanding of the struggles in the larger works, which often seem so forbidding.

B. D. K.

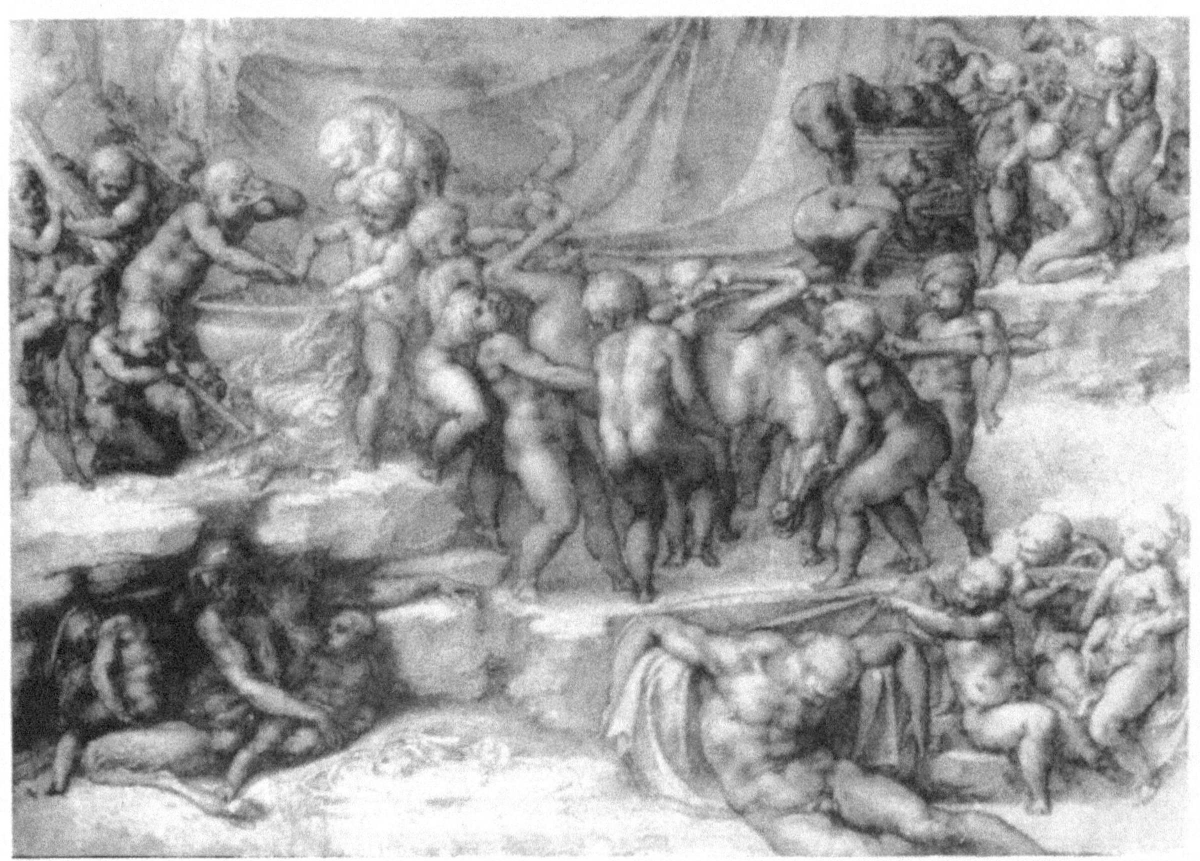

FIG. 7.—Michelangelo (?), *Children's Bacchanal*. Royal Collection, Windsor Castle. Copyright reserved.

REFLECTIONS ON MICHELANGELO'S DRAWINGS FOR CAVALIERE 109

RÉSUMÉ : *Quelques réflexions sur les dessins de Michel-Ange pour Cavaliere.*

Durant les années 1532 et 1533, Michel-Ange fit présent à Tomasso de Cavaliere, jeune noble romain, d'une série de dessins mythologiques. Six d'entre eux qui ont été identifiés : *Ganymède, Tityus*, trois versions de la *Chute de Phaeton*, et une *Bacchanale d'enfants*. Dans leur ensemble, ces dessins constituent un aveu poétique de l'amour de Michel-Ange pour Cavaliere. En même temps, par leur sujet et par la façon dont ils sont traités, ils expriment le sentiment que le positif et le négatif sont toujours liés de façon inextricable, dans toute expérience. Michel-Ange reprend la même idée dans deux sonnets d'amour écrits pour Cavaliere, qui peuvent être comparés avec les dessins de *Ganymède* et de *Tityus*, l'un représentant l'ascension, l'autre la chute. Ce rapprochement d'éléments antithétiques est encore plus fortement exprimé quand il est combiné en un seul thème, la *Chute de Phaéton*. Les trois versions de ce dessin révèlent la propre lutte de l'artiste pour parvenir à l'équilibre et à l'acceptation. Les lettres qu'il écrivit à Cavaliere montrent que ces sentiments étaient réels et personnels, et non pas une invention artistique désintéressée.

Quand le conflit entre positif et négatif s'applique à la création artistique, il devient alors la lutte entre les forces créatrices et destructrices, que l'on reconnaît si souvent dans les œuvres de Michel-Ange connues du grand public.

NOTES

1. Benedetto VARCHI, *Lezzioni*, Florence, 1590, p. 183. Translation from Giovani Papini, *Michelangelo : His Life and His Era*, trans. Loretta Maunane, New York, 1952, p. 299.

2. Giorgio VASARI, "The Life of Michelangelo," *The Lives of the Painters, Sculptors, and Architects*, trans. A.B. Hinds, New York, 1950, IV, p. 172.

3. For a discussion of some of these distortions see J. A. SYMONDS, *Life of Michelangelo Buonarroti*, London, 1893, II, p. 127 ff.
One of the best statements on the subject that I have come across is Marcel Brion's :
In Michelangelo's life, Cavaliere represented all that was finest and most complete in friendship in love too, perhaps. With him the great sculptor was purged of all the ambiguity of his relationships with young men of doubtful morality. His passion for Cavaliere was one of great intensity and great nobility; it was one in which his heart, mind and senses could have equal share, since he found his idea of perfect beauty in a living body.
(BRION, *Michelangelo*, trans. James Whitall, New York, 1940, p. 251.)

4. Vasari, "Michelangelo," p. 172. Besides these, Vasari mentions a life-sized portrait of Cavaliere; but he does not expressly state that it was given to Cavaliere. In another context Vasari mentions the drawing the *Saettatori*, or *Archers Shooting at a Herm* (p. 175), which is sometimes connected with the Cavaliere drawings. There is no proof, however, that this is one of the presentation series. A copy of the drawing is at Windsor, the Royal Library. See Charles DE TOLNAY, *The Medici Chapel*, Princeton, 1948, fig. 157.
For problems and history of attribution see de Tolnay, *Medici Chapel*, pp. 111-115 and notes 199-200.

5. For classical prototypes of these drawings see de Tolnay, *Medici Chapel*, plates 299 and 300; Anton Hekler, "Michelangelo und die Antike," *Weiner Jahrbuch für Kunstgeschichte*, VII (1930), pp. 201-223, and Alois Grünwald, "Zur Arbeitsweise einiger hervorragender Meister der Renaissance," *Münchner Jahrbuch der bildenden Kunst,* VII (1912), pp. 165-177.

6. There are many versions of this work both in drawing and in engraving, several of which show the lower half. Among these are : a drawing of Ganymede at the Fogg Art Museum, Cambridge, Massachusetts, attributed to Venusti by Bernard BERENSON (see *The Drawings of the Florentine Painters,* 2nd ed., Chicago, 1938, no. 1614, and II, p. 218); a Beatrizet engraving at the Boston Museum of Fine Arts; and a drawing at the Uffizi catalogued as Cristofano Allori.

7. Erwin PANOFSKY, "The Neo-Platonic Movement and Michelangelo," *Studies in Iconology,* New York, 1939, p. 218.

8. De Tolnay, *Medici Chapel,* p. 217.

9. *Phaedrus,* 1. 79; *De Rerum Natura,* III, 1. 982 ff.; see also Panofsky, *Iconology,* p. 217.

10. Varchi bears witness to this sonnet as meant for Cavaliere : *Lezzioni* p. 183. The English translation is from Symonds, *Life,* II, p. 127. The Italian can best be found in Carl FREY. *Die Dichtungen des Michelagniolo Buonarroti,* Berlin, 1897, no. CIX.

11. The literature does not reveal any tradition of an eagle in the Tityus myth. The original Homeric version (*Iliad,* XXI, 1. 407 ff.) of two vultures gave way to the later Roman story of the single bird, which might have been confused with the eagle of Prometheus. (See W. H. ROSCHER. *Ausführliches Lexikon der griechischen und römischen Mythologie,* V, cols. 1037-1038.) Nowhere, however, have I found the mention of an eagle. It is safe to say, then, that continuing tradition assigns a vulture as the retributive force for Tityus.

12. Panofsky, *Iconology,* p. 217, note 149.

13. This sonnet too Varchi documents as meant for Cavaliere : *Lezzioni,* p. 183. The English translation is from Symonds, *Life,* II, p. 127; for the Italian, see Frey, *Dichtungen,* no. LXXVI.

14. Panofsky, *Iconology,* p. 218.

15. For synopsis of opinions on dating problem see Panofsky, *Iconology,* p. 219, note 157.

16. Ovid, *Metamorphosis,* trans. Frank J. Miller, New York, 1921, II, 1. 319 ff.

17. Panofsky, *Iconology.* pp. 219-220.

18. Symonds, *Life,* II, p. 134. Also G. Milanese (ed), *Le lettere di Michelangelo Buonarroti,* Florence, 1875, pp. 462-464.

19. Milanese, *Le lettere,* nos. cdxi, cdxii, cdxiii, pp. 462-464.

20. See Henry THODE, *Michelangelo : kritische Untersuchungen über seine Werke,* Berlin, 1908, III, p. 159, no. 363.

21. *Ibid.,* III, p. 241, no. 518.

22. Panofsky, *Iconology,* p. 220.

23. Opinions differ as to the authenticity of this drawing-See V. THIEME and F. BECKER, *Allegemeines Lexikon der bildenden Künstler,* Leipzig, 1910-1950, XXIV, p. 522; Panofsky, *Iconology,* p. 221; Johannes Wilde, "The Drawings of Michelangelo and His School." *The Italian Drawings of the XV and XVI Centuries in the Collection of His Majesty the King at Windsor Castle,* ed. A. E. Popham, London, 1949, p. 255; and Berenson, *Drawings,* no. 1618.